DEMYSTIFYING THE CHINESE ECONOMY

China was the largest and one of the most advanced economies in the world before the eighteenth century, yet it declined precipitately there-after and degenerated into one of the world's poorest economies by the late nineteenth century. Despite generations of efforts for national rejuvena-tion, China did not reverse its fate until it introduced market-oriented reforms in 1979. Since then it has been the most dynamic economy in the world and is likely to regain its position as the world's largest economy before 2030. Based on economic analysis and personal reflection on policy debates, Justin Yifu Lin provides insightful answers as to why China was so advanced in premodern times, what caused it to become so poor for almost two centuries, how it grew into a market economy, where its potential is for continuing dynamic growth, and what further reforms are needed to complete the transition to a well-functioning, advanced market economy.

JUSTIN YIFU LIN is Senior Vice President and Chief Economist of the World Bank. He obtained his Ph.D. in economics from the University of Chicago in 1986 and returned to China in 1987, the first Ph.D. in social sciences to return from abroad after China started its economic reform in 1979. He was the founding director of the China Center for Economic Research at Peking University from 1994 to 2008 and is the author of seventeen books, including *The China Miracle* (1996), *State-Owned Enterprise Reform in China* (2001), and *Economic Development and Transition* (2009).

Demystifying the Chinese Economy

Justin Yifu Lin

CAMBRIDGE UNIVERSITY PRESS

Cambridge, New York, Melbourne, Madrid, Cape Town,
Singapore, São Paulo, Delhi, Mexico City

Cambridge University Press
The Edinburgh Building, Cambridge CB2 8RU, UK

Published in the United States of America by Cambridge University Press, New York

www.cambridge.org
Information on this title: www.cambridge.org/9780521181747

First published 2012
Reprinted 2012

Printed and Bound in the United States of America

A catalogue record for this publication is available from the British Library

ISBN 978-0-521-19180-7 Hardback
ISBN 978-0-521-18174-7 Paperback

Translated from the original Chinese by Stephanie Wang with further updates and revisions by Francesca Yu Sang and Bruce Ross-Larson

Contents

Figures

Tables

Preface

The book is based on my lecture notes for the course on China's economic development and transition at Peking University. I started to offer this course each semester when I founded the China Center for Economic Research at Peking University in 1993. Before I took the job as the Chief Economist and Senior Vice President of the World Bank in June 2008, I turned the notes into a book, and the Chinese edition was published by Peking University Press in 2009. The book covers the reasons for China's decline from its zenith before the eighteenth century, China's efforts to reverse that decline ever since, and the reforms necessary for China to complete the transition to a well-functioning market economy. In the English edition, I have updated the relevant chapters and included an appendix on global imbalances.

Sustained economic development relies on continual technological innovation and structural transformation. In premodern times technological inventions were based on the experience of farmers and craftsmen. The rate of technological innovation was slow and structural transformation was unperceivable. Most people at that time lived on subsistence agriculture, and only a few of them were ruling class, warriors, and craftsmen. With a large population, China naturally had a large number of farmers and craftsmen and thus enjoyed certain advantages in invention and technological innovation. What's more, China had a relatively advanced market system and upheld Confucian philosophy and a civil service examination system, which improved resource allocation, allowed social mobility, and facilitated national unity. That is why China led the world in many aspects for a very long period.

In the fifteenth century the Scientific Revolution in the West was characterized by mathematics and controlled experiments, in time leading to the Industrial Revolution in the mid-eighteenth century. When scientific experiment became the basis of invention, technological development in western countries accelerated at an amazing pace, as did their structural transformation and economic development. Many countries in Africa, Asia, and Latin America, defeated in conflicts, were reduced to colonies of western powers and left far behind.

The civil service examination system, based on Confucian classics, repressed Chinese intellectuals' incentives to learn mathematics and how to conduct controlled experiments, so a scientific and industrial revolution could not take place spontaneously in China. Within decades after the onset of the Industrial Revolution, China was no longer a leader in technological and economic development – but was instead left behind. After the Opium War in 1840 China suffered repeated humiliations by western powers, and its national sovereignty faced lethal challenges.

Under the influence of Confucianism, China's intellectuals regarded national prosperity as their responsibility, and generations of social elites and patriots strived unremittingly for national salvation. But it was not until the founding of the People's Republic of China in 1949, or actually not until the reform and opening program started in late 1978, that China began to change its course of poverty and backwardness.

After World War I nationalist movements surged around the world and after World War II the former colonies in Africa, Asia, and Latin America won their independence one after another. As in China, these newly independent countries, under the leadership of their first generation of revolutionaries, began to pursue modernization guided by the then-mainstream theories, hoping to build up advanced capital-intensive industries on their agrarian base. The priority industries went against their countries' comparative advantages and were not viable in open, competitive markets. The establishment of those industries and their continued operation relied on government protection and subsidies through various distortions to the market system. Despite the tireless efforts of a generation or two, economies stagnated, social and political crises broke out, and the gap with the developed world in per capita income grew even wider. By the end of the 1970s only a couple of East Asian economies succeeded in catching up with the developed countries.

In the 1950s and 1960s the international academic community criticized the market-based, export-oriented development strategy that the governments of East Asian economies adopted. The same thing happened when China initiated its reforms in the late 1970s. China's reform and opening program embarked on a gradualist dual-track approach. On the one hand, the government continued to provide necessary protections to the state-owned firms in old priority sectors, and on the other hand, it liberalized the private enterprises' entry to the new labor-intensive sectors, which were consistent with China's comparative advantage. From day one the policies elicited widespread skepticism in international academic circles. But against a wave of criticism China's economy notched up one amazing achievement after another, producing the "China miracle," with thirty consecutive years of rapid growth.

When China initiated its reform and opening in the late 1970s, other developing countries, in both socialist and non-socialist camps, were also undergoing various reforms, guided by the then-prevalent

Washington Consensus. Despite much effort, the growth rates of these economies were lower than those before the reform era. Many of them ended up in economic collapse and long-term stagnation.

This experience shows that there was no good theory to guide developing and transition countries in promoting their economic, social, cultural, and political development and transformation – and to realize modernization quickly and soundly. Why might this be?

Theories proposed by social scientists are usually based on phenomena in the countries they are from. Take economics. Since Adam Smith published *The Wealth of Nations* in 1776, laying a foundation for modern economics, the prevalent economic theories have been proposed mainly by economists from developed countries, interpreting the phenomena and resolving the problems of developed countries. But the opportunities and challenges facing developed countries differ from those of developing countries. So the theories tailored for the former are not necessarily applicable to the latter. And because the socioeconomic conditions and problems in developed countries are constantly evolving, their dominant theories changed from time to time. So, when attempting to adopt theories from developed countries to guide their policies, developing countries may be at a loss about which one to pick. Even if they select one, the theory may not fit their conditions.

Social science is by nature a simple logical system of causes and effects. Whether the theory is applicable to a country depends on whether the basic assumptions of the theory align with the socioeconomic conditions in that country. Usually only the scholars in that country have a good understanding of its history, culture, and realities – and thus can find the key variables among complex socioeconomic conditions and build a simple logical system capable of explaining the causes of problems and predicting the effects of actions in their countries.

The intellectuals in China and other developing countries should thus deepen the understanding of their own countries in all aspects, including in political, economic, and other social dimensions. Through that they may creatively construct a theoretical framework capturing the nature, challenges, and opportunities of their countries' modernization. This book is an attempt in that direction. By demystifying China's successes and failures, I hope the book will shed light on China's as well as other developing countries' future development.

Justin Yifu Lin

ONE

Opportunities and challenges in China's economic development

China was one of the most advanced and powerful countries in the world for more than a thousand years before the modern era. Even in the nineteenth century it dominated the world economic landscape. According to Angus Maddison, the famous economic historian, China accounted for a third of global GDP in 1820 (Figure 1.1). But with the Industrial Revolution in the eighteenth century, the West quickly rose, and China slid. And with a weaker economy, it was defeated repeatedly by the western powers, becoming a quasi-colony, ceding extraterritorial rights in treaty ports to twenty foreign countries. Its customs revenues were controlled by foreigners, and it surrendered territory to Britain, Japan, and Russia.

Since China's defeat in the Opium War in 1840, the country's elites, like those in other parts of the developing world, strived to make their motherland a powerful and respected nation again. But their efforts produced little success. China's share of global GDP shrank to about 5 percent and stayed low until 1979 (Figure 1.1).

China's economic fate then changed dramatically at the end of the 1970s when it started to implement the reform and opening strategy. Since then, its economic performance has been miraculous. Annual GDP growth averaged 9.9 percent over the next thirty years, and

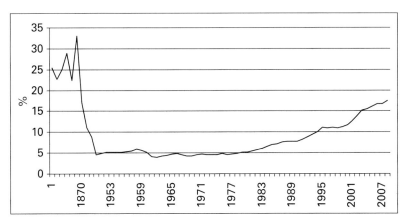

Figure 1.1 China's share in global GDP (%)
Source: Maddison (2006).

annual growth in international trade, 16.3 percent. In 1979 China was one of the poorest countries, with a per capita income of $210, a third of the average among the developing countries in sub-Saharan Africa, the poorest continent in the world.

Today China is a middle-income country, with a per capita GDP of $3,744 in 2009. It overtook Japan in 2010 as the world's second largest economy and replaced Germany as the world's largest exporter of merchandise. It is now the world's largest car producer, and Shanghai has been the world's busiest seaport by cargo tonnage since 2005. If China can sustain the current pace of growth, it will again become the world's largest economy by 2030 or even earlier.[1]

Against such a historical background, this chapter focuses on the opportunities and challenges in China's economic development. It sets the stage for answering five questions in the following chapters.

- Why was China the largest and most advanced civilization before the Industrial Revolution, yet lagging far behind western countries after it?
- Why was China's economic performance so poor before its reform and opening at the end of the 1970s, yet so miraculous after the reform?

- Why is China plagued by fluctuations in the economic cycle, fragility in the financial system, difficulty in the reform of state-owned enterprises (SOEs), widening in the gaps between regions, and unfairness in the distribution of income in the reform and opening process?
- To sustain rapid and sound growth in the twenty-first century, which aspects of China's economy should be reformed?
- Is China's economic growth real? Where is the exchange rate heading? And what about other issues of common concern, like the construction of a new socialist countryside and a harmonious society?

By reviewing both successes and failures of economic reform and development in China, as well as in other countries and regions, I put forward a general theory of economic transition and development. Based on this theory, I analyze China's achievements during its reform and opening, its major economic and social problems, the reasons for those problems, and the suggested solutions.

Fruits of China's reform and opening

The change in China's fate started in December 1978 when the Third Plenary Session of the 11th Central Committee of the Communist Party of China ushered in the reform and opening strategy – to reform the economic structure and open the economy to more foreign trade. An economy's openness is usually measured by the ratio of foreign trade-to-GDP, the "foreign trade dependency ratio." Mainland China's foreign trade at $20.8 billion in 1978 was 12% less than that of Taiwan, China. China's imports accounted for 4.8% of GDP, exports, 4.7%, and total trade, 9.5%.[2] Early in 1980, Deng Xiaoping, the architect of China's reform and opening strategy, proposed a target for that program: to quadruple China's 1980 GDP by the end of the twentieth century, possible only with average annual growth of 7.2 percent. Then a major in economics at Peking University, I doubted the attainability of the target. According to the theory of natural rate of growth, then widely acknowledged, no country can sustain long-term annual growth above 7 percent, except after a war or natural disaster. True, Japan and the four Asian Tigers managed it over two decades since the 1960s but their stunning performance was regarded as exceptional: the East Asian Miracle.

At the end of 1978 China had a population of 1 billion, with farmers accounting for 80 percent of the total, and a huge number of illiterates. So it was less than credible that a country as backward and impoverished as China could sustain 7.2 percent growth for two decades. But as an old Chinese saying puts it: "Striving for the best, you will be an average at worst; striving for the average, an under-achiever at best." Quadrupling GDP was seen more as a slogan than an attainable target.

Two decades later Deng's aim turned out to be timid. As stated, in the thirty years from 1979 to 2009, China's average annual growth was 9.9 percent, 2.7 percentage points higher than the targeted 7.2 percent.[3] Those added percentage points, seemingly small, translate into an aggregate economic volume 18.6 times that in 1978, more than twice the sevenfold increase from quadrupling GDP at 7.2 percent. Since 1978 the average annual growth of foreign trade has been 16.3 percent, 6.4 percentage points higher than GDP growth. By 2009 the volume of foreign trade exceeded $2.2 trillion, a 107-fold jump in thirty years.[4] Deng was thus a true statesman with great vision. Embarking on a seemingly impossible mission, he would prove that his ambitious targets were attainable.

When I returned to Peking in 1987 after finishing my doctorate at the University of Chicago and a year of postdoctoral work at Yale, China was embarking on a globalization strategy, "attending to the international economic circulation" through trade.[5] Specific practices included: "encouraging sizable exports of processed products while promoting sizable imports of raw materials" and "processing

imported material according to supplied samples, assembling supplied parts, and compensation trade." The topic of the first policy
brainstorming I took part in was: What would China's foreign trade
dependency ratio be if the strategy of attending to the international
economic circulation was implemented?

That ratio can be pretty high, even above 100 percent for small
economies, such as the four Asian Tigers. But for larger economies, it
is usually much lower. Among countries with a population over 100
million, Indonesia's dependency ratio was 23 percent in 1984, according to the 1986 *World Development Report*, an annual publication of
the World Bank.[6] In my opinion, China could do better if it tried
harder; so I argued that China could hit 25 percent. But that number
was dismissed, for most people did not believe that I, educated in
America, truly understood China's affairs. China's dependency ratio
had grown from 9.5% in 1978 to 16% in 1984. In the same year,
the ratio was 15.2% for the United States, and 23.9% for Japan.[7]
So, popular sentiment was that 25% was not a reasonable target,
even with the new strategy. My prediction proved as conservative as
Deng's in 1978. By 2008 the ratio reached 62%.

Besides expanding foreign trade, China has been vigorously attracting foreign investment. In 2008 foreign direct investment flows to
China were $692 billion, making it the world's number two invest-
ment destination, second only to the United States.[8] And thanks
to continuous economic growth and ever-expanding foreign trade,
China has amassed the largest foreign exchange reserves, approaching
$3 trillion, giving it more bargaining chips in the international arena.

Stabilizing and driving the world economy

China's rapid economic growth since its reform and opening has
exerted great influence at home and abroad. Domestically, the most
visible outcome is that living standards have dramatically improved.
In the 1980s those who returned from overseas were allowed to bring

home "three major items" duty free. With an overseas stay of more than half a year, six items were allowed. When I prepared to return in 1987, eight items were allowed in an effort to encourage more overseas graduates to come back to China. My eight-item package included a color TV, a refrigerator, a washing machine, an electric water heater, and four electric fans for my family. It was unimaginable in those days that school offices and almost every household in town would one day be equipped with air conditioning.

The living standards of both white-collar workers and farmers have been greatly enhanced. In 1978 an estimated 30 percent of rural residents, about 250 million, lived below the poverty line, relying on small loans for production and state grants for food. Contrast that with 36 million in 2009.[9]

Chinese people are not the sole beneficiaries of its reform and opening. China's exports of consumer goods and life's necessities, inexpensive and of good quality, improve the living conditions of the poor in many other countries.

Another contribution of China to the world economy is its stabilizing effect, as in the East Asian financial crisis starting in October 1997. During that crisis, countries in the region devalued their currencies one after the other. The South Korean won fell from 770:1 against the US dollar before the crisis to 1,700:1, the Thai baht from 25:1 to 54:1, and the Indonesian rupiah from 2203:1 to 11950:1.[10] East Asian economies were similar to China in their stage of development and export mix. And the substantial depreciation of those currencies made their products a lot cheaper in world markets, putting great pressure on Chinese exporters. The international financial community then expected China to follow suit, since exports meant so much to the country. But devaluing the renminbi (RMB) could induce "competitive devaluations," putting the crisis-afflicted countries in an even more precarious position.

The economic outlook in East Asia was even gloomier than in the United States during the Great Depression of 1929. Many experts in international economic and financial circles felt it would take a decade – or even longer – for the East Asian economies to recover. The world's eyes were on China and whether it would devalue. Despite the doubts and suspicions, China put the stability of neighboring economies high on its agenda, committed not to devalue its currency, and then honored this commitment, contributing much to Asia's rapid recovery in just a couple of years. What made that contribution possible? The substantial foreign exchange reserves that China had piled up since the reform and opening – and its enormous imports from East Asian economies.

Similarly, when the global financial crisis erupted after the collapse of Lehman Brothers in September 2008, China, counting on its large fiscal space and abundant foreign reserves, immediately adopted a stimulus package of $685 billion. The Chinese economy started to recover in the first quarter of 2009. Its GDP growth rate reached 9.1% in 2009 and 10.1% in 2010 despite global GDP's contraction of 2.2% in 2009 and growth of only 3.9% in 2010. China's strong growth during the crisis was the most important driving force for the global recovery.

Indeed, China's economic growth has benefited far more countries than just its neighbors. Over 2000–07 two-thirds of the economies in Africa grew at more than 5.5 percent a year, and nearly one-third reached 7 percent. Again, such unprecedented growth in Africa was in large part thanks to China. Its massive raw material imports have boosted prices in world markets, good for resource-rich African countries.

The same is true for many Asian and Latin American countries. Take Japan's Nippon Steel Corporation. Booming in the 1950s and 1960s, it waned when iron and steel became a sunset industry in the 1970s in Japan. Yet in the 2000s, its profits have been on the rebound. The biggest reason: rising international steel prices driven by Chinese imports. Argentina, Brazil, Chile, and other Latin American countries have also benefited from trading with China.

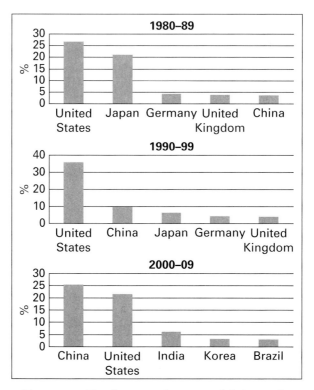

Figure 1.2 Top five contributors to global growth,
1980–2009
Source: World Bank, World Development Indicators.

China has thus become a major driving force for the world economy. In the 1980s and the 1990s, except for China, the other top five contributors to the growth of global GDP were all members of the G7 industrialized countries; in these two decades China's contributions were respectively 13.4 percent and 26.7 percent of the contributions of the United States. But in 2000–09 China became the top contributor, exceeding that of the United States by 4 percentage points (Figure 1.2).

Despite the rapid growth over the past three decades, China's per capita GDP was only $3,650 in 2009, about 8 percent of that in the United States. There is also a yawning gap between China and the rest of the developed world in per capita income, which China can narrow only with sustained growth, also critical to job creation for China's growing urban and rural workforce.

Reform could have undermined the interests of some groups, leading to social tensions. But China averted social unrest during its reform by not repeating the failures of the former Soviet Union and Eastern Europe. How? Rapid growth created resources for the government to compensate those groups.

The potential for China's continuing economic growth

Before the Industrial Revolution of the eighteenth century, growth across the world was rather slow – 0.05 percent a year. After that, growth accelerated but was quite unbalanced, and the differences between some countries were huge, with one or two as the locomotives of the world economy. First to take the lead was Great Britain, where the Industrial Revolution originated. But it was overtaken by the United States sometime between the end of the nineteenth century and World War I. After World War II Japan and Germany recovered rapidly, injecting new vitality to the world economy. But in the twenty-first century those four developed economies have had great difficulty in finding new areas for growth. And political and social issues in those countries have hindered their growth. Meanwhile, China has come to the fore as a new locomotive. How far China's train can roll will hinge on its fuel – on its potential for growth.

Opinions about the potential for China's growth vary greatly, with two typical takes. One holds that China will outpace the United States by 2030 or even earlier. The other is that China's economy could collapse at any time.[11] Which view is more sensible? Answering this question requires understanding the key determinants of economic growth. From the perspective of production functions, it is determined by the following:

- *Factors of production.* In economics the factors of production include natural resources, labor, and capital. If the factors of production increase in proportion, so will output. But in modern society, since natural resources are restricted by the area of the country, they can be regarded as fixed. The increase in labor is limited by population growth. So capital is the most variable of the three. Since China's reform and opening, savings and investments have exceeded 40% of GDP annually. For some countries, the figure ranges from 10% to 15%; for some African countries, it is close to zero. Of the factors of production, capital is the most critical for economic growth.
- *Industrial structure.* If the factors of production are allocated to industries with higher value-added, output will also increase. So the industrial structure also determines economic growth – moving factors of production to sectors with higher value-added, the economy will grow even without increasing those factors.
- *Technology.* Technology is another big determinant. Technological progress means higher productivity. Even when the industrial structure and factors of production remain unchanged, with better technology, an economy's output and growth will improve as well.
- *Institutions.* With the foregoing productive inputs, industrial structure, and technology, one can construct a production-possibility frontier, an economy's maximum obtainable output in an ideal state. How close it approaches that maximum hinges on institutions, which can help in upgrading labor, using resources effectively, and adopting appropriate technology.

Among these four determinants, technology is the most important in practice. The other three are subject, to some degree, to the speed of technological change.

Technological progress and the accumulation of capital

Since land and natural resources are basically fixed, and the growth of labor is rather limited, even if capital accumulates at great speed, without technological progress, returns will decline, according to the law of diminishing marginal returns. So the enthusiasm for accumulating capital will decline as well. Only when technology progresses at a certain speed can the effects of diminishing returns be avoided to sustain the enthusiasm for capital accumulation.

Nobel Economics Laureate Theodore Schultz produced some brilliant treatises on the topic. One of his major contributions, which earned him the prize, is embodied in his book, *Transforming Traditional Agriculture*.[12] Before it was published, most economists held that peasants in traditional agricultural society were irrational, because they seldom saved or accumulated their money – but that farmers in modern agricultural society were rational, because they invested what they have saved. For instance, American farmers each invest on average more than $1 million in farm equipment. Based on this, those economists concluded that irrationality was the major cause of the poverty of peasants in traditional society.

Professor Schultz put forward an opposite view, arguing that the choices by peasants in traditional society are actually rational. Why? In olden times when technological progress was rather sluggish, the savings/investments of the peasants were in equilibrium. In such a case, accumulating capital could reduce productivity, and saving would mean tightening belts. That could increase costs without producing any benefits.

Consider a simple example. Chinese peasants grow paddy rice and wheat and use sickles for harvesting. In traditional agricultural society, each peasant had one sickle. Investing then would mean buying a second sickle. But reaping with two sickles is not efficient. So the majority of peasants saved only for a new sickle after the old one was broken and had little incentive for investing. That is why it was sensible for peasants not to save in traditional agricultural society. To change the status quo, the peasants needed new, better technology, so that investing would produce higher returns, increasing their enthusiasm for capital accumulation.

Technological progress and industrial upgrading

Without new technology, there would be no new industry with higher value-added, and industrial upgrading would be out of the question. Almost all of today's high-value-added industries, like electronics and bio-engineering, are the results of invention, innovation, and new technology. Only with constant technological innovation will there be a flow of new industries with high value-added. Driven by high returns, businesses will invest in these emerging sectors, eventually leading to industrial upgrading.

Institutional improvement

Unlike capital accumulation, industrial upgrading, or even technological advance, which are all driven by profit, institutional improvement is a passive process. Institutions cannot be judged in isolation. As Marx put it, the base determines the superstructure, and as part of the superstructure, institutions must correspond to actual economic conditions. As mentioned, technological changes will affect various aspects of the base, demanding institutional improvement. So technological progress is a prerequisite for institutional improvement (Chapter 2).

In sum, the potential for economic growth hinges mostly on technological progress. According to Angus Maddison's *The World Economy*,[13] in the period of more than one millennium before the eighteenth century, even for the most developed European countries, the fastest average annual growth in per capita GDP was only 0.05 percent, so it took 1,400 years to double per capita incomes. After the Industrial Revolution growth picked up across Europe, and in the eighteenth and nineteenth centuries the average annual growth of per capita income was 1 percent, so it took seventy years to double per capita incomes. In the twentieth century per capita income growth rose to 2 percent, forty times that before the Industrial Revolution. So it took only thirty-five years to double, just a bit longer than a generation. Such seismic changes illustrate the critical role of technology in economic growth. To understand the potential for China's future development thus requires exploring the possibility for technological change in China.

Technological innovation: borrowing is the preferred option

There are two types of technological innovation: product and process. With product innovation, new products replace old products, as with computers replacing the abacus. With process innovation, the product remains the same but is produced more cost-effectively and efficiently. Ford Motors in its early days is a good example. It adopted the high-efficiency assembly line to replace traditional handcrafting methods, producing affordable cars for the mass market.

Both product innovation and process innovation can come from research and development (R&D) at home or borrowing from abroad.[14] Innovation does not necessarily involve the latest technology, and different countries tend to choose different innovation mechanisms. For the most advanced countries – like the United States, Japan, and Germany, which enjoy not only the highest per capita income but also state-of-the-art technologies – R&D is the only option for innovation. But for developing countries, lagging behind the developed world, the options for innovation in most industries include importing technology, copying, and purchasing patent licenses.

Which option is better, R&D or borrowing? People in different industries and different jobs have different answers. Researchers, playing a major role in R&D, are often more concerned about the concrete results of R&D and the experience gained in the process, and much less about the commercialization of the results and how much funding the research institutions or the R&D departments of companies have to put in. For them, the results of R&D are always positive. Compared with borrowing technology, which requires much less of their contribution, most of them naturally prefer R&D.

Most economists and entrepreneurs would give a different answer, because their primary concerns are costs and benefits. First, inputs into R&D are huge – for IBM and Intel, billions of dollars each year. Second, the chances of success are slim. Of all research, 99 percent ends in failure, and even for the successful 1 percent, there is no guarantee that the result is marketable. True, if an innovation succeeds, the returns can be handsome during the term of the patent. That's why entrepreneurs are so obsessed with the high returns to the successful 1 percent but oblivious to the huge costs and risks of the failed 99 percent. An ancient Chinese saying describes the symptom: "The reputation of one great general is made out of the rotting bones of tens of thousands." Blind to the tens of thousands of dead soldiers, people hailed the general as a legend.

Both mechanisms have pros and cons, and should be judged on the basis of a country's conditions. For developing countries like China, introducing technology from developed countries is generally preferred, if it is available. Most patent protection for a new technology is for twenty years. In practice, because of rapid technological changes, it costs almost nothing to introduce most technologies in ten years' time. For more recent technologies, some data show that the cost of introduction is no more than 30 percent of the original R&D cost. So, taking into account the cost of all the failed experiments, it would be less than 1 percent of the R&D cost.

Technological borrowing and its advantages for a lagging country

By introducing advanced technologies and experiences from developed countries, developing countries can innovate faster and at lower cost. Technological innovation will lead to improved efficiency, higher returns on capital, faster capital accumulation, industrial upgrading and economic growth. Consider how long it took countries around the world to double their per capita GDP in the rapid growth phase after the Industrial Revolution: the United Kingdom, fifty-eight years (1780–1838), the United States, forty-seven years (1839–86), Japan, thirty-four years (1885–1919), Turkey, twenty years (1957–77), Brazil, eighteen years (1961–79), South Korea, eleven years (1966–77), and China, ten years (1977–87).[15]

So, the later the economy entered its rapid growth phase, the shorter the time to double its output. As mentioned earlier, per capita GDP grew at about 1 percent on average for the industrial countries in the century after the Industrial Revolution, and 2 percent in the twentieth century. By contrast, for the successful developing economies it grew at 8 percent a year in the second half of the twentieth century, including Japan, the four Asian Tigers, and post-reform China.

After World War II the four Asian Tigers and China were basically at the same starting line. But by the 1980s the Tigers had become emerging developed economies with per capita incomes about one-third that of the United States. The major reason: they were good at technological borrowing and industrial upgrading. In the 1950s most people in the four Asian Tigers were farmers. With the continuing introduction of new technology and the development of high-value-added industries, labor moved to those industries, including services. As the returns on capital in those industries improved, capital was accumulated rapidly, so economic growth snowballed.

The completely different economic performances before and after reform in China also demonstrated how critical borrowing technology is to the economy. Before 1978 a slogan quite popular in China was – "Overtake the United Kingdom in ten years and catch up with the United States in fifteen years." China tested an atomic bomb in the 1960s and launched a satellite in the 1970s, both cutting-edge technologies. But its economy was far from cutting-edge. Fortunately, China started down the same road as the other East Asian economies after 1978, introducing technology and capital and "attending to the international economic circulation" to export labor-intensive products and accumulate foreign reserves. The main reason for China's rapid growth after its reform and opening is borrowing technology at low costs to achieve rapid technology change.

The key is to maintain rapid growth

No country other than China has maintained annual growth of 9 percent for more than three decades. Can China keep growing that fast for another two decades or even longer? Yes. This answer is based not on some optimistic estimate, but rather on the potential advantages of backwardness.

In 2008 China's per capita income was 21 percent that of the United States, measured in purchasing power parity by Maddison's estimates.[16] The income gap between China and the US indicates that there is still a large technological gap between China and the industrialized countries. China can thus continue to enjoy the advantages of backwardness before closing the gap.

Maddison's estimates show that China's current relative status to the United States is similar to Japan's in 1951, Taiwan, China's in 1975, and Korea's in 1977. GDP grew 9.2% in Japan between 1951 and 1971, 8.3% in Taiwan, China, between 1975 and 1995, and 7.6% in Korea between 1977 and 1997. China's development strategy after the reform in 1979 is similar to that of Japan, Korea, and Taiwan, China. So it has the potential to achieve another twenty years of 8% growth. Japan's income per capita measured in purchasing power parity was 65.6% of that of the US in 1971, Korea's was 50.2% in 1997, and Taiwan, China's was 54.2% in 1995. Twenty years from now, China's per capita income measured in purchasing power parity may reach about 50% of US per capita income. Measured by purchasing power parity, China's economy in 2030 may be twice as large as that of the United States, and measured by market exchange rates, it may be about the same size as that of the United States.

Problems facing China's economy

Many non-economic factors will decide whether China can realize its full potential. Along with its rapid growth, China, as a developing country in transition, has encountered problems never seen before – problems that need to be addressed.

Ever-widening income disparity and the urban–rural gap

In the very early stages of the reform and opening, the gaps between the urban and rural areas and those among the eastern, central, and western parts of the country were narrowing. But after 1985 they widened. The Gini coefficient (a measure of income equality, with a coefficient of 0 as perfect equality, and 1 as perfect inequality) increased from 0.31 in 1981 to 0.42 in 2005, approaching the level of Latin American countries.[17] As Confucius once said: "Inequity is worse than scarcity." Indeed, a widening income disparity would cause bitter resentment among the low-income group. In addition, the educational, medical, and public health systems are underdeveloped. So the income gap could cause tensions, undermining social harmony and stability.

Inefficient use of resources and environmental imbalances

China's rapid growth has consumed massive energy and resources. In 2006, with 5.5% of the world's GDP, it consumed 9% of the world's oil, 23% of alumina, 28% of steel, 38% of coal, and 48% of cement. Natural resources are limited. So, if China doesn't change its growth pattern or reduce its resource consumption, the fallout will inflict harm on other countries for generations to come. In addition, rising resource prices will increase the cost of overconsumption, which runs counter to scientific development strategy promoted by the Communist Party.

The environmental problems caused by breakneck development are also serious. The mining disasters and natural calamities in recent years are testimony to environmental deterioration. There were three major floods in the 1990s, each called "once in a century." How could there be three "once in a century" floods in a single decade? Natural disasters can deliver fatal blows, so protecting the environment to prevent disasters is important in China as well.

External imbalances and currency appreciation

China has had both current account surpluses and capital account surpluses since 1994. Before 2005 the current account surplus was relatively small, but it reached 7.6 percent of GDP in 2007. As a result of the large trade surplus, China accumulated foreign reserves rapidly. In 1990 its reserves were $11.1 billion, barely enough to cover 2.5 months of imports. But its reserves today are nearly $3 trillion – the largest in the world (see the appendix).[18]

Accompanying the rising trade surpluses was the rising trade deficit in the United States. The imbalances received much attention before the global financial crisis in 2008. In a testimony before the United States Congress in 2007, C. Fred Bergsten of the Peterson Institute stated: "The global imbalances probably represent the single largest current threat to the continued growth and stability of the United States and world economies."[19] Throughout the crisis, there have been claims that the most severe global recession since the Great Depression was caused in part or wholly by global imbalances, especially the imbalances between the United States and China. Some economists, such as Nobel Laureate Paul Krugman, argued that the undervaluation of the renminbi caused the large US trade deficit and that the consequent Chinese purchases of US Treasury bonds lowered interest rates and caused the US equity and real estate bubbles, leading to the financial crisis.[20] Others argued that a revaluation of the renminbi to rebalance US and China trade was a prerequisite for a sustained global recovery.[21]

Corruption

Before the reform, when people from different social circles had but a single income source, corruption was visible and easy to prevent. But in the post-reform era, when material incentives became major tools to enhance efficiency, income sources became more diversified, and various gray and dark incomes harder to spot. Widespread official corruption has further widened the income gap, increasing resentment among the groups whose interests have been undermined and impairing the credibility of the government. Once that happens, it's hard to maintain social cohesion in a major crisis, and economic and social stability can be undermined.

Education

China's education policies focus more on quantity than quality, which is detrimental to training workers and to long-term social progress. No matter what form technological innovation takes, borrowing from abroad or conducting domestic R&D, China has to rely on talent, and without good education, innovation is impossible.

A caveat: The problems I have described are not the only ones. Others include underdeveloped social security systems, low levels of technology, rampant local protectionism, mounting challenges from globalization, inadequate legal systems, and many other political, economic, social, and even external problems, each of which needs to be identified and addressed. If they cannot be addressed promptly, any one of them could wreak social and economic havoc, even political instability. Without a stable political and economic climate, China will not achieve its goal of rapid growth nor fulfill its economic potential.

To conclude, China has great potential to continue the current dynamic growth for another two decades or more and regain its position as the world's largest economy by 2030 or even earlier. To achieve that, China needs to overcome many intrinsic problems.

The following chapters will analyze how to tap into China's potential and overcome those problems.

References

Bergsten, C. Fred. 2007. "Currency Misalignments and the U.S. Economy." Statement before the US Congress, May 9 (www.sasft.org/Content/ ContentGroups/PublicPolicy2/ChinaFocus/pp_china_bergsten_tstmny.pdf).

Chang, Gordon H. 2001. *The Coming Collapse of China*. New York: Random House.

Goldstein, Morris. 2010. "Confronting Asset Bubbles, Too Big to Fail, and Beggar-thy-Neighbor Exchange Rate Policies." Paper based on remarks delivered on December 15, 2009, at the workshop on "The International Monetary System: Looking to the Future, Lessons from the Past" sponsored by the International Monetary Fund and the UK Economic and Research Council, Peterson Institute of International Economics.

Groningen Growth and Development Centre. 2008. "Angus Maddison." Last modified September 3, 2008 (www.ggdc.net/MADDISON/oriindex.htm).

Krugman, Paul. 2009. "World Out of Balance." *New York Times*, November 15.

2010. "Chinese New Year." *New York Times*, January 1.

Lin, Justin Y. 2004. *Fa Zhan Zhan Lue Yu Jing Ji Fa Zhan* [Development Strategy and Economic Development]. Beijing: Peking University Press.

2005. *Lun Jing Ji Xue Fang Fa* [On Economic Methodology]. Beijing: Peking University Press.

2010. "Global Imbalances, Reserve Currency and Global Economic Governance." Paper prepared for the Closing Panel at the IPD-FEPS Global Economic Governance Conference at the Brookings Institution, Washington, DC, October 7.

Lin, Justin Y., Fang Cai, and Zhou Li. 2003. *The China Miracle: Development Strategy and Economic Reform*, revised edn. Hong Kong: Chinese University Press.

Maddison, Angus. 2006. *The World Economy*. Paris: Organisation for Economic Co-operation and Development.

Schultz, Theodore W. 1964. *Transforming Traditional Agriculture*. New Haven, CT: Yale University Press.

Smith, Adam. [1776] 1976. *An Inquiry into the Nature and Causes of the Wealth of Nations*. Chicago: University of Chicago Press.

[1776] 1981. *Guo Min Cai Fu De Xing Zhi He Yuan Yin De Yan Jiu* [An Inquiry into the Nature and Causes of the Wealth of Nations]. Beijing: The Commercial Press.

World Bank. 1986. *World Development Report 1986: Trade and Pricing Policies in World Agriculture*. Washington, DC: World Bank.

1991. *World Development Report 1991: The Challenge of Development*. Washington, DC: World Bank.

2010. *World Development Indicators 2010*. Washington, DC: World Bank.

2011. *Global Development Horizons 2011. Multipolarity: The New Global Economy*. Washington, DC: World Bank.

Notes

1. World Bank (2011).
2. National Bureau of Statistics of China.
3. *Ibid.*
4. *Ibid.*
5. "The International Economic Circulation Strategy" of economic development was put forward by Professor Wang Jian. It advocates further opening in the coastal area of China through developing labor-intensive, export-oriented processing businesses. The purpose is to absorb the surplus rural labor and to earn foreign exchange for economic development.
6. World Bank (1986).
7. *Ibid.*
8. National Bureau of Statistics of China.
9. *Ibid.*
10. Thomson/Datastream.
11. Chang (2001) was one representation of such views.
12. Schultz (1964).
13. Maddison (2006).
14. On technological changes and innovation, see my article "Ji Shu Chuang Xin, Fa Zhan Jie Duan Yu Zhan Lue Xuan Ze" ["Technology Innovation, Development Phase and Strategic Choice"] in Lin (2004).
15. World Bank (1991).
16. The national statistics used in this and the next paragraphs are taken from Angus Maddison's Historical Statistics of the World Economy: 1–2008 AD (www.ggdc.net/maddison/Historical_Statistics/horizontal-file_02–2010.xls).
17. World Bank (2010).
18. Lin (2010).
19. Bergsten (2007).
20. Krugman (2009, 2010).
21. Goldstein (2010).

TWO

Why the Scientific and Industrial Revolutions bypassed China

This chapter[1] analyzes why China, before the modern era, was more advanced than the West in its economy, science, and technology but was then left far behind. Constant technological innovation and upgrading are the basis for a nation's long-term economic development. In premodern times, when invention was based mostly on the experience of peasants and craftsmen, China enjoyed an enormous advantage because of its large population. But that advantage disappeared with the Industrial Revolution in the West. Why? Because controlled experiments by scientists in labs replaced experience as the basis of invention.

The precondition for the Industrial Revolution was the Scientific Revolution, which featured mathematics and controlled experiments. The Scientific Revolution did not take place in China because its civil service system discouraged talented persons from acquiring the capacity for mathematics and controlled experiments. For the same reason, technological innovation in China failed to change from an experience-based model to a science- and experiment-based model. So, it was left far behind when the West made that shift. But that does not mean however that the Chinese did not have the capacity for industrial and scientific revolution. In modern China the disincentive to learn mathematics and conduct controlled experiments has been removed, so China will again definitely contribute to scientific and technological progress, as it did in the old days.

China's achievements in premodern times

World's largest economy – then and soon

There is a good chance that China will someday become the world's largest economy. But that would not be a new phenomenon. The late Angus Maddison, an economic historian, conducted meticulous quantitative research on the economic histories of China, Europe, and many other regions and countries in his book *The World Economy*.[2] According to his analysis, China dwarfed other world economies for nearly two millennia and remained the largest economy until the middle of the nineteenth century.

In AD 1 Europe was in the heyday of the Roman Empire, while China was about to embrace the prime time of the Han Dynasty. The two powers never engaged with each other, so it would be difficult to tell which was richer and more powerful. But Maddison estimates that China's per capita income was on par with Rome's.

According to Adam Smith's first law of economic growth in *The Wealth of Nations*, the division of labor is one of the driving forces of growth: the greater the division of labor, the higher the economy's productivity.[3] But the division of labor is limited by market size. So the larger the market, the more specialized the labor. Otherwise, even if production increases, the market cannot absorb it. When the Roman Empire disintegrated into city-states, the markets shrank dramatically, as did the division of labor and productivity. Every city-state was a natural economy, with very few commercial exchanges between them. Thus, per capita incomes in Europe declined. China, by contrast, remained for the most part united from the Han Dynasty on. Its market was thus much larger than those in Europe.

Leading position in technology

Technological innovation is essential for long-term economic development. A major feature of developing economies that separates them from the developed is technological backwardness. Before the seventeenth century China's technology was the most advanced in the world. Francis Bacon, the renowned British statesman and philosopher (1561–1626), argued that the three most important inventions for Europe's transformation from the Dark Ages to the modern world were gunpowder, the magnetic compass, and paper and printing.

Gunpowder broke down the previously impregnable castles of the feudal aristocracy and unified national markets. Starting in the thirteenth and fourteenth centuries, independent city-states began to be unified into larger nation-states. So, national markets were expanded, the division of labor was increased, and economies grew.

Without the magnetic compass, Columbus would not have discovered the New World, which brought wealth (such as gold) and many new crop varieties to Europe, changing it profoundly. When corn, potatoes, and other high-yield or drought-resistant crops from the New World were introduced to Europe, agricultural output increased substantially. Surviving became easier, and the population expanded. Thanks to new kinds of crops, Europe's population grew rapidly in the sixteenth and seventeenth centuries.

Before paper and printing, words were recorded on very expensive sheepskins, and all books were written by hand (hence the word "manuscript"). To copy the Bible could take a monk a lifetime. So, the value of one book could be said to equal that of one human life. With paper and printing, the cost of books fell dramatically, and the accumulation and dissemination of knowledge accelerated, never to slow again.

Bacon understood the importance of the three inventions, but he did not know where they originated. Now we know that they all came from China, the technological leader in those days.

A dynamic market economy

China's superiority was also reflected in its dynamic market economy, based on private ownership, especially of land. As early as the Spring and Autumn Period in 770–476 BC and the following Warring States Period in 475–221 BC (here, the Two Periods), private ownership of land existed in China, and trade in land was allowed. But in Europe, during the entire feudal period, the land belonged to the aristocracy, so there was no land market.

The labor market in China was also very active. During the Spring and Autumn Period, thinkers like Confucius traveled from kingdom to kingdom to peddle their propositions, in much the same way today's executives go abroad for job experience. Words from the Guanzi, a compilation of writings by Guan Zhong (a Chinese statesman, militarist, and philosopher in about 716–645 BC), tell a similar story: "A wealthy nation attracts people from afar." Not only was there a booming labor market in the early days, but the free flow of labor was the same as today's. But in Europe the land belonged to the feudal nobility, and the serfs were bonded to their master's land and could not move freely unless they became freeholders. Only a few of them could aspire to that.

China also boasted active commodity markets. A speculative futures market operated in the Two Periods, and the speculation was similar in nature to that of today. A famous example is the story of Fan Li. In the fight between the states of Wu and Yue some 2,500 years ago, Fan Li was an advisor to Gou Jian, the king of Yue. After Yue defeated Wu with his help, Fan Li left office for business, very soon accumulating great wealth. And then for the sake of a harmonious society, he distributed all his wealth to the poor, not just once, but three times.

Fan Li is also known as Tao Zhu Gong. His biography is recorded in *Biographies of Merchants* in the *Historical Records*, the masterpiece of historian Sima Qian (c.145–87 BC). He collected a large fortune through speculation in a very short time, and he was a true master of the game. He espoused three principles: First, if you know the good is in surplus or shortage in the market, you can tell whether the price is high or low. Second, when the price rises, at some point it will drop, and vice versa. Third, when the price is low, one should hoard the goods, like treasure, but when it is high, one should get rid of the goods, like trash.

Fan Li understood that prices are determined by the law of supply and demand – and how the price mechanism regulates supply and demand. The producer of a commodity usually determines how much he will produce based on its price. When the price is high, the producer will produce more, increasing the supply. If demand remains unchanged, the price will at some point fall. The falling price reduces the incentive for production. So the supply will drop. If the demand remains unchanged, there will then be a shortage of supply, resulting in a price rise.

In the real world many people make the opposite move. When the price is high, they keep the goods like treasure and begrudge selling them. And when it is low, they won't buy the goods because they regard them as unworthy of investment. Many people speculating in the stock market today have a similar mind-set. They buy high and sell low, and always suffer great losses.

The most difficult part in speculation is to determine whether the price is high or low. Take the Nasdaq index, which rose from 1,000 in the early 1990s to 2,000 in 1998, and to 3,000 in 1999 and 4,000 in 2000. In March 2001 it hit 5,300. At that point, many people still kept buying, judging that prices were relatively cheap: they believed the index could reach 10,000. It turned out that 5,300 was the peak; it slumped to a little more than 3,000 in 2002. Many people thought the index had hit the bottom, and began to buy. But the bottom eventually reached 1,200. Indeed, a tough call!

More important than the price of goods is the trend in prices. As Fan Li put it, "When the price rises, at some point it will ultimately drop, and vice versa." When producers make decisions about production and investment based on market prices, if the price is high, they will produce a large quantity. But when the supply is increased to a certain point and demand does not increase anymore, the price will drop, which will lead to great losses for many producers. So, many of them will stop investing and producing those goods; supply will decline gradually. If the demand keeps going up, then at some point a shortage of supply will push up the price once again. For all this to happen, a flexible market system is needed, where the market price gives a true picture of supply–demand interactions.

The story of Fan Li tells us that as early as the Two Periods, China already had a very dynamic market economy. For its transition from a planned to a market economy in modern times, China looked to the West, oblivious of the fact that more than 2,000 years before, it already had fairly mature markets for land, labor, and commodities.

Flourishing towns

Until the sixteenth century China was the wealthiest, most advanced, and most urban country in the world. Towns in China were much more prosperous than those in the West. But as the saying goes, "Prosperity is as fleeting as a wisp of smoke."

We can glimpse that affluence from some rare art works handed down from earlier times. The painting *Riverside Scene at Qingming Festival*, by Zhang Zeduan during the Northern Song Dynasty (AD 960–1127), vividly depicts, in meticulous detail, the bustling capital city Bian Liang (Kaifeng in Henan province), then the world's largest metropolis. The artistic value of the painting has long been recognized, but the historical, social, cultural, and natural information in it is even more valuable. Five meters wide, the painting portrays more than 500 people engaging in different activities in a cityscape replete with carriages and vessels amid towers and bridges.

The poet Liu Yong also depicted life in Lin'an (Hangzhou in Zhejiang province), the capital city of the Southern Song dynasty, in one of his masterpieces, "Watching the Tidal Bore." Life as depicted in the poem would be fascinating even today.

> Scenic splendor to the southeast of River Blue
> And capital of ancient Kingdom Wu,
> Qiantang's as flourishing as e'er.
> Smoke-like willows form a wind-proof screen,
> Adorned with painted bridges and curtains green,
> A hundred thousand houses stand here and there.
> Upon the banks along the sand,
> Cloud-crowned trees stand.
> Great waves roll up like snow banks white,
> The river extends till it's lost to sight.
> Jewels and pearls at the Fair on display,
> Satins and silks in splendid array,
> People vie in magnificence
> And opulence.
> Lake on lake reflects peak on peak which towers,
> Late autumn fragrant with osmanthus flowers,
> Lotus in full bloom for miles and miles.
> Northwestern pipes play with sunlight,
> Water chestnut songs are sung by starlight,
> Old fishermen and maidens young all beam with smiles.
> With flags before and guards behind you come,
> Drunken, you may listen to flute and drum,
> Chanting praises loud
> Of the land 'neath the cloud.
> You may picture the fair scene another day
> And boast to the Court where you're in proud array.[4]

From the poem we can tell that Lin'an was a green city with many rivers. Over the rivers were bridges with carved pictures. Every house in the city was beautifully decorated, and even their curtains were delicate. The poem may not give us an exact number for the number of households, but a rough estimate is that the population of Lin'an was more than 1 million.

The reasons for the estimate are as follows: there was no family planning policy, and many households had more than one wife under the same roof. So 100,000 households could translate into 1 million people. The market was thriving; treasures were put on display in every household; wealth was always flaunted. From the line "Water chestnut songs are sung by starlight," we can see that the residents took pleasure in a colorful night-life. Although not everyone could enjoy the life described in the lines, "Drunken, you may listen to flute and drum, / Chanting praises loud / Of the land 'neath the cloud," they tell us how luxurious entertainment could be back then.

One might suspect that Liu Yong exaggerated for artistic flavor. So perhaps the descriptions by Europeans traveling to China are more objective. The Italian Marco Polo visited China in the Yuan dynasty (AD 1271–1368), engaging in trade in the city of Yangzhou and later serving as a local official. When he returned to Italy, he wrote *The Travels of Marco Polo*, mentioning the city of Suzhou: "Suchou is so large that it measures about 40 miles in circumference. It has so many inhabitants that one could not reckon their number." He also believed that Hangzhou was "without doubt the finest and most splendid city in the world … anyone seeing such a multitude would believe it a stark impossibility that food could be found to fill so many mouths."[5]

China's sudden fall

Before the eighteenth century China had eight cities with a population over 1 million. In the thirteenth and fourteenth centuries, not just Marco Polo but all his fellow Europeans regarded China as very affluent. The way they saw China was similar to the way Chinese view Europeans today. Adam Smith described China in *The Wealth of Nations* as a wealthy country with an advanced economy and high productivity.[6] Carlo Cipolla, an Italian historian and UC Berkeley professor, wrote a book (1980) about European society before the Industrial Revolution. He concludes that between 1000 and 1700 the West was basically a poor and backward agrarian economy while China was a rich and advanced industrial economy.[7] Note that switching the subjects in that sentence depicts the picture today.

The leading cause of China being quickly overtaken by Europe was the Industrial Revolution in the mid-eighteenth century in the West. "When China was using iron-tipped plows, Europe was using wooden ones. But when Europe was using steel plows, China was still sticking with its iron." In other words, Europe was going through great changes in a short period while China remained unchanged, leaving China far behind.

The Industrial Revolution began in Britain and soon spread across the continent. Characterized by the invention of the steam engine and broad use of iron and steel, it started with the mechanization of the textile industry. Many people are trying to find out why it originated in Europe, and more specifically in Britain. It is true that Britain enjoyed many favorable conditions. But scholars who study China's history have found that as early as the thirteenth century China already had all the favorable conditions in its economy, technology, and industry that Britain did not have until the eighteenth century. In other words, China was on the verge of an Industrial Revolution much earlier in history. Yet in the next centuries it did not progress.

The Needham puzzle

In the middle of the nineteenth century, when the Opium War broke out, China suddenly realized it was far behind the rest of the world. The story presents an interesting puzzle, the Needham puzzle, first mentioned by Dr. Joseph Needham, who conducted meticulous research on Chinese history of science and technology.

In the early twentieth century, when still very young, Needham earned renown as a biochemist at Cambridge University. There were three Chinese students in his lab, and he loved to chat with them during breaks, always about science and technology. With Britain as the biggest and most powerful economy and the cradle of the Industrial Revolution, Needham took it for granted that all the advanced technologies must have originated in Europe, most likely in Britain.

The father of one of his female students was a professor of history of science and technology at Peking University, so she had a lot of knowledge in that area. When Needham averred that a certain technology of early days was invented on the continent, she told him that it was actually invented in China. She also told him which literature recorded it. At first, Needham didn't believe her. But after much digging, he found that she was right.

His surprise and curiosity later led him to study the history of Chinese science and technology. During World War II, as British cultural counselor in Chongqing, he collected many historical materials. After the war was over, he first worked at the United Nations Education, Scientific and Cultural Organisation and then returned to the United Kingdom to set up the Needham Library at Cambridge University, which he stocked with Chinese historical and cultural relics. Compiling a history of Chinese science and technology, he carefully chronicled the year each technology, machine, and tool was invented and which books recorded the relevant information.

He also noted the lag between China and Europe. Before the fifteenth and sixteenth centuries technology flows were one-way from East to West. In the sixteenth and seventeenth centuries some technologies began to flow from West to East. After the middle of the eighteenth century, the flow again was all one-way, from West to East.

Against this backdrop, Needham posed a puzzle. First, why had China been so far in advance of other civilizations? Second, why was China not now ahead of the rest of the world? The puzzle indicates a dramatic change in China's technological history.[8]

Many civilizations have written a brilliant chapter in human history. Egypt was the most advanced economy in the world 5,000 to 7,000 years ago. Then 3,000 years ago, it was Mesopotamia, and after that, Greece, Rome, and China. The course of most civilizations runs thus: growing from weak to strong, staying powerful for hundreds or even thousands of years, and then dying out gradually. For example, although Egypt is still the same country as in the era of the pharaohs, ancient Egyptian civilization is no longer there. The same is true of Mesopotamia. But China's civilization of thousands of years has not died out. Will it eventually repeat the history of Egypt and Mesopotamia?

The answer, related to the two questions in the Needham puzzle, will help to show whether China has a good chance of revival. To answer the questions, we should first understand why China was once so prosperous and why it later went downhill. The answer is important for China's future, because it will identify unfavorable factors in regaining the creativity of the Chinese nation.

The Needham puzzle has attracted a lot of attention. Explanations and hypotheses are still proposed. But current hypotheses can answer only one of the two questions, not both. A valid hypothesis should answer both questions if it is to be instructive for China's comeback.

Hypotheses trying (in vain) to explain the Needham puzzle

Cultural determinism. Cultural determinists believe that Confucianism, for all its stress on social harmony and the harmony between man and nature, is rather conservative. But the cultural determinism hypothesis cannot explain why China, under the same cultural influence, led the world in many ways 1,000 years ago. Cultural determinists can answer only the "lagging-behind-now" part of the Needham puzzle, not the "in-advance-then" part.

National competition. Some scholars attribute Europe's power and prosperity to its division into many small nations and the competition among them. To outperform its competitors, every state in Europe attaches great importance to science and technology. By contrast, China is one big united country, so competition is not necessary. Due to such long-standing competitive deficiencies, technological innovation was dormant in China. The hypothesis sounds plausible, but again, it cannot explain China's leading position more than 1,000 years ago, when China was also one big united country.

Patent protection. Another hypothesis is that patent protection fostered the Industrial Revolution in Europe. As early as the fifteenth century Britain started to protect patents. This is plausible perhaps, but it fails to account for China's glorious history.

Because patent applications required the disclosure of technical information, others could have the technology with slight adaptation and without violating a patent. So patent protection then was rather inefficient because of the high cost of collecting information and enforcement. And for reasons of confidentiality, many inventors did not apply for patents – which is still the case today. So, even if the mechanism is critical today, we cannot conclude that it was a determining factor for the Industrial Revolution.

High-level equilibrium trap. The high-level equilibrium trap, widely accepted in academic circles, especially in the West, holds that insufficient demand for new technology is the major reason for China's sluggish progress. The Chinese obsession with male heirs to extend the family lineage resulted in a rapid expansion of population. Since the total land area remained almost the same, the man-to-land ratio fell. Mark Elvin[9] and other scholars believe that the lower man-to-land ratio reduced demand for technology through two main mechanisms. First, it reduced the agricultural surplus, so new machinery and equipment became unaffordable. Second, it lowered labor costs. With labor so cheap, people were not interested in replacing labor with machines.

Starting from the premise that there were no technological changes to conclude that there were no technological changes is a typical case of circular reasoning. In addition, the demand for labor-saving technology depends not only on the cost of labor but also on the cost of technology. If technology to replace labor develops fast enough, the declining rate of the cost of new technology can overtake that of the cost of labor held down by population growth. In other words, although labor costs fall, machinery is even more cost-effective, so labor would not replace it.

A new theory to explain the Needham puzzle

Finding the inadequacies of existing hypotheses is only the first step. The next is to develop a new theory that can truly explain the same phenomenon. Most scholars recognize that it was not until the Industrial Revolution that China fell behind the West. So, what is the Industrial Revolution? A traditional definition is: "The invention and use of the steam engine, the mechanization of the textile industry, and the mass production and use of iron and steel." But that simple description fails to capture its nature.

Since the mid-eighteenth century, technological innovation in the West has not only been fast, it has been accelerating. That is why, in such a short span, the gap between China and the West became so wide. In fact, the acceleration of technological innovation is the most important feature of the Industrial Revolution. If it is only about textiles, iron and steel, and the steam engine, then it should be noted that as early as the thirteenth century, China's textile industry was already pretty advanced, as recorded by Sung Ying-hsing in 1637 in *T'ien-kung k'ai-wu* [*A Volume on the Creations of Nature and Man*]. But after the mid-eighteenth century, the United Kingdom and Europe developed many more new technologies and new industries, such as the chemical, automobile, aerospace, and information technology industries.

To answer why the Industrial Revolution did not take place in China, we first have to understand why technological change accelerated in Europe.

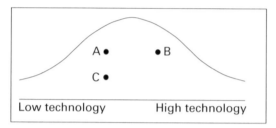

Figure 2.1 The technology distribution
curve

Three concepts

The technology distribution curve

First, look at the definition of technology and invention. Some research equates technology with machinery and equipment, but most economists see it as knowledge of how to allocate the factors of production. The difference between high-level and low-level technology is reflected in the relations between inputs and outputs. Suppose that productive inputs of a certain commodity include capital, labor, and land. For inputs of the same value, factors of production can be allocated in various ways. So, with productive inputs of equal value, the higher the value of output, the higher the level of technology, and vice versa.

Consider a left-to-right x-axis describing the state of technology (see Figure 2.1). The left side signifies lower technology, and the right higher. Above the x-axis are some points, each corresponding to a certain level of output value with the same unit value of inputs. Point A corresponds to an output value achieved by a certain way to allocate capital, labor, and land. Similarly, Points B and C also correspond to a unit cost with certain output values. In Figure 2.1, Point C has the same output value as Point A, whereas Point B has a higher output value than Point A and Point C. If we figure out all the possible allocation methods and show them on the graph, we may use distribution to show the collection of all the possible points, each standing for an allocation method. The boundary line

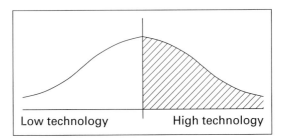

Figure 2.2 The invention probability curve

is the "technology distribution curve." Each point within the curve corresponds to a possible allocation; those beyond the curve signify an impossible allocation.

The invention probability curve

Invention can be defined as a possible allocation method, whose cost is the same as with the existing method but with higher output. Suppose that point A signifies the current technology. If we find a method of allocation with the same cost but less output value, then the method does not qualify as an "invention." If A is the reference point, then points like B qualify. Thus we can define an "invention probability curve." For a given technology distribution curve, every point to the right of the existing technology is a possible invention. For example, if A signifies the current technology, every point to its right and within the curve corresponds to a possible invention. The "invention probability curve" is the collection of all the points for possible invention, as shown in Figure 2.2.

The trial and error invention model

The invention probability curve can help us understand the invention model. In both premodern and modern times the invention model can also be called "trial and error." In premodern times suppose a peasant, due to laziness or other reasons, accidentally deviated from routines of his daily work, but it turned out his output was higher. The next year, the peasant might decide to do it again the "wrong" way. If the output was still higher, we could say that the peasant "invented a new technology." At first, he might not be willing to share his discovery, but others would be wondering why his output was always higher and would thus try every means to discover his secret. Sooner or later, the technology would spread. Modern times are just the same.

For example, Professor Paul Chu, president of China University of Science and Technology, is famous for his research on superconductivity. He has produced a variety of high-temperature superconductors in the lab. Just like the peasant in the old days, he also resorted to trial and error, trying all the possible combinations of materials to find the ones with superconductivity.

There are two types of trial and error. In premodern times it was usually experience-based. In those days it was peasants and craftsmen rather than intellectuals who engaged in production. As Mencius said, "The gentleman should avoid the kitchen." Intellectuals in those days would not even do the cooking, let alone plow the land. In modern times, however, trial and error is more experiment-based, with controlled experiments guided by science. Although the two share the same nature, their patterns are quite different. Trial and error is all about probability, just like the lottery. In this sense, the bigger the area to the right of the technology probability curve, the greater the probability of "winning."

Several factors can move the technology distribution curve to the right. One is individual talent. For example, Newton established the law of gravity after he was (supposedly) hit by a falling apple. Someone else would have only complained or been grateful for the free fruit. A second factor is the material. There are some preconditions for production. For example, to plow, a rake is a must. The iron rake has the same shape and function as the wooden rake; but the change in material still qualifies as technological progress, because the iron rake increases productivity.

A third factor is knowledge. Before the discipline of modern chemistry, many people believed that there was a magic way to turn stone into gold, yet no matter how hard they tried, stone remained stone. Now modern science tells us that we can extract gold only from stone with gold in it. With that knowledge, no one would ever now attempt to extract gold from stone without gold. So, with trial and error, knowledge-based experiments will enjoy a much higher probability of extracting gold.

A population may have 1% geniuses, 1% idiots, and 98% average persons. So, the bigger the population, the more geniuses there will be (and idiots), increasing the potential advantage in technological innovation.

Three hypotheses
Based on these concepts of technology, invention, and technological innovation, three hypotheses are proposed.

Hypothesis 1: Given current technology and the technology distribution curve, the invention probability curve can be decided. For a given invention probability curve, the more the trials and errors that are carried out, the greater the probability of inventing a new technology. Trial and error is like a random lottery: every ticket has a chance of winning, each with the same probability. So, ten tickets have a greater probability of winning than just one ticket.

Hypothesis 2: Given a certain number of trials and errors and the technology distribution curve, the more advanced the current technology, the lower the probability of inventing a new technology. The reason is simple. The more advanced the existing technology, the smaller the area under the invention probability curve, signifying a lower "winning" probability. Continuing with the lottery simile: suppose there are one first prize and a hundred second prizes. For any lottery ticket, the probability of winning the second prize is 100 times higher than winning the first.

Hypothesis 3: Given current technology and a certain number of trials and errors, the more the technology distribution curve is

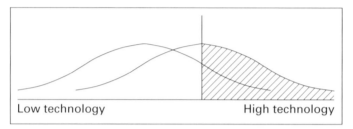

Figure 2.3 The more the technology distribution curve
moves to the right, the greater the probability of
inventing a new technology

to the right, the bigger the area under the invention probability
curve, increasing the probability of inventing a new technology (Figure 2.3). Deeper understanding of nature is essential to
human progress. For instance, alchemy was a craze in the Middle
Ages in Europe, but centuries passed and no one ever actually
extracted gold from simple stone. Today, guided by science, we
may conduct experiments intentionally and selectively, and the
chances for success become much greater than before. Similarly,
with different basic materials for invention, the invention probability will differ as well. For example, before steel was discovered,
the invention of the steel rake was not possible. With the discovery of steel, not only did the invention of the steel rake become
possible, but other steel tools were invented one after another.
With the technology distribution curve moving to the right, the
probability for invention is therefore increased.

Based on these three hypotheses, let's try to answer the Needham
puzzle.

Why China was so advanced in premodern times: invention based on experience

China has always been populous. Thanks to favorable natural conditions, the productivity of its arable land was always higher than
that of Europe. Due to lower costs of living, China's population

grew rapidly. By contrast, Europe, also one of the cradles of human civilization, did not have good conditions for high-yielding crops. Its carrying capacity of land was lower, so its population was much smaller than China's throughout history.

In premodern times technological innovation mainly relied on experience-based trial and error by craftsmen and peasants. The bigger the population, the larger the number of craftsmen and peasants, and therefore the greater chance for inventions in those days. Experience was a big part of technology, passed down from generation to generation. Hence the saying, "Those who will not defer to the elderly will suffer dearly." But occasionally there were cases of innovation in the overall climate of respect for tradition. An accidental trial found a way to improve productivity, and later the technology was popularized.

So, East or West, in premodern times, when invention was based mainly on experience, a big population conferred a considerable advantage, because there would be more trial and error, increasing the probability of invention. China is not an isolated case. Most ancient civilizations – ancient Egypt along the Nile valley, ancient Babylon in the Mesopotamian valley, and ancient India along the valley of the Indus River, invariably densely populated – had a large labor force. Those abundant human resources laid a solid foundation for technological progress for them.

Why technological change accelerated in the eighth to twelfth century in China

The major reason for the acceleration of technological innovation in China from the eighth to the twelfth century was the invasion by northern ethnic minorities, driving legions of people and the economic center southward. Like the northern part of the country, the south enjoys rainy seasons and a lot of sunshine between March and November, except that the south has even more rain. So, the north has wheat, sorghum, and grains as the staple crops, while the south has paddy rice. With the population moving southward and high-yielding rice becoming the staple crop, productivity rose.

A precondition for improving productivity is having appropriate tools. The farm tool used in the north was the rake, unfit for conditions in the south. The rake had to be adapted into the hoe, a technological change. Similarly, the major vehicle in the north was the carriage, in the south the boat. So with the migration, boat-related technologies sprang up. Where productivity is higher, there is a better chance of technological change. To sum up, favorable natural conditions in the south – like sunshine, water, and soil – made it possible to improve productivity. Therefore the technology distribution curve moved to the right, and new technologies mushroomed.

But the movement of the curve caused by massive migration could not go on for ever. After a period of acceleration, the pace of invention will slow, as described in hypothesis 2: with higher productivity and technology, the area on the right side of the given technology distribution curve gets smaller. When it reaches a certain point, even with increasing population and more trial and error, the pace of invention will eventually decelerate. Of course, if the population decreases, the pace will also decelerate, because a smaller population means fewer trials and errors. After the twelfth century China's population sometimes increased, sometimes decreased, but technological innovation never picked up again.

Why China lagged behind Europe in modern times: invention based on experiment

In premodern times, due to its smaller population, Europe was behind China in terms of technological innovation. The Europeans always admired China's sophisticated products and cutting-edge technologies brought to them via the Silk Road and sea routes. Then came the Industrial Revolution in the eighteenth century – the mechanization of textiles, the invention of the steam engine, and the production of iron and steel. But the most important feature was the acceleration of technological innovation, possibly because trial and error shifted from being experience-based to being experiment-based.

In premodern times experience was the byproduct of production. New technology was invented by the accidental trials and errors of peasants. After the eighteenth century, however, trials and errors were based mainly on intentional experiments. The number of experiments by a scientist in a lab could equal the trials of thousands of craftsmen and peasants in their lifetime. So, population was no longer a significant factor. For even with a very small population, intensive experiments could increase the probability of invention.

When experiments replaced experience as the basis for invention around the time of the Industrial Revolution, the number of trials and errors in Europe increased, and the pace of invention picked up accordingly. So Europe outpaced China and other places by a large margin. But according to hypothesis 2, when the pace of invention is accelerated to a certain point, due to a higher level of technology, the probability of success for invention will decline. This resulted in a bottleneck in technological innovation.

To release the bottleneck, Europeans increased their inputs in basic science, increasing their knowledge of nature and shifting the technology distribution curve to the right, further expanding the scope for technological innovation. This made it possible to maintain an ever-accelerating speed of technological innovation.

In the eighteenth century the role of science in technological progress was still disputable. For example, one of the disputed cases is the invention of the steam engine by Watt, a lab assistant rather than a scientist. Not until the nineteenth century was the importance of science established and accepted. Indeed, science provides enormous scope for technological innovation by enhancing people's knowledge about nature.

After the nineteenth century, whenever innovation bottlenecks occurred, the West overcame them by increasing inputs in basic science, constantly shifting the invention probability curve to the right and creating new scope for invention. The precondition for all this was the Scientific Revolution in the West in the fifteenth and sixteenth centuries. To find out why the Industrial Revolution did not occur in China, the key is to account for why the Scientific Revolution failed to materialize.

Why the Scientific Revolution did not occur in China: bureaucracy

We first have to understand the differences between primitive science and modern science. The definition of science is very simple: systematic knowledge about the world. Scientific discovery is similar to technological invention. The Scientific Revolution is not about the content, because just like modern science, primitive science is also systematic knowledge explaining natural phenomena.

Aristotle, the Greek philosopher and scientist, assumed all substances to be compounds of four basic elements: earth, water, air, and fire. Ancient China had "Five Elements": metal, wood, water, fire, and soil. In ancient times there was a "theory" explaining the origin of the mouse: it always emerged from a case containing cloth under a bed – a hypothesis at best. However ridiculous the hypothesis may sound, it seems to be supported by empirical evidence. Now we understand that mice, like human beings, also have parents. But even the early theory of the "origin of the mouse" was based on curiosity, observation, and induction.

Primitive science is a far cry from modern science, but both are about systematic knowledge of the world. Their major differences are the methods of advancing knowledge. Primitive science developed as the result of geniuses' casual observations of nature, whereas modern science uses mathematical models to formalize its hypotheses about nature and uses controlled or reproducible experiments to test them.

The advances in modern methodology are mainly manifest in accurate mathematical models and easier dissemination and accumulation of valid hypotheses. For example, the theory of "Yinyang" and "Wuxing" (translated as Five Movements or Five Elements) in ancient China is rather obscure, because what those five movements or elements actually refer to is extremely hard to grasp. According to the theory, we may describe someone as "having a big fire," but actually we see no smoke coming out of his or her body, so where is the "fire?" Plus, the theory has so many explanations, its dissemination meets obstacles.

Confucius once said that if, at age fifty, one can understand the *I Ching* (also known as *Classic of Changes*), one will understand one's fate decreed by Heaven. But the footnotes to the *I Ching* are so varied that it is hard to judge which ones rule. For another example, a line in *Tao Te Ching* (also known as *The Classic of the Virtue of the Tao*) reads: "*xuan* and *xuan* again is the door to all wonders." One explanation of the word "*xuan*" is "something abstruse and mysterious." Obviously such an explanation does not help.

But with the help of mathematical forms, the concepts and theories can be understood more clearly and easily, because mathematical symbols are unequivocal and their meanings will not change. In addition, it would be rather difficult to meet the three criteria for translation of literature put forward by Yan Fu, a famous translator and president of Peking University in the early twentieth century: faithfulness, expressiveness, and elegance. To be faithful alone, the least challenging of the three, has proved a tough job indeed. For starters, the translator could misunderstand the source text. To truly comprehend a language requires thorough understanding of the culture, for the language of any nation is infused in and with its culture. Even in the same language system, the same word can have different meanings over time. So, for disseminating knowledge, mathematical language can do a better job than natural languages.

The revolution in methodology is indeed of consequence. Both the Industrial Revolution and Scientific Revolution involved a methodological revolution. The Scientific Revolution contributed to the Industrial Revolution in two key ways: it introduced a revolution in methodology – controlled experiment replaced experience as the basis of trial and error – and it facilitated the rightward shift of the technology distribution curve.

Methodology itself is also a technology. Those who desire to grasp the special technology of scientific discoveries must be very curious about nature. In the West the Scientific Revolution was a combination of mathematics and controlled experiment. At first, those who were curious about nature occasionally combined the two, and they found that with mathematical models, laws could be described more precisely, and that it was easier to disseminate knowledge. What's more, controlled experiments could quickly separate acceptable hypotheses from the wrong and unacceptable.

Bureaucratic not mercantilist values

The number of people with great curiosity conforms to a normal distribution of the population; it may correspond to a tiny one-hundredth or one-thousandth on the right side of the distribution. In different societies the percentage is the same. As a populous country, China certainly has a large number of people who are curious about nature. It is not true that the Chinese were not good at math; nor is it true that controlled experiments were not their cup of tea. Then why did so many geniuses with intense curiosity in China fail to find that a combination of mathematical models and controlled experiments could satisfy their curiosity?

According to Needham, China had a bureaucratic system whereas Europe had a feudal aristocratic system, the latter more favorable to the cultivation of mercantilist values. With the collapse of the feudal system in Europe, capitalism and modern science emerged.

Needham was not a great economist or historian. He was good at enumerating phenomena, but logical consistency was not his strong point. According to him, the reason that Chinese feudal society was not friendly to mercantilism was that in the Confucian hierarchy, merchants ranked at the bottom below scholars (or nobles), peasants, and craftsmen. And according to official documents of all dynasties, merchants were not allowed to be part of the recommendation system (*Ju Xiao Lian* in Mandarin) or the civil service examination system (*Ke Ju*), so they could never be admitted into officialdom.

In reality, however, ever since the Tang Dynasty, merchants were allowed to take the civil service examinations. Some could even buy a position. As early as the Spring and Autumn Period and the Warring States Period traditional commerce thrived in China. Against that background, Fan Li was capable of piling up a huge fortune three times over. Even in the Han Dynasty, when Emperor Wu (156–87 BC) accepted Dong Zhongshu's proposal that "Confucianism alone should receive imperial sponsorship while all the other philosophies should be rejected," the merchant class was not stifled completely. Otherwise, it would be impossible to see such advanced commerce and capital markets in the Ming Dynasty. Many researchers hold that the Ming Dynasty already saw budding capitalism. Since it was not until after the fifteenth century that feudalism in Europe collapsed, it is fair to say that at least in the fourteenth and fifteenth centuries, "capitalism" in China was more advanced than its counterpart in Europe.

Patent protection?

Some believe that the Industrial Revolution originated in Britain because of its protection for inventions and patents. But since the Scientific Revolution preceded and determined the Industrial Revolution, we should focus on the actual conditions that prevailed when the Scientific Revolution took place rather than on what is important from today's perspective. The mechanism that China did not enjoy 400 years ago did not necessarily exist in Europe at the same time. Although property rights are a critical issue today, back in the Scientific Revolution in the fifteenth century, there was no mature mechanism for protecting property rights. Research at that time was undertaken more out of curiosity than from a commercial motive, and research results were basically public knowledge. Therefore, the commercial motive was not the reason for the absence of the Scientific Revolution.

Competition?

Another popular view in the West deems that competition has made all the difference. China has been a large and united country throughout its history, so competition among nations was not encouraged. Europe, by contrast, comprised many small nations, a breeding ground for competition. Competition leads to pressure, which turns into a driving force for technological progress. That is exactly why technology has progressed faster in the West today. Take the rivalry between the United States and the former Soviet Union. Due to the cut-throat competition between the two superpowers, science and technology, especially in space and military industries, received huge inputs and achieved impressive results. Even so, a more thorough analysis is required to test this competition hypothesis.

First, although China has been a united nation, China's control over ideology was not necessarily greater than Europe's. Although divided into many nations, Europe was united by religion, a major factor that needed to be taken into account in the attempt to understand nature. Back then, if anyone dared to propose something that ran against orthodox ideas, they could face death as heretics. China saw very little religious persecution except for the episode of "burning books and burying scholars alive" orchestrated by Emperor Qin Shihuang, the first emperor of a united China

(246–210 BC). But for exploring nature, the government was indifferent to any ideas. Even when someone held different views from the mainstream, they would not risk being burned at the stake. So, the united political atmosphere was not, at least in terms of ideology, a hindrance to exploring the nature of the world.

Second, competition between nations does not necessarily determine scientific progress. Even in modern times, without progress in the basic sciences, the chance of overcoming technological bottlenecks is slim. Understandably, 300 years ago, there was even less enthusiasm for investing in basic sciences for the sake of overcoming technological bottlenecks and making a nation more prosperous.

Third, scientific research consumes huge resources, so a large country obviously can do this better. In the Song Dynasty the government funded a water-driven clock. But state-funded projects were not common. Sometimes, wealthy families and royal or noble families in China also funded research, but not as fervently as their European counterparts.

Therefore, although the national competition hypothesis is plausible in modern times, it was not so 500 years ago. I would like to offer a new hypothesis.

Lacking people good at math and experiments

Since curiosity is an innate quality, China, as a populous country, has many curious people. The reason the Scientific Revolution did not take place in China was not because it lacked people with curiosity but because it lacked those who were good at math and experiments. Those abilities are acquired rather than innate. People with high levels of curiosity are often innately talented. However, in premodern times curious or gifted people in China, incentivized by the national civil service examination, simply did not have much incentive for learning math and controlled experiments. Without acquired human capital in those abilities, China could not have a Scientific

Revolution. Curious people in Europe had more incentive to acquire abilities in math and experiments because it had a different political system and official selection system. In Europe the titles of nobles were hereditary. So, even with a smaller number of curious people, Europe had more individuals who were both curious and good at math and controlled experiment. That is the major reason why the Scientific Revolution took place in Europe instead of China.

Before the Qin Dynasty (221–206 BC) feudal society in China was similar to Europe's. But in the Qin Dynasty the nobility system was scrapped, with a system of prefectures and counties established instead. According to the new system, the central government directly dispatched local officials at all levels. The Qin system was copied by the following dynasties. In the Sui Dynasty a civil service examination system was introduced. Later in the Song Dynasty the Four Books and Five Classics of Confucianism were designated as the textbooks for the selection exam.

Back then there was a saying, "Studying classics is superior to all the other trades." The reality behind the saying is that securing an official position produced the highest returns. Hence another saying, "If one studies hard enough, wealth, high-paying jobs, and beautiful women will all come your way." Another plus of being a civil servant was the great honor it was supposed to bring to one's whole family. Under such circumstances, talented persons naturally showed abundant passion for the exams, which promised handsome returns.

A talented person is not necessarily curious, but people who are curious, observant, and good at formulating scientific theories from their observations must be very talented. Because the incentive mechanism has a great influence on people's behavior, talented people were naturally drawn to civil service examinations, which promised the highest returns. Even if people were passionate about scientific research, they would not find much time for it.

The Four Books and Five Classics

There are more than 400,000 words in the Four Books and Five Classics, the designated textbooks for the civil service exam. Suppose one can memorize 200 words a day (and suppose those words are not forgotten afterwards), to learn all the books by heart would take more than six years. On top of that, candidates needed to read history books and learn to write poems and "eight-part essays." Altogether, it would probably take ten years to prepare for the exam, hence the phrase "a decade of sweat" to describe how tough it was to be ready to sit it. Back then, study was much more strenuous than today.

For those lucky enough to pass the exam and secure a position, to get promoted, they had to discipline themselves in accordance with the bureaucratic assessment standards – the values and theoretical systems advocated by the Four Books and Five Classics.

There is another puzzle in Chinese history: when information collection and supervision were rather primitive, how did the emperor control officials across the vast territory and maintain national unity? It had a lot to do with the nation's bureaucratic system established in the Qin Dynasty. Before the Qin, like their European counterparts, Chinese rulers did not have much control over local officials, as witnessed by the rivalry between the kingdoms in the Spring and Autumn Period and Warring States Period. But because the civil service examination system, introduced in the Qin Dynasty, provided opportunities for the smart and ambitious to be admitted to the bureaucratic system, they no longer had to resort to violent means to be part of the ruling class. That practice was carried on by dynasties following the Qin for the sake of national unity.

Confucian values

The Chinese system differed from the European, which was based on hereditary principles rather than the bureaucratic norms of the civil service system. Starting in the Song Dynasty the Confucian philosophy highlighting loyalty to and reverence for the emperor and one's father has been deeply implanted in the candidates for civil service examinations. They have long been exposed to that philosophy when preparing for the exams through the designated Four Books and Five Classics. One would be wracked with guilt if one was not loyal to the emperor.

Meanwhile all society placed a high moral value on Confucian philosophy. A highly informative book about the political and social systems of ancient China is 1587, *A Year of No Significance: The Ming Dynasty in Decline*, by Ray Huang.[10] The book tells the interesting story of Zhang Juzheng, the premier of Emperor Shenzong. Zhang introduced a government reform, but at a very critical moment, his mother died. According to Confucian values, he had to resign and mourn for his mother for three years. If he did so, the reform would very likely be aborted; he would have hated to see that happen, and Emperor Shenzong was also reluctant to let him go. In the end he was impeached for not resigning. The authority of the emperor came from officials' deference to Confucian values. If the premier, the head of all officials, chose not to uphold those values, it would have sent the message that disloyalty to the emperor was acceptable, threatening the very basis of the nation. So, in traditional society the cost of ruling the country was very low, and that is exactly why China has remained a large unified country for so long.

When the civil service examination was introduced, mathematics was one of the subjects. But the emperor soon decided that math was of little help to his rule and removed the subject from the curriculum. An essential work in China's history of science and technology is *Exploitation of the Works of Nature*, published in 1637 by Song Yingxing in the Ming Dynasty. In the preface Song wrote that this book was not for those who were smart and ambitious, because it had nothing to do with the civil service examination.

Studying the Four Books and Five Classics was time-consuming; one could hardly squeeze in time for mathematics and controlled experiments. Even if a handful of people were smart enough to juggle the exam preparation with scientific observation, without mathematic tools, the Scientific Revolution was not likely to take place. Wang Yangming (1472–1529), the greatest Ming Dynasty philosopher, politician, and general, wrote a poem, which reads: "The mountain is close whereas the moon is far, it seems that the mountain is larger by far. But if one's eyes were sky-large, one would find that the moon is far larger." Wang's observation certainly conforms to modern science, but he did not develop a scientific system because he lacked appropriate mathematical tools.

From experience to experiment

The prosperity of ancient China has everything to do with the civil service system. But when the basis for technological innovation shifted from experience to experiment, the system lost its superiority and hindered scientific and technological progress.

Institutions superior under certain technological and physical conditions can turn out to hinder social progress under other conditions – what we call "institutional traps" in economics. For example, when the means of collecting information were limited and the cost of supervision was rather high, the system of civil service examinations was superior, because it made it possible for the ambitious to be admitted to the civil service through strenuous efforts. The system was relatively fair and objective thanks to its objective assessment criteria. It also helped to maintain the vitality of officialdom because it made room for people with great ability. If those people did not revolt, the state would be stable, enjoying political and ideological unification.

Max Weber noticed that capitalism sprouted in China as early as the Ming Dynasty, and asked why it failed to thrive in China.[11] Weber's question is related to the Needham puzzle. After careful analysis, we shall find that the key issue again is the absence of the Scientific Revolution, without which the Industrial Revolution could not take place. Between the eighth and twelfth centuries, technological innovation progressed rapidly in China, but after the twelfth century, it stagnated. Under such circumstances, capital could not be deepened, and capitalism could not fully develop. Capitalism is about capital deepening and a deepening relationship between capital and wage labor.[12] In premodern China the traditional technology made it impossible to hire a large labor force for mechanized mass production, so capitalism could not take shape. For this reason, the answer to Weber's question is again the absence of the Industrial Revolution in China. Without that revolution, technology would not progress constantly, nor would capital be deepened continually. That is why capitalism, though sprouting in China, failed to develop fully.[13]

References

Cipolla, Carlo M. 1980. *Before the Industrial Revolution: European Society and Economy, 1000–1700*, 2nd edn. New York: Norton.

Elvin, Mark. 1973. *The Pattern of the Chinese Past*. Stanford, CA: Stanford University Press.

Huang, Ray. 1981. *1587, A Year of No Significance: The Ming Dynasty in Decline*. New Haven, CT: Yale University Press.

Lin, Justin Y. 1995. "The Needham Puzzle: Why the Industrial Revolution Did Not Originate in China." *Economic Development and Cultural Change* 41: 269–92.

2008. "The Needham Puzzle, Weber Question and China's Miracle: Long-Term Performance since the Sung Dynasty." *China Economic Journal* 1(1): 63–95.

Maddison, Angus. 2006. *The World Economy*. Paris: Organisation for Economic Co-operation and Development.

Needham, Joseph. 1981. *Science in Traditional China: A Comparative Perspective*. Cambridge, MA: Harvard University Press.

Perkins, Dwight H. 1969. *Agricultural Development in China, 1368–1968*. Chicago: Aldine.

Polo, Marco. 1908. *The Travels of Marco Polo*. Trans. and ed. William Marsden. Introd. John Masefield. London: J. M. Dent.

Smith, Adam. [1776] 1976. *An Inquiry into the Nature and Causes of the Wealth of Nations*. Chicago: University of Chicago Press.

Weber, Max. 1930. *The Protestant Ethic and the Spirit of Capitalism*. London: Allen & Unwin.

Weber, Max. 1997. "Confucian Politics in China and the Sprout of Capitalism in China: Cities and Industrial Associations." In *Collected Works of Max Weber: The Historical Steps of Civilizations*. Shanghai: Shanghai Sanlian Bookstore.

Xuanchong, Xu. 2007. *100 Tang and Song Ci Poems*. Beijing: China Translation and Publishing Corporation.

Notes

1. This chapter draws on Lin (1995).
2. Maddison (2006).
3. Smith ([1776] 1976).
4. Liu Yong, "Watching the Tidal Bore." This *ci* (poem) is translated by Professor Xu Xuanchong (2007).
5. Polo (1908).
6. Smith ([1776] 1976).
7. Cipolla (1980).
8. Needham (1981).
9. Elvin (1973).
10. Huang (1981).
11. Weber (1997).
12. Weber (1930).
13. Lin (2008).

Source: Maddison (2006)

THREE

The great humiliation and the Socialist Revolution

China was regarded as a great power until the end of the seventeenth century. But by the mid-nineteenth century it was a backward agrarian country. Europe caught up with China, not because of higher productivity but because of the discovery of the New World, which brought piles of gold and silver to Europe. The new wealth dramatically enhanced living standards there. When the Industrial Revolution started in the eighteenth century, technological innovation accelerated in Europe, soon leaving China behind, and the gap continued to widen.

Beginning a history of humiliation

China's per capita income in 1820 was 523 international monetary units, much less than the 1,287 for the United States and 1,756 (then highest) for the United Kingdom.[1] In 1950 China's per capita income was 614, a small fraction of the 9,573 (then highest) for the United States and 6,847 for the United Kingdom. So China's per capita income had fallen to one-fifteenth of that of the United States and one-tenth of the United Kingdom.

China's position in international politics also plummeted. Before the mid-Qing Dynasty (1644–1911) China was still the most powerful country in the world and the suzerain of its neighboring countries, which paid it tribute. When Great Britain first dispatched its envoys to China, China gave it a pejorative name suggesting that it was a country of barbarians with no respect for protocols. But less than a century after the Industrial Revolution, China was soundly defeated by Britain in the Opium War of 1840. After that it was successively defeated by France, Japan, and the Eight-Power Allied Forces, inflicting unspeakable injury and insult.

Successive defeats not only cost China its neighboring tributary countries (its protectorate Korea was reduced to a colony of Japan), but also demoted China to a semi-colony. It was forced to sign unequal treaties with more than twenty countries, grant concessions in many cities, and cede territory to Japan, Russia, and the United Kingdom. In no time the sovereignty of the former superpower had been violated in every possible humiliating manner.

Some believe that rampant corruption of the Qing Dynasty led to the sudden downfall of the Celestial Empire. But that conflicts with the empirical evidence: not a single emperor in the Qing Dynasty was so mindless or corrupt as to leave his people in dire poverty. True, there were anti-government sentiments among some Han people. But the hostility was born of nationalism not of complaints against the emperor. The bureaucracy may have been corrupt, but crooked officials were common in other dynasties as well. So it is not fair to blame the Qing Dynasty entirely for China's gradual weakening.

While Europe was accelerating its technological innovation and economic development and busily engaging in scientific experiment, China was stuck with its old technologies and productivity because the civil service examination system and the traditional education system stifled the Scientific Revolution and later the

Industrial Revolution. So the gap between China and Europe grew wider, culminating in the cruelest manner, with China's consecutive bitter defeats on the battlefield.

Chinese intellectuals, nurtured in Confucianism, had a strong sense of responsibility. They regarded the well-being of their fellow countrymen as their mission. And faced with the seismic shifts for the nation, they wanted to rejuvenate it. But they could not help feeling an acute sense of frustration seeing their nation humiliated and deteriorating. Their motherland, with its history and culture still fresh in memory, was crushed by "the barbarian countries" in less than a century. Therefore national rejuvenation became an urgent task for the political and cultural elites.

To understand their sentiments is the foundation to comprehending the modern politics, economics, and history of China. China, as an ancient civilization, collided with an emergent civilization; the war between the two was the culmination of that collision. As Huntington mentioned in his book *The Clash of Civilizations*, understanding and responding to foreign powers requires delving into the meaning of culture and civilization.[2]

The early search of Chinese intellectuals for national salvation and the Westernization Movement

The definition of culture and civilization varies from scholar to scholar. According to Marx the cultural system consists of the base and the superstructure, with the former determining the latter. But when it comes to the study of Chinese modern history, I am more inclined to the definition from Bronislaw Malinowski, teacher of Fei Xiaotong, a famous Chinese sociologist. According to Malinowski culture comprises three integral components. The first is inherited artifacts and technical processes, including all visible material objects, such as swords, guns, carriages, chopsticks, knives, and forks, and their production technologies. The second is social organizations – such as the banking system, education system, and political system. The third is ideas, habits, and values – that is, codes of conduct distinguishing between good and bad.

Malinowski's categorization is not in conflict with Marx's. The base in Marx's system corresponds to that of inherited artifacts and technical processes, and the superstructure corresponds to the sum of the other two components – the social organizations and codes of conduct. Malinowski believes that the three components of culture are integrated organically. When two civilizations clash, we have to understand the responses of both the masses and the intellectuals – to understand the causes of the clash.

China suffered a humiliating defeat in the Opium War of 1840, the first war that the Qing government had lost to a foreign rival. Before then, defeat was unimaginable. Naturally the thrashing led the intellectuals into serious reflection; they concluded that the loss was due to the huge difference in artifacts between China and the West. Therefore, during the reign of Emperor Tongzhi (1862–74), famous officials advocating national rejuvenation – such as Tseng Kuo-fan, Li Hongzhang, Zuo Zongtang, and Chang Chih-tung – launched the Westernization Movement (*Yang Wu Yun Dong* in Mandarin).

The slogan of the Westernization Movement was, "Chinese learning for fundamental principles and western learning for practical application." It meant that China should adhere to its old social system and ethical values based on Confucianism but also make use of western artifacts and the products of their civilization – for example, by purchasing their guns, cannons, and warships. They believed that with these artifacts, China could be strong and prosperous again. Apparently, the Celestial Empire mentality of these intellectuals remained unchanged: they still believed in the superiority of Chinese social organizations and values. Indeed, after three decades of efforts, the Westernization Movement did result in a considerable achievement. Three naval fleets were established at Weihaiwei in Shandong province and at Quanzhou and Mawei in Fujian province.

The culmination of the second clash was the Sino-Japanese War of 1894. Around that time Japan, an emerging power after the Meiji Restoration, attempted to colonize Korea, then under the suzerainty of China. Hence the conflict. Japan had also kept its doors closed to the outside world until the mid-nineteenth century, when the American navy knocked it open. That change also provoked serious reflection in Japan, which resulted in the political slogan, "Sonnō jōi," or "Revere the Emperor and Expel the Barbarians," advocating that the Tokugawa shogunate should give way to imperial rule. When Emperor Meiji was restored to power, he initiated a chain of reforms. In the end Japan established a "constitutional monarchy," like Britain, and introduced modern schools, army, banks, factories, and other social, political and economic organizations. The Meiji Restoration coincided with the Westernization Movement in China.

Before the Sino-Japanese War of 1894 the international community generally expected that China would win, because it then had the most advanced warships and weapons bought from the United Kingdom and France. Japan could not afford large tonnage warships and had to make do with the smaller ships that it produced. Plus, the guns and cannons of Japan were a far cry from those of the Middle Kingdom. An anecdote gives us some idea of the situation at that time.

Before the Sino-Japanese War of 1894 the Qing government tried a tactic proposed by Sun Tzu: "The supreme art of war is to subdue the enemy without fighting." The Chinese navy held a grand parade along the Huangpu River in Shanghai and invited foreign military attachés in China to watch, including the Japanese attaché. The hope was that by flexing its military muscle it could deter Japan. The tactic backfired. After watching the show the Japanese attaché was convinced that his country could win a war, despite China's superiority in weaponry, because he found the Chinese army disorganized and undisciplined.

The anecdote, not verified, tells us that in the Westernization Movement, China's effort was only artifact-deep and that there was no organizational reform in the fields of education, politics, economy, and so on. Without appropriate organizations, modern weaponry would not help much.

Not just artifacts and organizations but ideas and values

After the war the Qing government was forced to pay huge indemnities and cede Taiwan province to Japan, leading to another wave of social reflection. The intellectuals believed China lost to Britain in the Opium War because it lacked advanced weaponry. But it lost again to Japan, whose equipment was inferior to China's. So there must be something else. When reviewing what was going on in Japan, Chinese intellectuals found a quite different story. Also faced with western threats, Japan opted to open its door and embrace sweeping reforms. In three short decades it outpaced China.

So Chinese intellectuals came to a new understanding: to catch up with the West, China should follow Japan's example of abolishing the civil service examination system and establishing a constitutional monarchy. As seen in Chapter 2, the problem with the civil service examination system lay in its content not its form. The form is great, for it allowed capable people to be admitted into the bureaucratic system. Actually the United Kingdom copied the form to set up its own civil service, but it discarded the Four Books and Five Classics. The constitutionalists initiated the Reform Movement of 1898 to establish a constitutional monarchy. But the reform was quickly suppressed by conservative officials. The only result that remained was the Metropolitan University (*Jing Shi Da Xue Tang* in Mandarin), Peking University's predecessor.

Meanwhile, Chinese overseas students and other Chinese overseas, exemplified by Dr. Sun Yat-sen, had different propositions. Sun was born in Guangdong province, and later emigrated to Hawaii and received an education in the United States and a medical doctoral degree in Hong Kong. When he saw China humiliated by the western powers, he was also desperate to make his motherland strong again. Believing that the presidential system was superior to a constitutional monarchy, he proposed to overthrow the Qing government and form a democracy. So both constitutionalists and revolutionists proposed a major organizational reform in the social and political systems.

After China was invaded by the Eight-Power Allied Forces in 1900, even the hard-core conservative Empress Dowager Cixi realized that the government could not afford to delay reform any longer. But it was too late; the Qing government was soon overturned.

China participated in World War I as an ally of the Triple Entente. But at the Paris Peace Conference of 1919, instead of rewarding China for its contribution to the victory, the Treaty of Versailles transferred the concession of Qingdao from Germany to Japan, one of the great powers, rather than return it to China as agreed before the war. This utter humiliation provoked a strong backlash against the then-Northern government (*Beiyang* in Mandarin) by young intellectuals, including the students of Peking University.

Thus started the renowned May Fourth Movement against imperialism and feudalism. The old political and social institutions were reformed. The civil service examination was abolished. And an education system was established comprising junior high schools, senior high schools, and universities. Even so, China remained backward, weak, and bullied by the western powers. The reason again was that modern artifacts and institutions were not enough to turn things around; modern ideas and values still had to be introduced. Hence the slogan for the May Fourth Movement: "Democracy and Science."

The rise of socialist ideas in China and China's Socialist Revolution

It was a gradual and long process for the Chinese to recognize the role of weaponry, to understand what organizations can put it to best use, and finally to see the importance of values and ideas. After the May Fourth Movement, Chinese intellectuals were divided into two groups. One advocated westernization, arguing that all values, codes of behavior, social institutions, and even artifacts should closely follow the West. The other advocated socialism. After the Communist Party of China was founded in 1921, the socialist movement rapidly developed into a sweeping nationwide social and political movement. Here's why.

First, there was an obvious western phobia among the Chinese people. China had been beaten and humiliated by western powers in successive wars. Although the Chinese people had to bow to western weaponry, they never admitted defeat spiritually. So if they believed that an institution was superior to the western one in both theory and practice, they would be open to it. The western world, then in the early stages of capitalism, was plagued by social unrest caused by the miserable living conditions of workers. Thanks to industrial development, the level of urbanization was pretty high in the West, but most laborers were in the countryside. The huge income gap attracted a heavy and steady flow of rural laborers migrating to cities.

According to Marx's theory, the oversupply of the migrant population would result in a huge unemployed populace. Against that backdrop capitalists suppressed wages to the minimum, without fear of labor shortages, because living standards in cities were still much better than in the countryside. Therefore, the capitalists' revenue grew exponentially as the income of workers hardly improved. The ever-widening wealth gap inevitably led to frequent conflicts between the two groups. Observing these problems, Marx put forward the theory of historical materialism and identified five stages for society to pass through: primitive communism, slavery, feudalism, capitalism, and eventually communism.

In China Dr. Sun developed the Three Principles of the People, also known as San-min Doctrine: the principle of government of the people (Minzu), by the people (Minquan), and for the people (Minsheng). According to Sun, the principle of government for the people is communism in essence. Since there are so many problems in capitalist society, Sun called for a thorough revolution to root out all the problems once and for all, hence his famous slogan, "Accomplish all the tasks in one battle." The fact that even Sun, an advocate of capitalism, embraced socialism, gives some idea of the popularity and impact of socialist ideas at that time.

Second, when Russia established its first socialist regime, it unilaterally withdrew all the unequal treaties it had signed with China. At that time most Chinese were hostile to the great powers, for they had humiliated China by imposing so many unfair treaties. Therefore, a major purpose of various social movements was to put China on an equal footing with developed countries. In this context a socialist country treated China like its brother by spontaneously canceling all the unequal treaties. It is like when a landlord shows up out of the blue at a peasant's house and tells him that all of his debt is forgiven. Naturally, the peasant would be impressed.

The favor cost Russia nothing. As the first socialist country in the world, the USSR, besieged by capitalist countries, was too weak to claim the benefits from treaties signed during the era of the tsar. But most Chinese took it as a friendly gesture, and Sun also decided to ally his Kuomintang Party (KMT) with Russia and its Communist Party. In the 1930s the USSR grew stronger and made itself a great example for China – and for Chinese intellectuals striving for national salvation and prosperity.

Meanwhile, the western world was suffering the decade-long Great Depression, starting with the Wall Street Crash of 1929. During the depression the unemployment rate soared everywhere, the economy slumped by 30–40 percent, and no capitalist country was spared. It seemed that Marx's prediction about the crash of capitalism was about to come true. In sharp contrast the USSR under Stalin's leadership transformed from a poor and backward agricultural economy to an industrialized military world power in a dozen years. Doubtless, the USSR model was enormously appealing to Chinese intellectuals.

Marxism and the Communist Party of China

When the victory of the 1917 October Revolution in Russia brought Marxism-Leninism to China, Li Dazhao and some other intellectuals at Peking University began to spread the new theory, which laid an ideological foundation for the founding of the Communist Party of China. The May Fourth Movement of 1919 facilitated the integration of Marxism with the Chinese labor movement, providing both an ideological underpinning and personnel for the new party.

When the party was created in 1921, the socialist movement in China was facing a series of theoretical issues. According to Marx's historical materialism, the Socialist Revolution would break out only when the conflict between capitalists and the working class intensified to a certain level. Since capitalists have control over power and wealth, a single worker could never resist capitalist exploitation and oppression. Therefore, the whole class should be united, not just in one country but across the world. Why? When the working class in one country is united to overthrow the capitalist regime, its neighboring capitalist countries would lend a hand for fear that the working class in their countries would follow suit. The working class of a single country is not strong enough to resist the combined forces of the capitalist world. So Marx suggested that to win the Socialist Revolution, it must take place simultaneously in all the developed capitalist countries, because it was impossible for any country to accomplish it alone.

Leninism held instead that it was possible, that the revolution did not have to first take place in an advanced capitalist country. But for Lenin the precondition was that the revolution had to be led by a communist party organized by elites. The elites were not necessarily members of the working class, but they had to be well organized and educated. With the elites as the hard core and with the solidarity of the proletariat, it would be possible to accomplish the revolution in an isolated country.

That was exactly the case for Russia. First, the Communist Party was set up. Then the party organized city workers to stage uprisings. Finally the tsarist regime was overthrown. When the Communist Party of China was born in 1921, it followed Marxism and Leninism closely, and the Communist International dispatched representatives to guide revolutions in China and other countries. Guided by Leninism, the Communist Party of China's leaders constituted a party consisting of elites to spark uprisings in cities. But the uprisings were not as successful as those in Russia. Without exception, every one of them was crushed.

Why the Leninist model failed in China

The Communist Party of China staged many movements and uprisings as instructed by the Third International, but every one ended in failure. In my opinion, it was the different conditions in the two countries that produced the opposite results. For starters, China had many concessions whereas Russia had none. In the reign of the tsar, industries in Russia were concentrated in cities; enterprises were mostly owned by the nobility, except for a few owned by professional entrepreneurs or foreign capitalists. In China, by contrast, industries were concentrated in foreign concessions in the cities of Tianjin, Shanghai, Wuhan, Fuzhou, and so on.

In the reign of the tsar the government would send troops to quell riots of workers. The working class, as a vulnerable group, easily aroused sympathy in society, which would direct its anger and resentment toward the government and regard it as unfair to protect the capitalist against the poor worker. In China, with major factories situated in foreign concessions, the story was totally different. Take the appalling May 30th Massacre in 1925: the riot of textile workers was brutally crushed by Japanese troops. And later, when the rioting spread to British concessions, it was again quelled by British police. The massacre of unarmed workers ignited indignation in society, but anger was targeted toward foreign governments, not the ruling KMT party. In fact, the KMT government exploited popular anger and called for solidarity of workers around the leadership of then-president Chiang Kai-shek.

To sum up, riots of workers in different conditions produced totally different results. In Russia, when the tsar sent troops to quell the riots, he lost both the popular support and the legitimacy of his regime. In China, when foreign governments in the concessions sent troops to do the same, it made the ruling party all the more popular. The example tells us that *we can never be too careful when it comes to the application of a foreign theory, because with different preconditions, no matter how trivial they seem, the result can be very different.* Never worship a theory as absolute truth. To successfully apply and implement any theory, certain conditions must be satisfied, as the failure of the Leninist model in China confirms.

The success of Mao's strategy of "Encircling the Cities from the Rural Areas"

With one fiasco after another under the guidance of Leninism, some insightful Communist Party of China members came to realize that China's revolution could not succeed if it relied completely on overseas experience. So they started exploring new ideas. Mao Zedong developed the strategy of "Encircling the Cities from the Rural Areas." According to Marxism-Leninism, the preconditions for social revolution are social inequality and an unequal distribution of wealth.

In rural China there were landlords, poor farmers, and landless peasants. According to data for the 1950s, the landlords (3% of the total population) possessed 26% of arable land, yet poor farmers (68% of the total) possessed only 22%, a big gap in land allocation.[3] The income gap between capitalists and workers also existed in cities, but not as obviously as in rural areas. According to Marxism, peasants do not belong to the most advanced class. But considering the huge gap in rural China, the Communist Party of China's decision to confiscate the land from landlords and give it to peasants won big support from the latter. Plus, the government's control had been rather weak in rural areas.

In traditional China the county was the bottom level of administration. Grassroots administration usually fell to local gentry (the landlords). Therefore, the land reform targeting local tyrants had the same result as the workers' riots in Russia. When the KMT government sent troops to crush peasants, it also lost its legitimacy for having protected wealthy landlords rather than poor peasants, who won the sympathy of those who believed in justice.

According to Leninism, the Socialist Revolution should be carried out by the working class, the most advanced class, rather than more conservative peasants. Mao Zedong was flexible and pragmatic, applying the theory ingeniously instead of mechanically. The strategy of "Encircling the Cities from the Rural Areas" was the result of his extensive research in rural areas and thorough analysis of all social strata in China. It achieved remarkable success.

Guided by Mao's strategy, the Communist Party of China first established revolutionary bases in rural areas and then gradually targeted capitalists in cities. "Encircling the Cities from the Rural Areas" is of military significance. A political strategy also developed by Mao was "Unite the Majority and Fight against a Handful." At that time, numerous small industries and commerce in cities were owned by national capitalists. Compared with factories in the concessions, the businesses of national capitalists were smaller and vulnerable in the market. Mao suggested that these national capitalists also deserved protection, and the target was "a handful" of bureaucratic capitalists, the Four Big Families of Chiang, Soong, Kung, and Chen.

Before World War II Japanese and European capitalists built quite a few factories in China. Those factories, together with those built by the Japanese puppet government, were confiscated by the KMT government when the war was over. The confiscated property was later transferred to high-ranking officials of the KMT, turning them into bureaucratic capital.

In 1947 the Communist Party of China put forward its New Democracy Policies, which translated the two strategies into three guidelines:

- Expropriating the land of landlords for redistribution to poor peasants.
- Expropriating monopolistic bureaucratic capital for national property controlled by the socialist government.
- Protecting industries and commerce owned by national capitalists and guaranteeing them a golden age of at least half a century under socialist leadership.

The rapid transformation from an agrarian economy to a socialist country, as China desired, entailed a transition for China to catch up in industrialization and modernization. In this process, national capitalists could play a critical role. According to the New Democracy Policies, national capitalism could enjoy a golden age of at least five decades, during which time, free from the oppression of foreign governments and enterprises, it could develop much faster than before. The three guidelines won huge popular support, and guaranteed the Communist Party of China's victory over the KMT and the establishment of a socialist regime.

There is a saying in China: "Scholars are not capable of rebelling even if they are given three years to prepare." But in a generation's time (1921–49) the Communist Party of China grew from a small "social movement" started by several intellectuals to a party that united the whole country, unprecedented in Chinese history.

Reasons for copying the Soviet model

As soon as the People's Republic of China was founded, the socialist construction kicked off. Under the leadership of Chairman Mao, China implemented a planned economy, which existed for twenty-nine years from 1949 to 1978, as long as it took the Communist Party of China to found a new China. But the planned economy did not work.

Critics generally tend to blame Mao for copying the Soviet model of a planned economy. But why did Mao, so pragmatic and flexible during the revolution, slavishly copy the Soviet model after the People's Republic of China was founded? Some argued that he did not have any experience in industrialization. But he had no experience in revolution or war either, so that argument is flawed. In fact, copying the Soviet model was a smart and practical option. *China took a different road to revolution despite having the same goal as Russia, but the two had different conditions. When the People's Republic of China was founded, the two shared the same goal and similar conditions. So it was natural for China to take the same road to industrialization.*

The main motive for the older generation of revolutionaries was to make China rich and strong. On October 1, 1949, Chairman Mao, at the Tian'anmen Tower gate, declared to the world, "The Chinese people have stood up!" I believe he gave much thought to this statement: it expressed not only his own feelings but also the aspiration of the whole generation. Indeed, to help Chinese stand on their own feet was not only the underlying motive for the Socialist Revolution, but also the shared aspiration of generations of revolutionary pioneers, who had given up their lives to this cause ever since the Opium War.

Prioritizing the development of heavy industries

The Chinese people had long realized that without a strong national defense, they would be beaten. To have a strong national defense, they needed a strong military industry and thus strong heavy industries. So China launched a massive national construction program in 1952, initiating the strategy of prioritizing heavy industries. The purpose was to make sure that China would no longer be bullied and would rank among the world powers as soon as possible.

The Soviet Union gave China a great model. China was a poor and backward agrarian economy, just like the USSR before 1929. But under Stalin's leadership, the USSR witnessed rapid industrialization and quickly built its own industrial and national defense system. Meanwhile, the American and European markets were still suffering from the Great Depression. All these facts made the Soviet model of prioritizing heavy industries appear feasible and likely to satisfy the aspirations of the developing world.

China was not the only country interested in the Soviet model. Many leaders of newly independent nations after World War II in Asia, Latin America, and Africa opted for the same strategy, among them India's Nehru, Egypt's Nasser, Indonesia's Sukarno, and Tanzania's Nyerere. In the 1940s Latin America put forward the Dependency Theory, which categorized countries around the world into two groups: core countries and periphery countries.[4] The former refers to advanced capitalist countries, and the latter to backward and poor developing countries. According to the theory, developed countries produce industrial products and export them to developing countries that export primary commodities. In the 1930s the prices of raw material exports dropped sharply while the prices of industrial products remained stable. According to this theory, the developing country that exports natural resource products and imports manufactured products will be exploited.[5]

Dependency Theory was widely received, and most developing countries became reluctant to export their natural resources, preferring instead to produce manufactured goods that they once imported. That strategy, called import substitution, implies that a country has to produce not only its consumption goods but also the equipment and machinery for producing those goods. Nor is it that different from prioritizing heavy industries. The then-mainstream development economics also tried hard to help the developing world establish their own systems of heavy industries. With few exceptions, almost all developing countries committed to prioritizing heavy industries, China among them. Because as Mao put it, without a military industry, there would be no national defense to speak of, and China would surely be beaten. So China decided to implement this popular strategy to build its own heavy and military industries.

Departing from China's factor endowments and comparative advantage

China in 1952 resembled the USSR in 1929. Both were backward and poor agricultural economies, and both opted for prioritizing heavy industries, which have three major features. First, the construction period is very long – as long as five to ten years. Light industries may start production and receive returns the same year of investment, but it takes much longer for heavy industries to see returns. Second, backward and poor developing countries have to import equipment and machinery for heavy industries. Third, the initial capital outlays for heavy industries are huge. Projects of billions or even tens of billions of renminbi are not uncommon (1 dollar = 3.36 renminbi in 1952).[6] For light industrial projects, by contrast, 1 million or 10 million renminbi is considered big.

A backward and poor developing country also has three major features. First, the surplus is small. In developing countries most workers are farmers, and production disperses in rural areas and agriculture. Most agricultural products are consumed by farm households, with a small part for fodder and seeds, and surplus products are minimal.

The surplus can be sold in markets and turned into capital. But due to the very small social surplus, the capital available is also minimal. Scarce capital then leads to high capital costs. And interest rates in developing countries are generally very high. In most, the monthly interest rate for private lending can be 2–3 percent or higher.

Second, exports from these countries are also minimal, which leads to expensive foreign exchange and limited forex reserves.

Third, savings are too scattered to be raised. The agricultural region is spread across a vast area, and so are the savings, so it is difficult to raise already small scattered savings for investment. Due to meager incomes, farmers usually won't deposit savings in a bank. They would have to travel tens of kilometers on foot to county banks to deposit several dozens of renminbi, and when they need to buy soy sauce, vinegar, or matches worth several fen (100 fen = 1 renminbi), they would have to travel a long distance again to withdraw it. Even the pluses of safety and interest cannot compensate for the trouble of traveling. So most farmers preferred to hide their cash under their pillows or sew it into quilts.

From this analysis of the conflicting features of heavy industries and backward agricultural economies, we can conclude that it was impossible for a developing nation to embark on a major heavy industry project that has a long construction period, relies on substantial imports of equipment, and requires a sizable initial capital outlay. If the monthly interest rate of private lending is 2.5 percent, the yearly rate is 30 percent. Suppose that a project will take ten years to finish and will see no return before it is put into production. With a 30 percent yearly compound interest rate, an amount 13.7 times the original loan will have to be paid when the project is finished ten years later. Projects with returns that high are rare.

Added to this, building heavy industries entails importing equipment and machinery, which China did not have at that time. Limited forex reserves make foreign exchange expensive. As with high interest rates, it also leads to prohibitive costs for heavy industries. It was nearly impossible to raise sufficient capital from rural areas if the initial capital outlay of a heavy industrial project required hundreds of millions or even billions of renminbi.

The next chapter shows how China, an agricultural economy short of capital, pursued its priorities for capital-intensive heavy industries.

References

Huntington, Samuel P. 1996. *The Clash of Civilizations and the Remaking of World Order*. New York: Simon and Schuster.

Lin, Justin Y., Fang Cai, and Zhou Li. 1996. *The China Miracle: Development Strategy and Economic Reform*. Hong Kong: Chinese University Press.

    2003. *The China Miracle: Development Strategy and Economic Reform*, revised edn. Hong Kong: Chinese University Press.

Maddison, Angus. 2006. *The World Economy*. Paris: Organisation for Economic Co-operation and Development.

Malinowski, Bronislaw. 1944. *A Scientific Theory of Culture and Other Essays*. Chapel Hill, NC: University of North Carolina Press.

Prebisch, Raúl. 1950. *The Economic Development of Latin America and its Principal Problems*. New York: United Nations.

Singer, Hans W. 1950. "The Distribution of Gains Between Borrowing and Investing Countries." *American Economic Review* 40: 473–85.

Notes

1. Maddison (2006).
2. Huntington (1996).
3. National Bureau of Statistics of China.
4. Prebisch (1950) and Singer (1950) are two major proponents of this theory.
5. Dependency Theory was based on the experiences of price movements during the Great Depression. From what I see the different price changes for different types of products in the 1930s were actually due to the price elasticity of supply. Because of the Great Depression, the world's total demand was shrinking. Under these circumstances, the higher the price elasticity of supply, the less the price will drop – and vice versa. Products of different natures respond differently to shrinking demand; so it was not a case of exploitation.
6. The renminbi exchange rate of 1952 is calculated based on trade data of 1952 from the National Bureau of Statistics of China.

FOUR

The comparative advantage-defying, catching-up strategy and the traditional economic system

China, so powerful and prosperous for so long, waned after the Opium War in 1840, falling prey to western powers. Ever since then, many patriots have been striving, unflinchingly and ceaselessly, to revive the nation's past glory. In 1949 the People's Republic of China was founded to realize the long-cherished dream of its people. The leaders of the new regime had to decide which development strategy and administrative system to adopt. Considering that China was a backward agrarian economy lagging far behind the world, the leaders decided to adopt a strategy of prioritizing heavy industries so that the country could leapfrog into an advanced industrial economy and achieve full independence and great national strength. This strategy was the logical starting point for the traditional economic system.

This chapter explores the institutional formation under the development strategy of prioritizing heavy industries and the economic logic underlying the traditional institutional arrangement. It then discusses the causes of the Agricultural Crisis (1959–61) and briefly reviews China's economic development before 1978.

The development strategy of prioritizing heavy industries and the traditional economic system

Chapter 3 provided a possible explanation as to why Chairman Mao Zedong copied the USSR's strategy of prioritizing the development of heavy industries after the founding of the People's Republic of China. In 1949 China very much resembled the Soviet Union of 1929 under the leadership of Stalin: both were backward agrarian economies aiming to rapidly develop heavy and military industries. Since the two shared similar conditions and goals, it was sensible and practical for China to follow the example of its socialist brother to prioritize heavy industries and speedily establish a comprehensive industrial system. But it is hardly feasible for a developing country to turn to market forces in order to implement that strategy.

As I mentioned in Chapter 3, heavy industries, which are capital-intensive, had three major features for China. First, the construction period was rather long. Second, the key technologies and equipment had to be imported. Third, the initial capital outlays were huge, involving up to tens of billions or even hundreds of billions of renminbi. But most developing countries are agrarian economies and have little surplus for capital accumulation. So those countries have high capital costs due to severe scarcity, limited foreign exchange reserves and expensive foreign exchange because of limited exports, and difficulties raising capital because of dispersed production.

The features are indeed incompatible. First, a developing economy cannot afford the high interest cost entailed by a project with a long construction period. Second, limited foreign exchange reserves and expensive foreign exchange make it extremely difficult to import expensive equipment and machinery. Third, it is very difficult for an agricultural economy with little surplus to raise capital for developing heavy industry.

The internal logic of the trinity of the traditional economic system

For the government of a fledgling developing economy, whether socialist or capitalist, to prioritize capital-intensive industries implies that its most pressing task is to suppress the interest rate well below the market through administrative measures.[1] Meanwhile, to solve the problem of expensive machinery imports, the government also has to directly and artificially intervene in its exchange rates – to overvalue its currency and undervalue foreign currencies so that the imports are affordable. And to mobilize a surplus for capital accumulation, the silver bullet is to guarantee that the existing enterprises enjoy handsome profits and use them in the next round of production.

The government can increase the profits of those enterprises through two main means. It can grant them a monopoly, so that they can set monopolistic prices for their products and thus harvest handsome profits. It can also suppress the prices of all productive inputs, including the prices of capital, raw materials, and wages. Since wages are so low, the government has to accordingly drive down the prices of food, clothes, housing, transport, and related services. So the internal logic of the planned economy is to artificially depress interest rates, overvalue the domestic currency, and suppress the prices of raw materials, wages, and all daily necessities.

For a non-socialist country to prioritize capital-intensive industries, the government has to at least lower the interest rate and undervalue foreign currencies. For other measures, it depends on the effectiveness of its administrative intervention. For example, countries in Latin America generally chose to lower the prices of raw materials, but the extent of lowering them differed from country to country.

The distorted price system is a distorted macro-policy environment, affecting every enterprise by its distorted price signals, which break the market equilibrium. When the capital price is depressed, the capital cost becomes cheaper not only for heavy industries but also for light industries and agriculture. As a result, the total demand for capital increases. At the same time, a low interest rate discourages savings and reduces the supply of capital. As a result, the supply of capital falls short of demand in the short term, and so does foreign exchange. With domestic currency overvalued and foreign currencies undervalued, the cost of importing equipment and other products is reduced, resulting in excessive imports and insufficient foreign exchange.

Because exports are the main source of foreign exchange, the artificially overvalued domestic currency drives up the prices of exports. The price hike reduces export volumes and foreign exchange earnings. Generally speaking, the demand for foreign exchange will exceed its supply by a large margin, resulting in supply shortages. Similarly, the distorted prices of daily necessities will also put those commodities in short supply. János Kornai, a Hungarian economist specializing in socialist economies, calls the planned economies of socialist countries the "Economics of Shortage."[2] He attributed the shortage to the nature of socialism, but I maintain that the shortage is caused by distorted prices. If the government suppresses the price of a certain production factor, its demand will exceed its supply, resulting in short supply. During World War II, typically capitalist countries like Britain and the United States adopted a rationing system. To curtail the spiraling consumer prices, they had to push down the prices of the daily necessities to an extremely low level, and soon demand overtook supply. To ensure basic necessities for every citizen, not even the prime minister could buy more than his ration allowance. Obviously, socialism was not responsible for that shortage. When resources are allocated by administrative directives rather than market forces, market competition disappears.

Artificially low prices result in shortages of basic necessities. They also lead to short supplies of capital, foreign exchange, and raw materials. To ensure that all the factors of production can be used in the priority industries, the government can never count on market forces to allocate resources. Under such circumstances, it has to make a national prioritized plan for industries and for projects in each industry. To support the plan, the government has to use administrative measures to allocate its scarce capital, foreign exchange, and raw materials. This distorted pricing and system of resource allocation facilitates the establishment of enterprises in the prioritized industries – it also guarantees them fat profits. Before the reform and opening, Liaoning province in northeastern China, part of the rust belt today, was the dominant economic region. Heavy industries were a major part of the province's economy, and the products were overpriced and the input prices deliberately suppressed. It was therefore no surprise that the province's revenue was among the highest in China.

To implement the strategy of prioritizing heavy industries in such an institutional environment, the government also has to create compatible micro-management institutions, which are not in line with the market mechanism. To make sure the surplus is channeled to heavy industries, the government has to apply tight controls. Had the enterprises been privately owned, and their surplus controlled by capitalists, they would have been definitely channeled to more profitable light industries.

The reasons for private capital to go to light industries are quite simple. First, they require less investment and earn a faster return. Second, against the background of a planned economy where shortages are commonplace, light industrial products are also highly sought-after, so capitalists can sell manufactured items at good prices in parallel markets, higher than the ration prices, and thus gain profits. That is exactly why the government made a move to nationalize light enterprises, so that it could enjoy absolute control over the surplus funds.

During the new democratic revolution period (1949–56), there was a policy that promised a golden age for national capitalists, protected from competition from foreign governments and enterprises. But in a matter of years, their enterprises were nationalized. The newly founded factories were of course dependent on the government for investment and owned by the state. Had the old factories remained privately owned, the owners would have invested the surplus in industries other than those high on the agenda of the national plan. So, to ensure full control of the entire surplus, all private enterprises had to be nationalized.

The government needed not only to directly own and allocate economic surplus, but also to directly intervene in the management of all enterprises, by depriving the directors and managers of their decision-making power.

Take the former Soviet Union. The Communist Party owed the success of the urban revolution to the city workers and directors of major factories. Yet after 1929 the directors and managers, mainstays of the revolution, were deprived of their decision-making power. Why? Because the market was monopolized and all the production factors were cheap in a distorted pricing system, the heavy industries could gain pretty high profits. When there is no competition, it is hard to decide how much profit is suitable. If the managers had a say in running the business – for example, if they could decide on worker salaries and benefits – they might abuse their power to gain wealth for themselves and workers at the expense of national interest.

Another possible scenario: despite their cheap productive inputs, some industries, such as transportation, whose products were considered as inputs for heavy industries, were always making a loss because the prices of their products were suppressed so much. A market devoid of competition could not calculate the exact loss. If the managers had decision-making power, they might have cooked the figures and exaggerated their losses, and the government would not have been able to verify the accounts. With opportunities to embezzle the earmarked surplus funds, the managers would have depleted the funds for national investment.

To ensure that the surplus funds were safe in its hands, the Chinese government had to nationalize urban enterprises and make the managers puppets of the government. In the era of planned economy, there was a saying mocking the management of state-owned enterprises: "Man, money, and materials, none of your business; producing, providing, and peddling, that's papa's call." This doggerel vividly depicts the real picture in those days. The enterprises had absolutely no say in either whom or how many employees to recruit. Nor did they enjoy any financial independence. All their profits were taken by the government, which decided how to allocate those profits according to national needs. Neither the directors nor the managers had any right to make policies for assets and investment. Nor could they decide what to produce, where to source, and whom to sell to. Clearly, the managers of nationalized enterprises were little more than figureheads.

The account here explains the root causes of the trinity of the traditional economic system characterized by distorted prices of factors and products, highly centralized and planned allocation of resources, and powerless managers at the micro level. Without knowledge of the logic behind this system, you may find it irrational. But if you have a clear picture of the rationale underlying the system, you may agree that under the restrictive circumstances, from the perspective of the national interest, the trinity system was indeed the best institutional arrangement available, if scarce resources and surplus funds were to be used to the utmost to prioritize capital-intensive heavy industries.

Within the framework of a planned economy, the trinity system was developed to facilitate an agrarian economy short of capital to prioritize capital-intensive heavy industries. This system affected not only the cities but also several major systems in the rural areas after 1952. Its influence on the rural economy remains even today. Those systems include the state monopoly over purchasing and marketing, the collectivization of agriculture, the regional grain self-sufficiency, and the urban–rural dichotomy in household registration.

The monopoly over purchasing and marketing
of agricultural products

In 1953 the Chinese government adopted the policy of monopo-
lizing the purchasing and marketing of agricultural products. To
understand why, we can find some clues in *The Selected Works of
Chen Yun*. Then the Minister of Finance, Chen discovered in 1953
that, in the past, whatever the Communist Party of China called on
the farmers to sell, they would readily rush to sell. But after 1953,
all of a sudden, they were reluctant to sell to the government. Chen
lamented the farmers' dramatic change.

What were the real reasons behind this reversal? It again comes
down to the policy of prioritizing heavy industries. Before 1953 the
government launched the campaign of "Overthrowing the local
landlords and distributing their land to farmers," for which the
farmers were grateful. And as there was no planned economy at that
time, the government conducted all its business with farmers based
on market prices and was never behind in payments. So, whatever it
called on the farmers to sell, they were ready to sell.

Then the first "Five-Year Plan" kicked off in 1953, and industrialization started in the cities. To create the high profits for urban
enterprises for the sake of expanded production, the government
had to suppress the cost of all productive inputs, many of which
came from rural areas, such as cotton for production and grains and
necessities for workers' lives. The government could have purchased
the agricultural produce at market prices and sold them at lower
prices to the city residents and enterprises, but that option did not
appeal to the government. If the surplus created by enterprises in
cities were transferred to the rural areas, suppressing the prices of
productive inputs in cities would not result in the accumulation of
surplus capital and would therefore be pointless. Even though that
option would please the farmers, it ran counter to the aim of prioritizing heavy industries. So the government had to purchase at low

prices from the farmers and sell again at low prices to the cities, to transfer the rural surplus to urban centers.

In 1949, when the People's Republic of China was newly founded, there were three types of grain and cotton businesses in the rural areas: government run, privately run, and jointly run. Privately run businesses purchased grain and cotton at market prices, but the other two types bought them at much lower prices set by the government. Under these circumstances, any farmers with a sharp mind would sell to privately run businesses.

To secure the steady supply of low-priced produce it needed, the government had to exercise a monopoly. In 1953 it started to monopolize the purchase of grain and cotton.

According to this mechanism, farmers had to fulfill the government's procurement quota before they could sell their products to the market. And if they failed to meet the quotas, they would end up with a sole buyer, the government, which set the prices. In the beginning only grain and cotton were purchased in this centralized manner. But soon after 1954 nearly all farm products were included, including sesame, peanuts, and eggs. The reason? If only the prices for grain and cotton were suppressed, sensible farmers would plant less grain and cotton and more products they were free to sell. Meanwhile, the government also carried out a planned marketing policy in cities: it decided which enterprises got which goods, and even living necessities like grain had to be purchased according to the national plan (with grain coupons, cotton coupons, cloth coupons, and so on).

Accelerating the collectivization of agriculture

Supported by the monopoly over purchasing and marketing agricultural products, industries in cities began to require more industrial inputs and workers, but the rural output could not keep up with the demand. The government tightly controlled the purchasing and selling prices, but it could not control farmers' freedom to decide when to work and when to rest. The lowered prices of the products dented farmers' enthusiasm, and they began to find more time to rest, for the opportunity cost of their rest time was the meager income from their production.

The rising demand from urban areas and the farmers' declining enthusiasm for production inevitably resulted in short supplies of farm produce. To solve this problem, there were two options. The first was to raise purchasing prices to boost farmers' enthusiasm, but this would contradict the goal of maximizing the surplus in cities. The second option was to increase investment in agriculture, such as stepping up infrastructure construction, improving agricultural productivity, and so on. But the funds for this would still have to come from government revenue, against maximizing the surplus for industrialization. How would it be possible to increase rural productivity without increasing inputs from the government? Economies of scale provided a solution.

By 1952 the land of the landlords had been distributed to each household. Due to the small size of the rural households, it was hard to achieve economies of scale. Here is how economies of scale work in rural China. Some factors of production like draft cattle and other draft animals are not divisible. If the scale is too small, productive factors of this kind cannot be fully used, resulting in certain waste. But if the scale expands, those productive factors can be fully used.

For example, in agricultural production, most locales in China have a double cropping system: soon after harvesting summer grain, new seeds must be sown. Delays of even a few days can leave crops vulnerable to frost before they mature. If the frost is too severe, there could be no harvest at all. Manpower may not be sufficient to ensure timely sowing, so draft animals become essential. When the land per household is limited, it would be a waste for each household to keep a draft animal. But if several households can share one, the cost for each household is greatly reduced – hence the economies of scale.

In addition, when agriculture was collectivized, field ridges were no longer necessary, so economies of scale help save some land too. That is why one year after land was distributed to each household in 1952, the agriculture collectivization campaign kicked off.

Regional grain self-sufficiency

The third institutional arrangement was regional grain self-sufficiency. For many who study China's economy, this is a confusing institutional arrangement – for if grain, unlike other commodities, is in short supply and cannot be produced locally, it has to be imported. But importing food is like handing one's bowl to someone else. Historically some countries did use food as a weapon and imposed embargoes against their rivals. So a common goal for many countries is to guarantee national self-sufficiency in grain.

China was a little bit different: it had to be self-sufficient not only on a national basis but also on a provincial basis. That policy remained until the 1990s in various forms. There was a saying then, "The mayor is in charge of the vegetable basket, and the governor takes care of the rice sack." China is a vast country, so production conditions vary substantially from province to province. For example, Henan and Hebei provinces in northern China, due to their dry weather, are suitable for cotton instead of grain. Historically, they traded cotton for grain with Anhui, Hubei, Jiangxi, and other provinces in southern China. Similarly, provinces in the southwest and northwest traded medicinal herbs and other cash crops for grain with inland provinces. Each produced farm products in which it had a comparative advantage and traded them for what it lacked.

Under the national purchasing and marketing plan of 1953, the grain price was artificially low. The more grain a province sold to the country, the more tax it had to pay. By contrast, the more a province asked for food from the state, the more subsidies it could get. That resulted in a dichotomy between the provinces short of grain and those enjoying a surplus. The former were thrilled to ask for more, but the latter were reluctant to produce more. With a growing population and ongoing industrialization, the demand for farm products (including grain) was increasing. But because some provinces that could produce more chose not to, other provinces, whose comparative advantage did not lie in grain production, had to produce their own food. That is the story of regional "self-sufficiency in grain." That rather rigid policy remained influential until the 1990s and comes into life again whenever there is a concern over grain shortage.

The urban–rural dichotomy in household registration

The household registration system, which made a sharp distinction between urban and rural residents, also started in 1953. Labor mobility and migration were fairly easy before the mid-1950s, but after that they became more difficult and remained so until 1978, at the start of the reform and opening. The reasons? As mentioned before, China introduced the strategy of prioritizing heavy industries in 1953. At the beginning of the big industrial push, migration from rural areas was still allowed. But very soon, capital-intensive heavy industries could not create enough jobs for the urban labor force. Back then, urban residents worked either at government agencies or state-owned enterprises (SOEs). The government was committed to taking care of all the employees in cities and providing jobs for their children. So, to prevent urban residents from losing their jobs and rural migrant laborers from enjoying various subsidies that only urban residents were entitled to, tight restrictions had to be imposed on rural-to-urban labor flows. Consequently, the root cause for the urban–rural dual system of household registration was underemployment in cities, closely related to the strategy of heavy industries.

To sum up, the above-mentioned systems took shape in 1953 when the first Five-Year Plan started. The core of the plan was to guarantee demand for 156 heavy industrial projects. The institutional arrangement in China was basically in line with that in the former Soviet Union, because the two shared the same objective and the same constraints. That is why they opted for the same measures.

The results of the Cooperative Movement and the traditional system

Without understanding the mechanism behind the Cooperative Movement that started in 1953, it would be difficult to understand its evolution. A popular explanation is that without such a movement, the landlords would re-emerge, and there would be a huge wealth gap in the rural area. If that were so, why did the movement not start immediately after the land of landlords was confiscated? Back then it would have met fewer obstacles, because for the former landless farmers, joining the cooperative with their fellows would definitely have been more desirable than being oppressed by landlords.

The evolution of the Cooperative Movement

The reason that the Cooperative Movement started a year after land was distributed to all farmers in 1952 is that a series of issues with heavy industries did not emerge until 1953, when the strategy of prioritizing heavy industries was enforced. To be specific, the government had to purchase farm produce at very low prices, while farmers had no incentives to expand production. Hence the Cooperative Movement.

The movement went through several stages. Between 1953 and 1954 "mutual aid teams" were a popular form. Land, draft animals, and output belonged to their respective households, but in a busy farming season a couple of households would cooperate voluntarily to aid each other. The mutual aid teams made some sense. For example, a household with a draft animal could lend it to those who did not have one. And mutual aid could greatly enhance the efficiency of harvesting, accomplishing a great deal of work in a short time.

The economic basis of mutual aid teams existed long before socialism took root in China. For instance, the common "exchange of labor" closely resembles the mutual aid team.[3] Thanks to the long tradition, the mutual aid team, introduced in 1953, was well received and soon popularized. The mutual aid team did achieve economies of scale, good for farmers in rush harvesting, rush sowing, and rush ploughing. Encouraged by increased output and farmers' enthusiasm, the government decided to scale them up to "primary cooperatives" in 1954.

More advanced than the mutual aid team, a primary cooperative comprised twenty to thirty households, similar to the size of a natural village in rural China (especially south of the Yangtze River). In a primary cooperative the land of different households was pooled, making field ridges unnecessary, thus saving some land. There were two ways to distribute output: one was based on land, farm tools, and draft animals, and the other on work. At the end of the year, after subtracting the cost of seed and fertilizer, net output was distributed on the basis of work points. The primary cooperatives were also well received; a lot of farmers responded enthusiastically to the government's call to join the cooperatives with a slogan: "Free to join and free to exit."

Again encouraged by the good results, the government decided to upgrade the primary cooperatives to advanced ones (1956–57) comprising 150–200 households, which usually made a natural village in north China, but included several natural villages in the south. In primary cooperatives land and farm tools belonged to each household separately, but in advanced cooperatives they were pooled, and the distribution of output was based totally on work. At that time, farmers were hardly affected by this new arrangement. Although some farmers reportedly killed draft animals secretly at night for food, those cases were rare, because after the land reform, there was little difference among rural households in land areas and farm tools.

In 1956 the articles of association of the advanced cooperative were approved by the National People's Congress, establishing the principle of "Free to join and free to exit." When any farmer decided to withdraw from the cooperative, his original land, farm tools, and draft animals had to be returned. In addition, any accumulation during the stay in the cooperative had to be converted to a certain value and distributed to him. With the economies of scale continuing to play their magic, the output from the advanced cooperatives (1956–57) also kept growing. By 1958 the government decided to scale it up even more. Hence the people's commune.

The first commune was formed in August 1958, and three months later the communes were popularized nationwide, covering 99 percent of all farm households. On average, one commune included 5,000 households, 10,000 farmers, and 60,000 mu of arable land (4,000 hectares). Part of the reason to scale up was irrigation, which was essential for sizable agricultural production. One household alone could not afford an irrigation project, but neither could 200 households, the size of an advanced cooperative. To build a small reservoir or irrigation canal, it would be better to mobilize the whole commune. So the commune became the production unit.

The agricultural crisis of 1959–61

The people's commune clearly showed more pronounced socialist features – the distribution of food based on need rather than performance, as had been the case in the advanced cooperative.[4] Farmers no longer needed to cook for themselves – they all dined at public canteens and could eat as much as they wanted. Cooking time and straw were saved – also a demonstration of economies of scale. But in 1959 grain output declined by 15 percent over 1958, and in 1960 by another 15 percent, with 1961 on par with 1960. The three-year agricultural crisis turned out to be a major human disaster, resulting in the unnatural deaths of 30 million.

In 1962 the people's commune remained, but the production unit was reduced to the production team, usually twenty to thirty households, the size of the primary cooperative. Distribution was based on work points. To sum up, the production team became the size of the primary cooperative, and the distribution mechanism that of the advanced cooperative. The production team remained until 1978.

The government no longer blindly worshiped scale. With ongoing industrialization and population growth, it still had to face the increasing demand for grain and other farm produce. Its response was to increase inputs into agriculture. Starting in 1962 it committed to increasing grain yields through scientific research. In 1964 dwarf rice, developed by the Chinese Academy of Agricultural Sciences, was popularized nationwide. In 1976 hybrid rice, developed by Yuan Longping in Hunan province, was popularized. The yield of dwarf rice is 30 percent higher than that of ordinary rice, and hybrid rice is 30 percent higher than that of dwarf rice. These modern varieties also require more chemical fertilizer, which also means more input. There was a slogan in the 1970s – "Mechanization is the answer to agricultural development" – signifying great progress in agricultural modernization during this period.

Traditional explanations for the crisis

The agricultural crisis of 1959–61, a major catastrophe resulting in massive famine and 30 million deaths, merits serious thinking and research by economists at home and abroad, especially by Chinese economists. Avoiding a similar disaster requires understanding the real reasons for the crisis. There are at least three hypotheses.[5]

First is the bad weather hypothesis. Although the probability of three successive years of bad weather hitting every part of such a large country as China was unlikely, this explanation was plausible due to the susceptibility of agriculture to climatic changes. But in real life, bad weather should not diminish yields nationwide. Take flooding:

although the area affected by floods may suffer from reduced yields, the neighboring provinces may actually increase their yields due to better availability of water. Even flood-afflicted areas, having more groundwater, may see better yields in the next year. Local floods will not have a major impact on the national yield – nor will drought. So, it is quite unlikely that bad weather could lead to yield declines of 15 percent and last for three years nationwide.

Second is the hypothesis of bad policies and bad management. When popularizing people's communes at the end of 1958, a communal kitchen program was introduced, with free meals for everybody, and food was quickly consumed. Most of the chiefs and party secretaries of the communes were not farmers, but cadres dispatched by the government. For example, those ill-informed cadres proposed "deep ploughing and close planting," which led to a dramatic drop in grain yields.

The third hypothesis, proposed by Dwight Perkins, a renowned economist specializing in China's economy, is the reduced incentive related to the unwieldy size of the commune. The average size of a commune was 10,000 farmers and 4,000 hectares of land, large indeed. If one farmer works very hard, the total output will increase, but this farmer can get only one-ten-thousandth of the increased output. By the same token, if another farmer deliberately slows down, he suffers only one-ten-thousandth of the reduced output. Such an incentive mechanism clearly discourages enthusiasm and eventually leads to declining output.

So, the three hypotheses are all logically plausible. But I personally think the probability of bad weather across a country as large as China is extremely low (although it cannot be ruled out). Mismanagement indisputably leads to shrinking output. Distribution according to need, especially the practice of providing free meals, may reduce enthusiasm and output as well. To conclude, the three hypotheses are all logically sound, but to decide which might be valid requires empirical testing.

In fact, the three factors were non-existent after 1962. If natural disasters were the cause, productivity should have recovered after 1962 to the pre-1958 level in no time. As regards mismanagement, the communal kitchens were abolished after 1959, three years before 1962, and the "deep ploughing and close planting" method was given up soon after its introduction. Especially after 1962 the communes were broken down to production teams (only twenty to thirty households), smaller than the successful primary and advanced cooperatives. So, mismanagement should not have been an issue. On incentives, in the days of the advanced cooperative, the size was about 150–200 households, and distributions were based on work. And there was no slump in productivity then. To sum up, the impact from the three proposed causes should have disappeared soon after 1962. Even taking land's recovery and labor's health into account, productivity should have recovered to the 1958–59 level in 1962 or 1963, or at the latest in 1964 – a reasonable inference.

Productivity is measured mainly by total factor productivity (TFP).[6] If the foregoing three hypotheses were valid, the TFP should have recovered in a couple of years after 1962. But despite considerable effort to introduce modern technology (tractors, chemical fertilizer, and improved varieties), it did not recover until 1984, when the production team system was replaced by the household responsibility system (Figure 4.1).[7] So, even if the three hypotheses were valid, they cannot be major determinants.

To prevent history from repeating itself, we must find out the major causes of the catastrophe. The topic of my doctoral dissertation at the University of Chicago was the household responsibility system. Starting in 1978, when the system was introduced, output increased by a large margin, and so did productivity. Interestingly, the same thing happened in 1953, when individual production turned collective. In other words, from 1953 to 1958, when individual production gave way to collective production, productivity increased, and from 1978 to 1984, when the system was reversed,

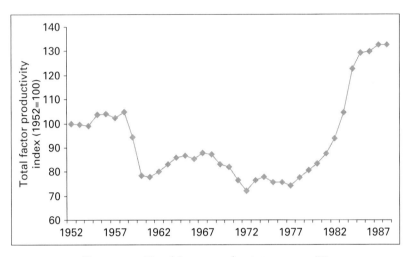

Figure 4.1 Total factor productivity, 1952–88
Source: Lin (1990).

productivity again increased. Now, I will focus on the connection between this phenomenon and the agricultural crisis – and offer another hypothesis.

Removing the right to exit

Before I elaborate on this hypothesis, allow me to introduce a little game theory. The economies of scale also apply to bank robbery. Cooperation between two robbers makes the job much easier than doing it alone, for while one man is breaking into a bank, the other man can look out and drive. Imagine two genius robbers who never get caught. The police have identified the two suspects, but for lack of evidence, they cannot arrest them or put them on trial. But the two robbers often get caught stealing, so the police are trying to find some way to get them to confess.

In the United States, if the suspect is willing to turn state's witness and testify against an accomplice, he or she may be exempted from execution. So the police have designed an incentive mechanism to encourage confessions. If the two robbers both confess to a bank

TABLE 4.1 *Prisoner's dilemma*

		Prisoner Y Stays silent	Betrays
Prisoner X	Stays silent	(2, 2)	(12, 0)
	Betrays	(0, 12)	(6, 6)

robbery, each gets a six-month sentence. If neither confesses, each gets a two-month sentence for stealing. If one confesses and testifies against the other, the former is acquitted, and the latter gets a twelve-month sentence.

This is the "Prisoner's Dilemma" (Table 4.1). From the individual's perspective, betrayal would be a rational option, for no matter what the other player does, this player will always gain a greater payoff. But from the perspective of the two, cooperating is more rational. Yet the two robbers still have to consider another scenario: they may continue to cooperate in the future, and they will probably be caught again. So if the game is played repeatedly, each player has an opportunity to punish the other player for a previous uncooperative play by tit for tat. The threat to punish is real, so in the end both might cooperate, achieving maximum payoff for the two of them.

So if the game is a one-off, the individual's payoff will trump that of the two, because either individual can pose a real threat to the other. If the two robbers plan never to cooperate again, they both will probably "betray," because the other one does not pose a threat. Cases like this are quite common in daily life. For example, commodities are more reliable from shops than from street vendors, for the former usually have fixed places of business and thus a reputation to maintain, but the latter engage in one-off deals. The same logic applies to the agricultural crisis in 1959–61.

The manifestations of economies of scale in agriculture are as follows. First, in a season of rush harvest and rush sowing, time will be a major issue, and group cooperation is usually more efficient than working alone. Also, the draft animals are expensive. If several households can share one, they can save on inputs. These are economies of scale in production. Second, in terms of security, everyone may fall ill sometime. When someone is sick, group members will make more effort to help them through. Then when you are sick, others will reciprocate.

But the nature of agricultural production makes supervising quality exceedingly costly, much more expensive than supervision over industrial production. For example, it is difficult to discern rice from weed when weeding. And fertilizing before or after rain makes a lot of difference. (It's better to fertilize after rain.) Of course, sensible distribution of the harvest should be based on the quality of work, but it is not practical to tell whether someone has mistaken rice for weed when weeding. So it is hard to translate the abstract work quality into concrete work points. Under these circumstances, distribution had to be based on how many days one has worked, so it inevitably led to equal distribution. Even a smaller production team had about twenty households and fifty farmers. So additional work input from one individual ended up with one-fiftieth of the benefits, inevitably reducing the enthusiasm to work.

In both risk-sharing and production, cooperatives enjoyed economies of scale. To realize the benefits of scale economies, a critical issue of supervision has to be solved. To sustain the cooperatives, everyone has to be self-disciplined. But some people are always lazier than others, and if people know they will not be punished, more people will choose to freeload. So, voluntarism is essential for the survival of the cooperative. According to the articles of association the National People's Congress passed in 1956, land and farm tools provided by farmers belonged to the group, but farmers enjoyed the freedom to withdraw from the cooperative at any time. With that policy as a precondition, when more freeloaders appear, productivity would decline to a level that is even lower than that of an individual household. When that happens, hard workers will decide to withdraw from the inefficient cooperative. The freedom to withdraw protects those who work hard but also constitutes a real threat to those who don't. And when more people choose to drop out, the cooperative will in the end disintegrate. Freeloaders will be forced to work individually and forgo the benefits of scale economies. If would-be freeloaders understand that being lazy will likely mean they have to say goodbye to the benefits of scale economies, such disintegration can be prevented.

Unfortunately, encouraged by the initial success of the cooperative, the government decided to make the policy compulsory. The article of "Free to join and free to exit" in the 1956 National People's Congress articles of association disappeared in 1958 and did not come back until 1978, when the Third Plenary Session of the 11th Central Committee of the Communist Party of China was convened. So the game changed after 1958, when the people's commune was popularized. When the right to exit was removed, dropouts of capable farmers and disintegration no longer posed a real threat. As a result, freeloaders took advantage of hard workers, and even formerly hard workers would not work hard any more. The reason is simple: in this one-off game, staying idle is the rational option. So productivity really fell as more farmers became sluggish.

Most collectivization movements around the world were initially voluntary, with a right to exit, like those in Africa and Central and South America. But in the end, the exit right was usually removed. The former Soviet Union was similar, with its collectivization movement depriving farmers of their freedom to withdraw in 1929. They were paid fixed salaries unrelated to their contribution. Without good supervision, no one would work hard. So the general pattern of collectivization movements was that productivity increased at the beginning when farmers were free to withdraw and the output was higher than when farmers worked individually. But when the right was suddenly deprived, as in the Soviet Union in 1929 and China in 1958, output plummeted. Depriving the right to exit led to a universal decline in labor input. When the declines reached a certain level, they offset all the benefits of scale economies, reducing productivity. The whole process unfolded rapidly, and the crisis in the Soviet Union took more than 5 million lives. Given that the Soviet Union's population then was one-fifth that of China, one can infer that severity of the crisis in the Soviet Union was close to that in China.

When the exit right was removed, whatever incentives were left would be less appealing. So in the compulsory cooperative, collective productivity should be lower than the average of individual productivity. But it is not easy to verify this assumption empirically, because after 1962 many modern technologies were introduced to agriculture. The resulting improvement in productivity could offset lost productivity as a result of the disincentives. Yet, even when those innovations increased after 1962, productivity was still 20 percent lower than in 1952. That is, despite the fact that new technologies improved productivity, the hypothesis that removing the exit right caused the crisis remains valid. The other three hypotheses, though plausible, cannot explain why productivity did not recover until 1984.

Deviations from comparative advantage?

Still another hypothesis argues that the state monopoly over purchasing and marketing made provinces deviate from their comparative advantages, resulting in a productivity slump. Not until after 1978, when the reform program revived local markets, was local production again based on their comparative advantages, and productivity improved considerably. But the centralized purchasing and marketing policy was introduced in 1953, and productivity actually improved between 1953 and 1958. So this hypothesis can hardly explain why the productivity suddenly slumped after 1959.

In addition, the differences in comparative advantage across the country should be diminished if each locale had to be self-sufficient

TABLE 4.2 *The capital accumulation rate, 1952–78*

	% of GDP
First Five-Year Plan (1953–57)	24.2
Second Five-Year Plan (1958–62)	30.8
(1963–65)	22.7
Third Five-Year Plan (1966–70)	26.3
Fourth Five-Year Plan (1971–75)	33.3

Source: *China Compendium of National Income Statistics (1949–85)*, compiled by Department of Equilibrium Statistics on National Economy, National Bureau of Statistics of China.

in grain and the local government increased inputs of infrastructure and science and technology for agriculture. The provinces short of grain would put in more related science and technology, so their productivity would be enhanced more than those with enough grain. So the comparative advantage of the latter will be less strong.

Producing in a comparative advantage-defying (CAD) manner would reduce output and productivity less than 3 percent. But the actual loss was 20 percent. So only 15 percent of the loss can be blamed on defying comparative advantage, and we must look elsewhere to explain the remaining 85 percent. Do not forget people's enthusiasm for work. In any economy, a rapid change in productivity is usually related to that enthusiasm.[8]

The performance and impact of the economy before 1978

The planned economy started with the first Five-Year Plan in 1953.[9] Assessing it should consider the following:

First, was the surplus mobilized to the maximum? From this aspect, the planned economy was pretty efficient. The capital accumulation rate reached 24.2 percent of GDP during the first Five-Year Plan (1953–57) and 30.8 percent of GDP during the second Five-Year Plan (1958–62) (Table 4.2).

TABLE 4.3 *Sectoral share of investment in capital construction, 1952–78 (%)*

	Agriculture	Light industries	Heavy industries	Other
First Five-Year Plan (1953–57)	7.1	6.4	36.2	50.3
Second Five-Year Plan (1958–62)	11.3	6.4	54.0	28.3
(1963–65)	17.6	3.9	45.9	32.6
Third Five-Year Plan (1966–70)	10.7	4.4	51.1	33.8
Fourth Five-Year Plan (1971–75)	9.8	5.8	49.6	34.8

Source: Statistics on China's investment in fixed assets (1950–78), compiled by the Department of Statistics on China's Investment in Fixed Assets, National Bureau of Statistics of China.

TABLE 4.4 *Sectoral share of revenue in national income, 1952–78 (%)*

Sector	1952	1957	1965	1970	1975	1978
Agriculture	57.7	46.8	46.2	40.4	37.8	32.8
Industry	19.5	28.3	36.4	41.0	46.0	49.4
Other	22.8	24.5	17.4	18.6	16.2	17.8

Source: National Bureau of Statistics of China (1992).

According to the hypothesis of take-off, an economy's investment has to exceed 11 percent of GDP to get out of a low-income equilibrium trap.[10] China was always above that before 1978, indicating very effective mobilization of the surplus during that period. Investment in heavy industries was always high: almost half of the investment in infrastructure went to heavy industries (Tables 4.3 and 4.4). Accordingly, their output grew at great speed, and by 1978 was close to half of national revenue. Heavy industries received a high priority while light industries were not so fortunate. On the surface China resembled highly developed countries in industrial structure. Its average industrial growth – at 6 percent a year – was not slow before the reform kicked off. China tested an atomic bomb in the 1960s and launched a satellite in the 1970s. So if the objec-

TABLE 4.5 *Sectoral employment structure, 1952–78 (%)*

Sector	1952	1965	1978
Agriculture	83.5	81.6	73.3
Industry	6.0	6.4	12.5
Other	10.5	12.0	14.2

Source: National Bureau of Statistics of China (1992).

tive is heavy industries, military industries, and aeronautics indus-tries, the economy can be regarded as very efficient, for it took only two decades for an agrarian economy to achieve a feat that only developed countries were capable of before.

But that achievement came at a heavy price. First, it resulted in an unbalanced economic structure. Although China was close to the developed world in its heavy industry, its employment remained that of a backward agricultural economy, with 70 percent of the labor force in agriculture – an irrational allocation of resources (Table 4.5).

Due to the strategy of prioritizing heavy industries, urbanization was impeded. Not only were farmers not allowed to migrate to cities – urban youth had to move to the rural areas. This unusual industriali-zation resulted in low urbanization, and with an imbalanced indus-trial structure, labor's enthusiasm to work was dampened as well.

The working capital in industrial sectors is usually used for inputs and inventories, so the more efficient a company, the less working capital it should require. According to the World Bank, working capital was close to 30 percent in China, India, and the Soviet Union (Table 4.6), with all three having a common strategy to prioritize heavy industries. Although all plans were directed by the state in practice, companies retained some inventories so that they could meet their quotas, even when raw materials did not arrive in time. There were also times when products did not sell well. For example, I visited a machine tool plant in Wuxi in 1980 and found

TABLE 4.6 *An international comparison of working capital ratios (%)*

Country	Year	Working capital ratio
China	1981	32.7
India	1979	27.9
South Korea	1963	7.0
Japan	1953	19.9
United Kingdom	1970	16.6
Soviet Union	1972	29.6

Source: World Bank (1985).

some machine tools marked as manufactured in 1978 still in inventory, taking up a lot of working capital. That was one reason for China's high ratio of working capital at the time (Table 4.6).

In addition to the inefficient use of capital, the efficiency of industrial production was also lousy. To produce one dollar of GDP output, the coal steel consumption and transportation distance was 3.1 ton-kilometers per dollar for China, 1.7 for India, and 1.8 for the United States. Clearly, for the same output, China took many more ton-kilometers per dollar than India and the United States.

On a field study, when I was a post-graduate student at Peking University, I heard a story that may help explain the discrepancy. Bao Steel was not yet built, and An Steel in northeast China and Wu Steel in Wuhan were two major steel production centers, with products allocated by a central planning body. The equipment industry in northeast China was supposed to get steel from An Steel, and Wuhan city was supposed to be supplied by Wu Steel. But a mismatch frequently took place. Why? Because only a couple of officials in the former State Planning Commission were designated to be in charge of steel, and they were overwhelmed by the large number of enterprises and their varied and complicated demands.

TABLE 4.7 *Living standards of urban and rural residents, 1952–78*

| Year | Income index (1952 = 100) | Consumption index (1952 = 100) | | |
		Total population	Urban residents	Rural residents
1952	100	100	100	100
1957	153	123	126	117
1978	453	177	212	158

Note: The income index and consumption index are calculated at comparable prices.

Source: National Bureau of Statistics of China (1993).

From 1952 to 1981 TFP grew 0.5 percent a year at best. Some research suggests that it even declined. According to the World Bank it grew at 2 percent in the developing world. So China's efficiency was much lower than even its peers'.[11] The Chinese people tightened their belts, and while China launched a satellite, average living standards scarcely improved between 1952 and 1978 (Table 4.7).

Compared with other countries, 6 percent economic growth was not bad, but as national income grew 400 percent, consumption grew only 77 percent. Clearly heavy industry, the atomic bomb, and the satellite took priority over people's well-being.

There was a huge urban–rural gap, too. As the consumption of urban residents grew over 100 percent, that of their rural counterparts grew only 57 percent. The reason for the jump in urban consumption was increased employment. In the 1950s most women were housewives, but by the 1960s and 1970s they began to be bread earners, "Supporting half of the sky," as Chairman Mao praised. The improvement in living standards came not from better salaries, but from more jobs. The working population in the rural areas increased as well, but due to the strict control over the labor flow to cities, improvements in rural living standards were sluggish.

So if the goal was to launch a satellite or develop heavy industries, the system was a big success. But if the goal was to improve living standards, it was barely satisfactory, especially when compared with neighboring economies. In the early 1950s per capita income on the Chinese mainland was on par with South Korea, Singapore, Taiwan, China, and Hong Kong, China. But by the end of the 1970s, when the four Asian Tigers took off and converged with developed economies, China was left far behind. To catch up with the developed world is a common and legitimate aspiration of all developing countries. But all the planned economies, socialist or not, eventually failed.

In 1995 the per capita income of Singapore already exceeded that of the United Kingdom, and was very close to that of the United States. Hong Kong, China, also surpassed the United Kingdom. The purchasing power of Japan was a little short of the United States, but in absolute terms the former outperformed the latter by a big margin.[12] In this sense, it is the first country to outpace both the United Kingdom and the United States. Together, these economies created the East Asian Miracle.

References

Kornai, János. 1980. *Economics of Shortage*. Amsterdam: North-Holland.

Lin, Justin Y. 1990. "Collectivization and China's Agricultural Crisis in 1959–1961." *Journal of Political Economy* 98(6): 1228–52.

Lin, Justin Y., and James G. Wen. 1995. "China's Regional Grain Self-sufficiency Policy and Its Effect on Land Productivity." *Journal of Comparative Economics* 21(2): 187–206.

Lin, Justin Y., Fang Cai, and Zhou Li. 1996. *The China Miracle: Development Strategy and Economic Reform*. Hong Kong: Chinese University Press.

   2003. *The China Miracle: Development Strategy and Economic Reform*. revised edn. Hong Kong: Chinese University Press.

National Bureau of Statistics of China. 1987. *The Statistical Data of Fixed Asset Investment in China (1950–1978)*. Beijing: China Statistics Press.

   Various years. *China Statistical Yearbook*. Beijing: China Statistics Press.

National Bureau of Statistics of China, National Economic Accounting Division. 1987. *A Compilation of National Income Statistics Data (1949–1985)*. Beijing: China Statistics Press.

Rostow, W. W. 1960. *The Stages of Economic Growth: A Non-Communist Manifesto*, 3rd edn. New York: Cambridge University Press.

World Bank. 1985. *The 1984 Economic Study Tour. China: Long-term Issues and Options*. Washington, DC: World Bank.

2011. *World Development Indicators 2011*. Washington, DC: World Bank.

Notes

1. For more information, see Lin, Cai, and Li (1996, 2003).
2. See Kornai (1980).
3. The exchange of labor means that several households join hands to reap crops of one household after another.
4. This section draws on Lin (1990).
5. For more information about the three hypotheses, see Lin (1990). The bibliography related to the three hypotheses will not be listed here. Those who are interested may see the bibliography of Lin (1990).
6. Total factor productivity is the difference between output growth rate and the weighted average rate of growth of inputs. If the growth rate of inputs is, say, 10% and the growth rate of output is 12%, 10%, or 8%, the corresponding total factor productivity will be 2%, 0%, or −2% respectively.
7. China was the first country to popularize dwarf rice, and the planted area was the largest in the world.
8. See Lin and Wen (1995) for the discussion of this hypothesis and its refutation.
9. This section draws on Lin, Cai, and Li (1996, 2003).
10. Rostow (1960).
11. World Bank (1985).
12. Because of the Lost Decades after the burst of the real-estate and equity bubbles in 1991, Japan's per capita income fell below that of the United States again after 2000 (World Bank 2011).

FIVE

Enterprise viability and factor endowments

Soon after its founding, the People's Republic of China implemented a CAD, catching-up strategy, prioritizing heavy industries. The purpose: to develop, as soon as possible, advanced capital-intensive and technology-intensive industries that would keep China competitive with the developed world. China tested an atomic bomb in the 1960s and launched a satellite in the 1970s. It is fair to say that the initial goal was largely realized – but at a huge cost. For a long time living standards in the country remained repressed. By the end of the 1970s a third of China's people were still struggling for food and clothing.

Between the 1940s and 1960s, the CAD strategy was embraced not only by China and other socialist countries but also by some newly independent, non-socialist countries, such as Egypt, India, Indonesia, and some in Latin America. Like China, these economies also bit the dust. The first years after the strategy was implemented usually witnessed rapid growth driven by investment, but after a while growth would slow and crises would break out.

It is a natural and legitimate aspiration for developing countries to catch up with the developed world, yet almost none of the countries that adopted the CAD strategy did this. Only a few realized that dream: Japan and the four Asian Tigers, together creating an "East Asian Miracle." In per capita income, Japan exceeded the United States in 1987. Singapore, one of the four Tigers, also surpassed the United States in 1996. Hong Kong, China, was around 80–90 percent of the United States in the early 1990s. Taiwan, China, and South Korea were close to 50 percent and 40 percent respectively, of the United States in the mid-1990s.[1] Can those success stories provide an alternative development strategy for developing countries? To answer that question, we first have to figure out the reasons behind the "East Asian Miracle."

This chapter proposes a theoretical framework of factor endowments and enterprise viability. The next one explores the relationship between the comparative advantage-following strategy (hereafter CAF strategy) and economic development.

Interpretations of the East Asian Miracle

Cultural determinism

The earliest explanation for the East Asian Miracle focuses on Japan's history and culture. Before the advent of capitalism and the Industrial Revolution, feudal Europe comprised a large number of city-states of all sizes, each a small natural economy. Later, thanks to gunpowder from China, boundaries between city-states were broken, and unified nation-states were formed. The first law of economic growth put forward by Adam Smith in *The Wealth of Nations* is that the division of labor is one of the driving forces: the greater the division of labor, the higher the productivity.[2] But the division of labor was conditional on the size of the market. The larger the market, the greater the division of labor. When Europe transformed into nation-states, markets expanded, and labor's division and productivity were enhanced accordingly. Hence, the surplus for investment.

Some scholars believe that is why capitalism and the Industrial Revolution took place in Europe. They also believe that Japan, though a faraway oriental country, had one thing in common with Europe. Japan, before the Meiji Restoration, though ruled in name by a Mikado, was de facto ruled by the Shoguns and more than 200 dispersed aristocrats (daimyos) at all levels. Like in Europe, there was a hereditary system of aristocracy in Japan, and each aristocrat had his own castle. And each castle was a natural economy, with no unified national market. After the Meiji Restoration, Japan followed the western example and established a constitutional monarchy. Aristocrats were deprived of real power, and a national market was finally unified, exactly what happened after the breakdown of feudal society in Europe.

If that hypothesis were valid, other countries in East Asia could never be modernized. Take China. Back in the Western Zhou Dynasty (about 1000–771 BC), it was a typical feudal society. Under Emperor Zhou, hundreds of feudal states were established as hereditary fiefdoms. Later, when Emperor Qin unified China in 221 BC, a system of prefectures and counties replaced the aristocracy. Since then, China basically remained a big and unified country until modern times. In other words, unlike Japan and Europe, China's economy has long been unified. So, if the hypothesis were correct, modernization for other East Asian economies, or for that matter other developing countries, meant copying a Japanese model of first forming a feudal society with dispersed natural economies and then building a unified national market. But it is unrealistic to ask an already unified economy to disperse.

In the 1960s and 1970s four other emergent economies – the four Asian Tigers of South Korea, Singapore, Taiwan, and Hong Kong – made their presence felt. Unlike Japan, the four have always been unified. And by the 1970s they developed into modern industrial economies attracting worldwide attention. What's more, they maintained rapid growth for more than two decades and bridged the income gap with the developed world. The success of the Asian Tigers proves the foregoing hypothesis was ill-founded.

By the early 1980s, however, no other economies had closed the gap with the developed world. Thus emerged another culture-based hypothesis. Because Japan and the four Asian Tigers are greatly influenced by Confucianism, some scholars attribute their success to Confucian philosophy. This hypothesis is influenced by Max Weber's proposition of the Protestant ethic, featuring diligence, frugality, and a willingness to save and invest as the major reasons capitalism developed in the West.[3] The Confucian culture also stresses social order and deference to authority. Diligence and frugality help accumulation and investment, and deference to authority facilitates social stability. Together, they laid the social and economic foundation of industrialization.

But if Confucianism were truly responsible for the success of Japan and the four Asian Tigers, China should have been all the more successful, since it is the cradle of that philosophy. And during the May Fourth Movement in 1919, Confucianism was actually held responsible for China's failure to modernize. It was labeled as "man-eating," to be beaten down. Such a view was shared by many elites in East Asia, holding ground long after the May Fourth Movement, until South Korea and Taiwan, China, became modern industrial economies.[4]

Confucianism barely changed from traditional to modern times, and so cannot be held responsible for either the success or failure of economies. So, although apparently common to Japan and the four Asian Tigers, it is not the major reason for their success.

The Cold War

Some scholars of international politics attribute the success of East Asian economies to the Cold War. After World War II the world was divided into two camps: capitalist and socialist. Japan and the four Asian Tigers were on the edge of the Iron Curtain, close to the socialist camp and the first line of containment of socialism and communism. So the United States offered them many benefits – for starters, military and economic aid. In the 1950s and 1960s aid from the United States helped South Korea and Taiwan, China, accumulate sufficient capital to maintain peace and stability and lay the foundation for their economic take-off.

Because poverty is usually the cause of a Socialist Revolution, the United States wanted those economies to thrive. But for them to get rich on their own, not just direct financial assistance but also technical support was essential. The United States thus facilitated technology transfers to those economies. Taiwan's most successful enterprise – Formosa Plastics Group, owned by Wang Yung-ching – was built thanks to financial supports and technology imported from the United States in the 1950s. The United States also opened its domestic market to those economies, importing huge volumes of their exports.

This hypothesis can perhaps explain why Japan and the four Asian Tigers were successful, but it falls apart in the Philippines, also an East Asian economy, and a failure. If American support were the major reason for take-off, the Philippines should have all the more reason to be in better shape. But the then-largest naval and air bases of the United States were in the Philippines. The United States granted the most financial assistance to the Philippines, its former colony, which won its independence in 1946. And there were no technology transfer restrictions or market access restrictions. The results? In the 1960s the Philippines was on the right track, a star of tomorrow in Asia, second only to Japan. But in the 1970s it was reduced to one of the least advanced countries, with the worst economic performance in Asia. Even today, the Philippines remains a backward country.

So, even if the Cold War helped the growth of East Asia, it cannot be a determining factor. By the same token, if the Cold War was the determining factor, countries in Latin America should have developed even more than their East Asian counterparts. Although Latin American countries were not at the forefront of socialist

expansion, they have Cuba, a socialist country, as their neigh-
bor. Fidel Castro carried clout in Latin America. To shield those
countries from Castro's influence, the United States offered them
far more benefits than it did to East Asia – in capital, technology,
market access, and assistance. Even so, those economies were hit by
one crisis after another, especially in the 1970s and 1980s.

The market economy

The market economy hypothesis, proposed by researchers at the
World Bank and the International Monetary Fund, holds that the
success of East Asian economies should be attributed to the fact
that they all pursue a market economic system.[5] Indeed, these East
Asian economies, unlike socialist countries, all pursued a market
economy based on private property. The market economy – featuring market competition and effective allocations of resources – can
increase enthusiasm and efficiency. With reasonable allocations of
resources, greater enthusiasm, better management, and more technological progress, the economy is guaranteed to succeed. In the
words of those economists, the success of the East Asian economies
is "getting prices right." To get prices right, market competition
must be given full play.

True, the East Asian economies are market economies based on
private property. But those with a thorough understanding of these
economies will see the inadequacy of the hypothesis, because the
governments of these economies did much more than simply give
the market full play. Japan's Ministry of International Trade and
Industry has always been actively formulating industrial policies to
support the development of certain industries. Its practices resem-
ble the planned economy. It artificially lowered the interest rate to
support the development of certain industries with cheap capital.
It also imposed barriers on imports to protect the domestic market.
Except for Hong Kong, China, the other three Asian Tigers all
greatly intervened in their markets. Even Hong Kong, China, is not

a full market economy, because it also intervened in the real estate and financial industries. So the market economy hypothesis is not the complete story.

The government intervention hypothesis

Some other scholars hold exactly the opposite view: those economies "got the prices wrong" to support some competitive industries. This hypothesis is proposed by Alice Amsden, a scholar at MIT, who studies the economies of South Korea, Japan, and Taiwan, China, and by Robert Wade, a British scholar who studies the economy of Taiwan, China.[6] The detailed analysis of how these governments distorted prices to support certain industries leads them to conclude that distorting prices is the major reason for their success. But that conclusion is also flawed. Socialist countries and some non-socialist countries (China, India, some in Latin America and Africa) also distorted prices to mobilize resources for their strategic industries. Yet their economies did not thrive at all. So, the government intervention hypothesis is too simplistic.

The export-orientation hypothesis

Some scholars of international trade suggest that one of the major reasons for the success of East Asian economies is their export-oriented policies.[7] They argue that an export orientation is essential for economic growth. With such a policy, the economy has to make products competitive in the international market by constantly improving technology and management. In addition, such a policy facilitates frequent contact with the developed world, making it possible to learn advanced technology and managerial expertise. In addition, exports earn foreign exchange to pay for imports of technology and machinery.

On the surface, the East Asian economies are more export-oriented than other countries and regions. But is their high export orientation the cause of their success or the consequence? If it is the cause, the higher the export orientation (thus more exports) of an economy, the better. But as long as the government is willing to sub-sidize, it can export as much as it wants. Yet subsidized exports are not necessarily conducive to economic growth. So, export-oriented policies are more likely to be the result of economic growth rather than the cause.

Each of the foregoing three hypotheses – market economy, gov-ernment intervention, and export orientation – captures an aspect of the East Asian economies. But on closer inspection they are all superficial, not the true underlying reasons. It's like the story of the "Blind Men and an Elephant." Each blind man bases his percep-tions of what the elephant looks like on the part he touches. No one is completely right or wrong, but no one has a full picture of the elephant. Similarly, a valid hypothesis to pinpoint the true reason(s) for the success of these economies should be able to explain all the aspects of the issue instead of just one aspect.

A proposed theory of enterprise viability and comparative advantage

Concepts and models

The definition of viability

Before I explain this new theory of comparative advantage,[8] the important concept of enterprise viability needs to be defined. "Viability" is the capacity of a normally managed enterprise to earn a socially acceptable normal profit in an open, free, and com-petitive market, without external support or protection. "Normally managed" means that there is no major problem in its operation or management. "Normal profit" refers to an average profit acceptable to the market. "Open" means that the domestic market is connected with foreign markets. "Free" means that there is free access to the market. "Competitive" means that there is no monopoly in the market.

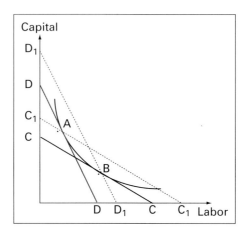

Figure 5.1 Relative prices of production factors and technology choices

The reason for defining viability is to set a standard, so that we can better understand enterprises that are not viable. A "non-viable" enterprise cannot earn a socially acceptable normal profit in a free, open, and competitive market, even if it is normally managed. Nobody would invest in a non-viable enterprise. Even if someone did so by misjudgment, the investors would eventually withdraw their investment. The external support and protection is, of course, that from the government. The reason a normally managed enterprise is not viable is that the government has intervened in its technology, product, and industry choices, so the government has to provide the support and protection that a non-viable enterprise needs.

Technology choice in a single-product economy
Consider the simplest economic model, with only one type of product produced with two factors – capital and labor. Each point on the isoquant in Figure 5.1 represents a specific technology required to produce a given amount of product. Point A represents a capital-intensive technology, while point B represents a labor-intensive technology. Both produce the same amount of product.

In an open and competitive market, the technology an enterprise should choose will depend on the isocost line, indicating the relative prices of capital and labor. If C is the isocost line in the economy, the technology represented by point B is the best, for it costs the least. Any other technology will make the enterprise incur losses in an open and competitive market. For example, if it adopts technology A, it would be expected to incur a loss equivalent to the distance from C to C_1. So, with the given amount of products, the least-cost technology is the best. By the same token, if D is the isocost line in the economy, technology A is the best.

To sum up, the best technology available hinges on the slope of the isocost line, which depends on the economy's factor endowment structure – the relative abundance of its capital and labor. When labor is relatively abundant and capital is relatively scarce (as in developing economies), the isocost line will be something like C rather than D. When capital becomes relatively abundant and labor relatively scarce (as in developed economies), the isocost line will change to something like D.

People generally assume that technologies adopted by the developed world are always better. For example, the output of an American farmer may be dozens of times that of a Chinese farmer. That is because the United States has adopted a capital-intensive technology according to its endowment structure, with relatively abundant capital and scarce labor. Under that circumstance, a capital-intensive technology is the most cost-effective choice – but not necessarily the best for any circumstance. Even so, many people believe that the technological choice of developed countries is the best no matter what, because they see only that more advanced technology in developed countries brings higher output per labor.

They thus assume that the capital-intensive technology is the best. Hence the slogan, "mechanization is the answer to agricultural development" in China in the 1970s, as mechanization was a common feature of all developed countries. But in an open competitive market, the isocost line of China should be C rather than D, because China, like other developing countries, had relatively abundant labor and scarce capital. In that case, only the enterprises that choose point B are viable, because technology B costs the least, and the enterprises choosing B can produce acceptable profits.

In a competitive market, if the government does not intervene, enterprises will choose technology consistent with the endowment structure for the sake of survival and profitability. But because most people (including national leaders) held the belief that the technology option of the developed world was always better, they wanted Chinese farmers to choose technology A, just as their American counterparts did. But in an open competitive market, choosing A means that the enterprise cannot make any profit, because this choice defies the comparative advantage determined by the endowment structure. So, the government's intervention makes the enterprise non-viable. To earn any profit under such circumstances, the enterprise has to be protected or subsidized by the government.

The product or technology choice in a single-industry economy
The foregoing discussion can be extended to an industry that has many different products. In international trade a product is always regarded as an industry, but in real life an industry always has multiple products. Take the information technology industry. It comprises not only multiple products but also multiple production sections. Some production sections specialize in creating new products and new technologies, such as IBM and Intel. Others specialize in producing OEM chips based on the designs from IBM and Intel. The production line is usually very expensive. For example, a production line of eight-inch wafer integrated circuits costs around $1.3 billion (about 10 billion RMB), capital-intensive indeed. But the cost of IBM's new technology is even greater: the annual R&D input at IBM is more than $5 billion, and at Intel more than $8 billion.

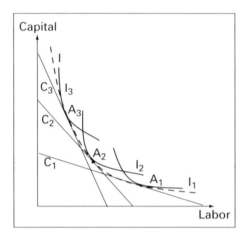

Figure 5.2 Relative prices of production factors and the product choices in a given industry

Now examine the single-industry economy. There are multiple types of products in the industry: some are capital-intensive, like new products and new technologies, which require enormous R&D inputs; others are labor-intensive, like components production and products assembly. Suppose that the information industry produces products I_1, I_2, and I_3. I_3 represents capital-intensive new products and technologies, such as those of IBM and Intel. I_2 represents products like chips, also capital-intensive, but not as much as I_3. I_1 represents component assembly, which is labor-intensive and does not require much capital. In Figure 5.2, lines I_1, I_2, and I_3 represent the isoquants of three different products I_1, I_2, I_3 that have the same output value. The *isovalue line* I is therefore the envelope of the isoquants of I_1, I_2, I_3 in the industry. Each point on the isovalue line represents a specific product in the industry that is produced by a specific technology and has the same value.

Which products, capital-intensive or labor-intensive, a country should produce hinges on the isocost line of the country. If the isocost line is indicated by C_3, the economy should produce product I_3. By the same token, if the isocost line is indicated by C_1, I_1 should be preferred. The discussion shows that in an open competitive market, a firm's viability and its choice of products and relevant technologies are determined by the economy's endowment structure.

The popular view in China is that its information industry, involving mainly labor-intensive components production and product assembly, is not worth mentioning. Although China ranks third in this industry next to the United States and Japan, it does not have much indigenous intellectual property. Intellectual property is a result of R&D, taking the form of new products and new technologies (I_3). Only enterprises that have invested hugely in R&D – like IBM, Intel, and Nokia – can create and own intellectual property. Now notice the huge gap between the isocost line of these companies and that of Chinese companies. In an open competitive market, a Chinese company producing products with indigenous intellectual property rights would not be viable without protection and subsidy from the state, even if well managed.

Product/technology/industry choices in an economy with many industries

The model can be further extended to the whole economy. Suppose that an economy has three industries I, J, and K, represented by the three isovalue lines I, J, and K (see Figure 5.3). Each industry produces multiple products, and each product can be produced with different technologies.

K_1 and J_2 are typical products of developed countries, because industry K is close to the capital axis, indicating that K is capital-intensive. The isocost line D indicates an endowment structure with relatively cheap capital and expensive labor. So, a developed economy with relatively abundant capital has comparative advantage to produce K_1 and J_2. But if the isocost line is C, typical of developing countries, the story is different. Products I_1 and J_1 in the labor-intensive industries I and J enjoy comparative advantage. In that context, if a firm instead decides to produce K_1, it will not

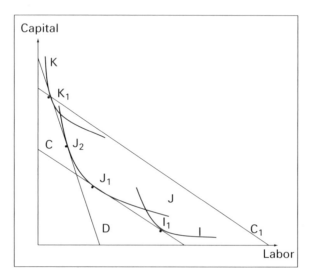

Figure 5.3 Relative prices of production factors and industry choices

be viable in an open competitive market; no matter how well it is managed, it cannot earn an acceptable expected profit. Generally, no one will invest in such companies. Even if someone did, based on false information, the companies would go bankrupt anyway.

Under the CAD strategy, some companies are asked to produce products and choose industries or technologies not consistent with their economy's endowment structure. Those companies are not viable. To save them from bankruptcy, the government has to protect them and provide subsidies.

Viability and comparative advantage

The concepts of viability and comparative advantage are closely related – but with a different focus. For starters, viability focuses on the expected profitability of a company, and comparative advantage examines the competitiveness of a product or an industry in an open competitive market. Simply put, the viability theory addresses enterprises while the comparative advantage theory studies industries. Even so, the endowment structure of an economy determines both.

In accordance with the strict definitions, the concept of comparative advantage applies only to open economies while the concept of viability applies to both open and closed economies. Suppose that the United States and China were the only two countries in the world and did not trade with each other. Comparatively speaking, the United States has abundant capital and a small population, and China has scarce capital and a big population. Both countries need to produce food to feed their people, but the technologies used are different. In the United States, where capital is relatively cheap and labor expensive, to save costs in a competitive market, a rational farm will choose capital-intensive technology. Similarly, a rational farm in China will opt for labor-intensive technology. So, the concept of viability also works in a closed economy.

The optimal industrial structure and policy burden

Now that we understand the concept of viability, it will be easier to comprehend the concept of "optimal industrial structure." An industrial structure consistent with the endowment structure is an optimal industrial structure; otherwise, its efficiency suffers.

The concept of optimal industrial structure may seem irrelevant, but it can actually extend to many areas in economics. For example, it can extend to industrial organization theory, which does not yet have the concept, because it does not have the concept of viability. It can also extend to development economics. Most scholars of development economics define the object of development as upgrading the industrial and technological structure, taking no notice of the critical role of the endowment structure in the industrial structure in developing countries.

Based on the concept of viability, an economy's optimal industrial and technological structure and its optimal product mix are determined by the economy's endowment structure. Here I'd like to stress a basic principle: to change an endogenous phenomenon, one first has to change the exogenous cause of the phenomenon.

An economy's industrial and technological structure and product mix are determined by the economy's endowment structure. So, to upgrade the structure implies that the endowment structure – the relative abundance of capital and labor – must be changed first. More specifically, the relative capital abundance should be increased. If that is achieved, capital will become cheaper, and labor more expensive.

To stay competitive in a competitive market, a company has to take the initiative to change the mix of input factors, replacing labor with capital. As a result, the intensity of both capital and technology will increase, as will the marginal productivity of labor and labor's income. The whole process happens spontaneously as a result of companies' normal response to market prices, and no government intervention is needed. But if a government implements a CAD strategy by altering the industrial and technological structure without first changing the endowment structure, it defies its optimal structure. The companies in that economy will not be viable or efficient, and they will pay a dear price.

The traditional view holds that the major gap between the developed world and the developing lies in their differing industrial and technological structure. But it fails to see that industrial and technological structure is determined by the factor endowment structure. Therefore, the development objective should be to upgrade the endowment structure, not the industrial and technological structure.

Unfortunately, many economists who have been studying development economics for decades in top-class universities (like Harvard and MIT) are still focusing on upgrading the industrial and technological structure. For an economy implementing the traditional CAD strategy for some time, the technology in that economy could show some progress, and its products could become more capital-intensive. But companies in the prioritized industries would not be viable in an open competitive market and could not survive without the government's protection and subsidy. If the government demands that those companies continue, it has to bear some "policy burden," that imposed by the government's development policy. For instance, companies in developing countries should concentrate on industries I or J (see Figure 5.3), but the government might demand that they engage in industry K. In an open competitive market, those companies would suffer losses. Because the losses are caused by the state policies, the state should be accountable to the relevant companies and give them policy support.[9]

Policy support has several manifestations. First, the state can grant direct subsidies to – or develop preferential tax policies for – those companies. If only a small number of prioritized industries are supported by the state, subsidies and tax incentives will work. But if the number is big, they will not work. In the days of the planned economy in China, there were eight ministries for the machinery industry, each supervising many subsectors of heavy industries. Apparently, the state subsidies could not cover them all.

Direct financial subsidies can work in some developed countries. For example, producing rice is not consistent with Japan's comparative advantage. But to ensure food security, the government grants a large amount of direct financial subsidies to that sector. The case is similar in Europe and the United States. But keep in mind that agriculture accounts for less than 5 percent of the national economy in developed countries, so they have little problem in covering the subsidies. For developing countries, by contrast, the story is totally different. With the colossal heavy industries that have to be subsidized, it is unlikely that the government can collect enough taxes from other sectors to subsidize the prioritized industries.

Alternatives to subsidies include creating trade barriers to keep similar products from developed countries from entering the domestic market, imposing prohibitive tariffs, and eliminating competition by establishing monopolies for the supported companies in the domestic market.

Second, policy support can derive from distorting factor prices – lowering interest rates, overvaluing foreign exchange, and even lowering the prices for raw materials, wages, and daily necessities. By pushing up product prices and cutting costs, the government can help non-viable companies survive and even make handsome profits. A telling example: before 1978 Liaoning province ranked fourth in economic size, next to three municipalities (namely Beijing, Shanghai, and Guangzhou). The major reason is that all of its pillar industries enjoyed both monopolistic product prices and cheap factor prices. With China's accession to the World Trade Organization, the interest rate is still low enough, but other factor prices have been liberalized. In the new circumstances those heavy industries are not viable anymore; hence the recent national strategy to rejuvenate the northeast's rust belt.

As mentioned, price distortions are another form of policy-backed subsidization. In socialist countries the subsidized companies are usually owned by the state. In non-socialist countries subsidies can lead to even worse consequences. The companies that would not be viable in an open competitive market can earn handsome profits in an environment distorted by policy-backed subsidies.

Generally only two types of people can invest in these capital-intensive industries: the rich and the powerful – hence, crony capitalism. The prioritized industries are controlled by the rich or those who have close connections with government officials. Since these people have shouldered the "policy burden" by helping implement the national development strategy of prioritizing heavy industries, they earn profits with the government's protection and subsidy. Capitalists certainly welcome profits, and the more the better.

There are two ways to earn more profits: one is to improve management and operating efficiency, and the other is to ask for more protection and subsidies from the state. The second requires less effort, so rent-seeking and corruption take place. And whenever companies incur any loss in a competitive market, they will bargain for more subsidies. Due to asymmetrical information, the government cannot verify their statements, creating a soft budget constraint. Without a hard budget constraint, irregular behavior would occur. So, even if some industries were established and survived for a while, thanks to huge resources mobilized by the state, in the end their low efficiency is bound to create economic, social, and political problems. That is exactly what happened in the countries implementing the CAD strategy in Eastern Europe, Asia, Africa, and Latin America.

References

Amsden, Alice H. 1989. *Asia's Next Giant; South Korea and Late Industrialization.* New York: Oxford University Press.

Chang, Ha-joon. 2008. *Bad Samaritans: The Myth of Free Trade and the Secret History of Capitalism.* New York: Bloomsbury Press.

Kruger, Anne O. 1992. *Economic Policy Reform in Developing Countries.* Oxford: Basil Blackwell.

Lin, Justin Y. 2003. "Development Strategy, Viability and Economic Convergence." *Economic Development and Cultural Change* 53(2): 278–309.

Lin, Justin Y. 2009. *Economic Development and Transition: Thought, Strategy, and Viability.* Cambridge: Cambridge University Press.

Lin, Justin Y., and Guofu Tan. 1999. "Policy Burdens, Accountability, and the Soft Budget Constraint." *American Economic Review: Papers and Proceedings* 89(2) (May): 426–31.

Smith, Adam. [1776] 1976. *An Inquiry into the Nature and Causes of the Wealth of Nations.* Chicago: University of Chicago Press.

Wade, Robert. 1990. *Governing the Market.* Princeton, NJ: Princeton University Press.

Weber, Max. 1930. *The Protestant Ethic and the Spirit of Capitalism.* London: Allen & Unwin.

World Bank. 1993. *The East Asian Miracle: Economic Growth and Public Policy.* New York: Oxford University Press.

2010. *World Development Indicators 2010.* Washington, DC: World Bank.

Notes

1. World Bank (2010).
2. Smith ([1776] 1976).
3. Weber (1930).
4. Chang (2008).
5. These viewpoints are expressed in World Bank (1993).
6. See Amsden (1989) and Wade (1990).
7. A representative of this hypothesis is Kruger (1992).
8. This section draws on Lin (2003, 2009).
9. Lin and Tan (1999).J_1

SIX

The comparative advantage-following development strategy

Empirical facts have proved the futility of a development strategy directly aiming at upgrading the industrial and technological structure. The reason is that artificially upgrading the industry and technology structure defies the comparative advantage determined by the existing endowment structure and will result in distortions and low efficiency.[1] So, to upgrade that structure and ensure the maximum efficiency, the cause – the factor endowment structure – must be changed.[2]

Factor endowment refers to an economy's relative abundance in capital, labor, land, and natural resources. Usually land and natural resources are given, for countries can no longer have colonies in foreign lands, as in the eighteenth and nineteenth centuries. The gap between labor growth in developing and developed countries is minimal: labor growth in developing countries is usually 2–3 percent, and that in developed countries is also above zero. The major difference comes from capital accumulation. For some countries, the rate is as high as 30–40 percent, but for others, it is less than 10 percent.

So, upgrading the endowment structure refers to increasing the relative abundance of capital. For any production period the factor endowment structure determines the sum of the resources, capital, and labor available to an economy and the relative prices of capital and labor. In the longer term the endowment structure can change with changes in population and capital accumulation. And the capital accumulation rate determines the upgrading of the factor endowment structure.

The determinants of capital accumulation are the following. First, the economic surplus from each production period can be accumulated as capital if it is used for the next period of production rather than being consumed. The key to upgrading the factor endowment structure of an economy is to increase the surplus of each period of production and the proportion of the surplus accumulated as capital. With more surplus and a bigger proportion of it accumulated as capital, upgrading the factor endowment structure is faster.

Note that if, at every point in time, a person's private production activities increase not only his own income but also the output of products and services of the society, that person's private production activities are consistent with the social production activities, creating more surplus. But sometimes a person's private productive activities increase his own income but not necessarily the social output, as in rent-seeking. Rent-seeking is based on government protection and subsidies, which are channeled from other sectors' income, so the total social output is not increased. In other words an economy where the private productive activities conflict with the social ones produces less surplus than the economy where the two types of activities are in agreement.

In addition, in an open competitive market the economic surplus also depends on the competitiveness of the companies engaging in social production activities. The more competitive the company, the more market share it will claim. It will also produce more surplus because it can sell all its products and services.

In sum, the economic surplus is determined by two factors: first, whether the private productive activities of a person are in line with the social production activities, and second, whether these social production activities are competitive in an open competitive market. With a given surplus, the rate of capital accumulation also hinges on whether people are willing to accumulate. If they are willing to save instead of consume the surplus, there will be more surplus for investment, and the rate of accumulating capital and upgrading the endowment structure will also pick up.

Based on an understanding of these determinants, upgrading the factor endowment structure boils down to increasing the economic surplus and accumulating capital. The traditional development strategy is to readjust the industrial structure through government intervention. But a CAF strategy aims at changing the endowment structure.

First, if an economy develops in a manner consistent with its endowment structure at every stage, companies will be viable without government protection and subsidies. There will be no rent-seeking, and the private production activities of every person will be consistent with the social production activities. Second, the CAF strategy can make companies more competitive in an open competitive market. Third, because developing countries are short of capital in relative terms, a CAF strategy will maximize the returns on capital. And with the possibility of borrowing new technologies from developed countries at low costs, the rate of technological change will accelerate. So even if capital accumulates at great speed, it will not lead to diminishing marginal returns. With higher returns on capital, the enthusiasm for saving and investment will also be greater, stimulating capital accumulation and upgrading the endowment structure.

Upgrading the endowment structure means that the relative abundance of capital increases, so the relative prices of factors will change, and the isocost line will shift from C to D (see Figure 5.3). In an open competitive market, when the isocost line changes, the existing industry/product/technology options will not be optimal for the next period of production, because they will no longer represent the least cost. In this context, intelligent entrepreneurs will use more capital to replace labor, develop new products, engage in new industries, and use more capital-intensive technologies to save on cost. That is how change in the cost structure leads to industrial and technological upgrading. At the end of the production period, the entrepreneurs who have made changes accordingly will see reduced costs and more profits, both an incentive for them and a challenge for others.

This competitive pressure, together with accelerated technological changes, drives the whole industry to upgrade. In an open competitive market the upgrading is spontaneous. And during the whole process the industrial and technological structure should be consistent with the economy's endowment structure and comparative advantage. Companies that follow the comparative advantage of the economy are viable, bear no policy burden, and have no excuse for rent-seeking. Nor does the government have to subsidize them. When private production activities are consistent with social production activities, the economy performs with high efficiency, and the surplus and capital accumulate at the greatest pace. And the new endowment structure will push for another round of industrial upgrading and technological progress. That is how the CAF strategy works.

Now let us revisit three hypotheses mentioned in Chapter 5: market economy, government intervention, and export orientation. They are actually describing the endogenous requirements or results of the CAF strategy. Next, we will study the role of markets, governments, and exports in the CAF strategy.

The CAF strategy
and the market mechanism

In an open competitive market, entrepreneurs will spontaneously and constantly adjust the production structure according to price signals to adapt to the changing endowment structure, upgrading the economy's endowment structure and industrial and technological structure. For entrepreneurs, what concerns them most is how to reduce costs and increase profits according to the price signals in the market. A prerequisite for companies to make correct decisions is that relative factor prices should truly reflect their relative abundance. If they do, entrepreneurs will spontaneously choose the product, technology, and industry that are consistent with the economy's comparative advantage. The only way to ensure this is with full competition in the product and factor market. To conclude, the market mechanism with full competition is a basic institutional arrangement for the CAF strategy.

The CAF strategy
and the government

When it comes to economic development, the role of the government may differ significantly between developing and developed economies, even if both are based on the market. For developed countries the government should interfere less, as long as it fulfills its basic functions of a minimum government – maintaining public order, providing public goods, compensating for externalities, and so on. But for developing countries, a minimum government is not optimal. Here's why.

Developed countries lead the world in technology and boast the best available product and industry structures. So, it is hard for them or their firms to see where their product/technology/industry should head at the next stage. They have to make their decisions at their discretion. Most of the firms will fail in this mission, and only a couple of them will succeed and thus lead in developing the economy. In this process the government enjoys no advantage in information and has little role.

At the end of the 1990s the Iridium Satellite Constellation project, launched by Iridium Communications Inc., a subsidiary of Motorola in the United States, attracted a lot of attention worldwide and was recognized by the Chinese Academy of Sciences as one of the top ten technological achievements of 1998. As part of the project, Motorola launched more than forty satellites in the four corners of the earth and developed satellite phones for use anywhere in the world. The telecommunications technology was quite something. But so was the prohibitive cost of the cell phone: the subscriber had to pay $50,000. In the end the project failed because there simply weren't enough users. So, when it comes to R&D for cutting-edge technologies, there are no ready-made examples to learn from and certainly many uncertainties and risks.

For developing countries, things are quite different. The products, technologies, and industries they develop already exist in the developed world. They can thus learn from their more advanced peers and even import their technologies, the advantage of latecomers. But what pace is appropriate? Which industries should be prioritized? The old comparative advantage-defying (CAD) strategy prioritizing heavy industries and aiming at fast pace has proved to be of low efficiency, and a CAF strategy will be a better choice. Because the development path of a developing country is largely predictable, the government can and should play a role in information collection, coordination, and compensation for externalities.

Information collection

The first function for government implementing a CAF strategy is to collect and disseminate information. To give full play to the latecomers' advantage, the government has to find answers to the following questions: Is it easy for the existing product, technology, and industry to be upgraded to the next stage? What is the market size for the new products? How many developing countries at the same development stage are on the same road?

Collecting and processing information is costly, yet disseminating processed information costs almost nothing. In this sense, information is a kind of public good. If each company collects its own information without sharing it with others, it will lead to repetitive information collection and huge waste. Since information has features of public goods, the governments of developing countries can collect relevant information on the product, technology, and industry according to the changes in their endowment structure and comparative advantage. If multiple products are consistent with their comparative advantage, the government should also get to know their respective market size and supply to avoid diminishing profits from overinvestment. The information collected by the government can provide a reference to companies in the form of industrial policies.

Coordination

The second function for government is coordinating investments by relevant companies. Industrial upgrading and technological innovation require not only investment in production but also improvement in education and access to finance and infrastructure, such as power, roads, and port facilities. Many companies cannot internalize those improvements. So, the government should step in to coordinate private investments in those improvements or provide those services itself.

Compensation for externalities

The final function of the government is to compensate the externalities for companies, but such compensation is conditional. The government develops industrial policies in accord with the information collected, but these policies are not necessarily correct. If they are incorrect, companies that responded first to the government's call will suffer a loss or even go bankrupt. Their bankruptcy can serve as a warning to other companies, which will shun investment in the same fields. But if the industrial policies are correct, and the companies that have made the first move are phenomenally successful, more companies will follow suit. And increased competition will dilute the profits of the pioneer companies.

Either way, the pioneers can provide useful information to the whole community. But the costs of failure and the benefits of success are not symmetrical. If the cost has to be borne by an individual company and yet the benefits can be shared by the whole society, no company will be willing to be the "white mouse." Considering these information externalities, the government should encourage companies to be the "first crab-eaters" by providing them subsidies, benefiting all of society. The subsidies can take the form of tax breaks or lower interest rates in accordance with industrial policies.

The industrial policies under a CAF strategy are quite different from the policies prioritizing heavy industries under the CAD strategy. The former ensures that companies are viable, while the latter cannot. Under the CAD strategy, companies rely heavily on government protection and subsidies, because they are not viable. But under the CAF strategy, the government has to provide only a small amount of protection and subsidies to help businesses compensate for the externalities, because they are viable. Two examples will illustrate the distinction.

Why prioritizing heavy industries succeeded in Germany but failed in China and India

After World War II many developing countries adopted the CAD strategy. Germany, with its amazing development in the late nineteenth century, is always the poster child for the strategy. In 1870 Bismarck, "the Iron Chancellor," developed the "Blood and Iron Policy" to support heavy industries and the military industry, aiming to transform Germany, in a very short period, from an agrarian economy to a modern industrial economy, and from a relatively backward country to a European power.

The Blood and Iron Policy looks very similar to the CAD strategy many developing countries adopted after World War II: both prioritized heavy industries. But those policies were implemented under different endowment structures, hence the opposite results.

According to the data from Maddison's *The World Economy: A Millennial Perspective*, Germany's per capita income in 1820 (in purchasing power parity) was about 62 percent of Britain's, and when Bismarck introduced the Blood and Iron Policy, the figure was 57 percent.[3] Per capita income is a good indicator of the factor endowment structure: the higher the income, the more abundant the capital.

It is true that heavy industries such as iron and steel are capital-intensive and require a large amount of capital, but they were not the most advanced industries at that time, with their development traced to the Industrial Revolution. Nor was Germany really short of capital: given that Britain was the most advanced economy at that time, 57 percent did not look bad. But with dispersed financial services and poor resource mobilization capacity, the state had to step in to overcome difficulties in financing heavy industries. That strategy was consistent with Germany's latent comparative advantage determined by its endowment structure and a good example of government coordination of industrial policies.

By contrast, when China and India proposed prioritizing heavy industries in the 1950s, their per capita incomes were between 500 and 600 international dollars (based on 1990 purchasing power parities), only about 5 percent of the United States in the same year, and a third of Germany's in 1870. The data demonstrate a glaring disparity in factor endowments between Germany on the one hand and China and India on the other. To sum up, Germany implemented a CAF strategy with the government playing a coordinating role, while China and India implemented a CAD strategy.

Automobile industry policies and per capita income

Japan developed its iron and steel and shipbuilding industries in the 1950s. And by the 1960s, with the accumulation of capital and technology, it was ready for some industrial upgrading, and the Ministry of International Trade and Industry (MITI) developed policies to prioritize the automobile industry. US per capita income in 1965 was $13,419 in purchasing power parity 1990 international dollars, and Japan's was $5,934, about 40 percent of the US level. In the 1960s aerospace and computer industries emerged in the United States and the automobile industry was no longer the most advanced.

MITI's original purpose was to protect Toyota and Nissan, yet more than a dozen heavy industrial enterprises planned to enter the automobile industry, including Honda (then engaging in motorcycle production), Mitsubishi (in iron and steel), Suzuki, Mazda, Hino, and others. At the beginning, MITI discouraged these enterprises from entering for fear of overcrowding and did not give them any protection or subsidy. But in the end they all thrived in the global market without the government's support.

According to the definition of viability, a company is viable if in an open competitive market it can make profit and survive by normal operation and without government support; the industry in which those successful businesses are engaged is also consistent with the comparative advantage of the economy. So, the automobile industry policies of Japan in the 1960s were consistent with its comparative advantage.

In the 1950s China and India also developed auto industry policies. But their per capita incomes were a far cry from that in the United States: China's was $575 and India's $676. China's iron and steel industry was yet to be developed, not to mention parts manufacturing. Changchun First Automobile Works in northeast China employed more than half a million people; the plant was equivalent to a city. Why? Because there was no industrial base to speak of and the plant had to produce all the related parts on its own. India's story was the same. In sum, Japan's auto industry thrived because it was consistent with its comparative advantage, whereas the same industry in China and India had to rely on government protection and subsidies, because it defied the comparative advantage of the time.

In the 1970s South Korea also introduced an automobile industry policy. Its per capita income was 30 percent of Japan's, and 20 percent of America's. Its industrial foundation was not as good as Japan's, but better than China's and India's. Accordingly, the protection and subsidy provided by the Korean government was less than in China and India. As a result the auto industry policies of South Korea in the 1970s were partially successful. It built three auto plants: two of them went bankrupt, and only one survives today – Hyundai – and it is doing well.

Sitting next to me at an international conference in the United States in 1991 was the president of Hyundai's American branch. I told him that South Korea must be the envy of other developing countries, selling cars in the American market. To my surprise, he told me that Hyundai had been suffering losses in the United States for many years in a row. The fact that a business is losing a lot of money in a foreign market suggests that it is receiving a lot of protection and subsidy from its home government, including trade barriers. In other words the prices of the products are artificially raised in the domestic market so that the company can use the money from domestic consumers to subsidize the non-viable branches in the foreign market. In this sense the success of South Korea's automobile industry has a big cost.[4]

From these stories we can see that the same industrial policy produced totally different results in different countries. The results were determined by whether the policy was consistent with the comparative advantage as determined by its economy's existing factor endowment structure. If it was, it would succeed – like the industrial policy of iron and steel and heavy machinery developed by Germany in 1870 and the automobile policy of Japan in the 1960s. If not, it would fail.

Whether a government protects or subsidizes an industry once it has been set up is a good indicator of whether the policy is consistent with the comparative advantage. A business that has to rely on government protection or subsidy to survive is not viable. In fact, a viable business only needs the government to play its role in information collection, coordination, and compensation for externalities at the budding stage, because it is supposed to earn a normal profit through good management in a competitive market.

To conclude, there is a glaring technological gap between developing and developed countries. Developing countries can make full use of the gap to reduce the cost and accelerate the pace of technological innovation, giving full play to the advantage of late starters. Specifically the governments of developing countries can play their role in information collection, coordination, and compensation for externalities to improve the competitiveness of their enterprises, and to accelerate capital accumulation and industrial and technological upgrading. Again, any policy of the government should be consistent with the factor endowment structure and comparative advantage. Speed is not everything, and foreign stories are not all good. So it is essential to maintain a competitive market to ensure that the price signals are truly responsive to supply and demand.

The CAF strategy and export-oriented policy

Countries with a successful development strategy generally boast a larger proportion of exports. Take China. Its dependence on foreign trade was a mere 9.5 percent in 1978 but jumped to 70 percent in 2003, a substantial increase. But notice that how much a country depends on foreign trade is determined by the nature of its development strategy. Under a CAD strategy imports shrink because the country has to make products that enjoy no comparative advantage. But industries that do enjoy comparative advantage cannot export much either because resources have been transferred to the prioritized industries that have no comparative advantage. For example, China's labor-intensive industries have always enjoyed a comparative advantage. But before 1978 the main exports were agricultural products and processed agricultural products, and the growth in labor-intensive light industries was sluggish for lack of capital.

In sum, the CAD strategy reduces both exports and imports. But under a CAF strategy a country will import the products for which it does not have comparative advantage and prioritize industries that do, so that it can export those products in larger volumes.

Reflections on reality

Under a CAF strategy the industries with comparative advantage will be competitive. Enterprises in these industries can earn normal profit through good management. The government can reduce subsidies and the whole society can accumulate more wealth. On the flipside a CAD strategy undermines the economy's efficiency and stirs up all kinds of social issues. The question is why, after World War II, did so many political leaders and social elites follow the CAD strategy instead of the CAF strategy, despite the latter being obviously superior?

When analyzing this issue, we need to distinguish short-term and long-term results. Suppose we have two developing countries of the same economic size when they implement their development strategies. One adopts a CAD strategy, the other a CAF strategy.

In the short term the country with a CAD strategy will build its heavy industries very fast, seemingly fulfilling the dream shared by many newly independent countries that they could be prosperous and strong in no time. But in the long term those countries created very little surplus. The surplus created by their prioritized industries, if any, is actually transferred from other sectors, while the industries that could have created a lot of surplus were suffering from sluggish development, starved of capital. In this case, due to the lack of capital accumulation, the economy will grow very slowly, or even face stagnation and crisis. That is why economic development supported by a CAD strategy is not sustainable.

By contrast, the country with a CAF strategy can eventually grow rapidly because it can produce plenty of surplus. So, judging from long-term performance, the CAF strategy is more desirable. There is a clear conflict between the short-term catching-up and long-term development strategy. Unfortunately, many leaders and elites are blind to the conflict. All they see is the yawning gap in the industrial and technological structure between the developed world and their countries. They are desperate to bridge the gap, unaware of the fact that the industrial and technological structure is an endogenous variable that cannot be changed by direct intervention.

Another question: Why did East Asian economies that shared the same catching-up dream as other developing countries opt out of the traditional development strategy and choose the CAF strategy instead? With efforts over three to four decades, they eventually caught up with and even overtook many developed countries.

It is not that the political leaders or social elites in those economies were more visionary. Actually they did not have much of an alternative. In the 1950s, just like other developing economies, the East Asian economies also wanted to implement a CAD strategy. When the Chinese mainland launched the first Five-Year Plan prioritizing the development of heavy industries, Japan's MITI produced a report suggesting that Japan should follow suit, otherwise in two to three decades, when China would be an advanced industrial power, Japan would be left far behind. At that time the Taiwanese authorities, hoping to retake the Chinese mainland, also aimed at building a strong army and national defense supported by heavy industries. Yet neither Japan nor Taiwan ended up with the CAD strategy prioritizing the development of heavy industries. Why? Because that strategy is inefficient – and requires enormous resources.

The capacity for resource mobilization depends on two factors: per capita resources and the size of the population. The Soviet Union, also a planned economy, maintained rapid growth for almost half a century until the 1960s, because its per capita resources were the highest in the world, and it had a population of more than 200 million. China had a vast rural area and a huge agricultural population, so the price scissors easily transferred the rural surplus to the cities for industrial development. By contrast, the East Asian economies had small populations, were medium-sized, and had scarce natural resources per capita. Investment in heavy industries against that backdrop could come only from deficit financing, which would lead to high inflation in a couple of years, costing the government popular support. So, to maintain political and social stability, these East Asian economies had to give up prioritizing heavy industries. Although Japan and the four Asian Tigers did not opt for the CAF strategy voluntarily, the results were good after all.

We scholars should trace the source and find out the ultimate reasons for economic development, to "leap from the realm of necessity to the realm of freedom," as Engels put it. When we study the "East Asian Miracle," we should see beyond the phenomenon itself and identify the driving forces behind the miracle so as to offer applicable successful stories for other developing countries.

Will the CAF strategy make a country always lag behind?

The first two questions to pop into people's minds are: Will the developing country that implements a CAF strategy always lag behind the developed world? Will it lose the ability of endogenous innovation because it is always importing technology and engaging in either labor-intensive industries or labor-intensive sectors in capital-intensive industries? The answers are easy. Whether it can catch up with developed countries hinges on the relative growth rate rather than its current level of economic development. If both developing and developed countries make their industrial and technological decisions based on their respective comparative advantage, the rate of technological change in developing countries must be higher than that of developed countries, because developing countries rely mainly on technology imports, which cost much less than R&D costs in developed countries.

Rapid technological innovation brings about higher returns on capital and more enthusiasm for accumulation. That is why the savings rate in successful developing countries is generally higher than in developed countries. With the continuing accumulation of capital, the factor endowment structure will be upgraded, as will the industrial structure. In other words developing countries can catch up with developed countries under the CAF strategy. Meanwhile, with the factor endowment structure of the developing country getting close to that of the developed countries, the need for industrial and technological innovation will increase accordingly. Although developing countries rely heavily on technology imports, innovation is not uncommon. Ever since China's reform and opening, its innovation capability has been increasing rather than decreasing.

For some industries in China, it is likely that no countries more advanced than China are still in the business because those industries do not comply with their comparative advantages any more. The industrial structure of developing countries usually lags behind that of developed countries. Some products may be no longer produced in developed countries, because they have been phased out or because they do not comply with their comparative advantage. When more advanced countries are no longer producing and innovating in those sectors, China will have to research and develop new technologies and products on its own strength if it wishes to become an industry leader.

Before the 1980s Japan and Germany led the world in motorcycles. So, after the reform and opening, China's motorcycle industry imported technology mainly from these two countries. China's first motorcycle manufacturer, Jialing, was a joint venture with Japan's Honda. Later, after Japan and Germany withdrew from the production of low-end, 200cc and smaller motorcycles, China evolved into the world's largest producer of those types in no time. China's annual production is now more than 10 million motorcycles, more than 4 million of them manufactured in Chongqing municipality. When I visited Chongqing in 2006, a local official mentioned that the number of patent applications exceeded 1,800 annually, on average five every day. Its leading position in the industry and the pressure on it facilitated innovation of such frequency.

In some high-end industries such as computers, despite a relatively large space for technology imports, adaptation always accommodates local conditions. This kind of innovation in the form of localization usually takes place in production. Automation is commonplace in developed countries, because labor costs are very high. But labor costs are much lower in developing countries, so they enjoy a comparative advantage in labor-intensive industries. If quality can be ensured, replacing machinery and equipment by labor can be more competitive.

Here is another story from China. Hangji town in the Hanjiang district of Yangzhou city, Jiangsu province has been a toothbrush production base since the Qing Dynasty, when Emperor Daoguang reigned (1820–50). Back then, the toothbrushes were made of pig bones and bristles. In the 1980s after the reform and opening, many people in this town re-engaged in this traditional industry under the government's call. Among them were the five Han brothers. In the late 1980s and early 1990s they found that the profit in this industry was rather limited and that it was extremely difficult to expand their market share, because there were too many competitors and because product homogeneity was a serious problem.

So, they started to search for some breakthroughs. In 1993 Han Guoping, one of the five brothers, noticed German-made toothbrush production equipment exhibited at the Beijing Agricultural Exhibition Hall. Chinese handmade toothbrushes then had two major drawbacks: the bristles fell off easily, and the sections were rough. The German equipment overcame these two drawbacks, but it cost RMB 3 million ($450,000), astronomical for a private business in the early 1990s. After careful study, Han found that only the final two processes were needed to solve the problems, and other processes could be replaced by manual work.

The two processes cost only RMB 800,000 ($120,000), RMB 2.2 million ($330,000) less than the total. If the depreciation period is ten years, it could save up to RMB 220,000 ($33,000) every year (with interest on loans, it can save even more). In the early 1990s the per capita monthly income in Yangzhou's rural areas was only RMB 300 ($45). The manual part involved four persons, and even with a RMB 500 ($75) basis, the average annual labor cost was only RMB 24,000 ($34,000), a fraction of the machine cost. So, with its equipment and competitive products, Han Guoping rapidly expanded production, built a national toothbrush brand – Sanxiao – and claimed 70% of the domestic market.

In some other fields the gap between China and the developed world is narrowing. Except for a couple of core technologies that developed countries are reluctant to share, China has mastered all the other technologies. And mastering the core technologies becomes immensely profitable. A Langfang natural gas company, Xinao, produces pipelines and bottled products. The bottled gas requires special steel to ensure safety. The steel bottle used to be imported. When China tried to produce it, the sealing technology critical to safety remained a mystery. Xinao had thought to introduce this technology from a US company and in return gave the company some Xinao shares. But the US company declined the offer on the grounds that it might earn bread today but that their sons would have no bread tomorrow. So, Xinao had no alternative but to research on its own. In less than a year it developed the sealing technology, leaving the US company regretting that it had lost its bread even for today.

Developing countries enjoy a comparative advantage in all the foregoing cases of innovation. Some other fields also require endogenous innovation by developing countries. Examples include some technologies that have huge demand in developing countries but fail to attract enough attention and input from developed countries due to insufficient demand – as well as technologies related to national defense and security.

In the end we cannot say that domestic innovation is better than technology imports, or the other way around. The purpose of the CAF strategy is efficiency, capital accumulation, and economic growth. When technology imports cost less and earn more profit than indigenous innovation, they are a better option. But when technology imports are not available or cost too much, indigenous innovation will be better. Developed countries invested heavily in cutting-edge technologies. It is not that technologies developed on their own are superior but that no better technology is available. Without R&D, there will be no technological progress to speak of, and economic development will hit bottlenecks at a certain stage and stagnate. That is why the rate of technological change and economic growth in developed countries is slower than that in developing countries. The success stories of Japan and the Asian Tigers give us every reason to believe that it is perfectly possible for developing countries with a CAF strategy to catch up with developed countries.

Will international capital flows fundamentally change the comparative advantage of developing countries?

The theory of the CAF strategy is about upgrading the factor endowment structure through capital accumulation so that developing countries can catch up with developed countries in terms of the relative abundance of capital. Is it possible to achieve this by attracting massive inflows of foreign capital? No. The inflows of foreign capital will increase the capital stock in developing countries, but it will not be large enough to put the relative abundance of capital in a developing country on par with that in developed countries.

Foreign capital flows into developing countries not to narrow the global income gap but to make profit. The first aim is to use cheap labor or resources and build export bases in developing countries. Apparently, the destination of foreign capital inflows is always labor-intensive or resource-intensive industries. The second aim is to penetrate the local market, based on their comparative advantage, so foreign-funded enterprises usually engage in industries more capital-intensive than the local ones. But they will use the local advantage, cheap labor, to reduce costs. They invest in industries that are not as capital-intensive as the same industries back in their home countries.

Wuhan Dongfeng Peugeot Citroën Automobile Company introduced a production line from French Citroën to produce Fukang cars, and Guangzhou introduced a production line from Japanese Honda to produce Accords. The Accord is more expensive than the Fukang. But the Fukang production line was imported entirely from France according to the request on the Chinese side. So, the production equipment and processes were exactly the same as the French ones, at a cost of RMB 10 billion ($1.15 billion). While the Accord production line was adapted to China's circumstances, manual work replaced some equipment. Therefore, the cost was only a little more than RMB 2 billion ($300 million). Naturally, Accord's profits exceeded Fukang's by a large margin. Again, keeping profit in mind, foreign companies will not use technology as capital-intensive as in their home countries unless they are subsidized by the local government, so the capital input will not be as great as might be imagined.

In addition, the legal, credit, and market environment in developing countries is not as mature as in developed countries, so the investment risk is much higher, another constraint on the inflow of foreign capital.

These factors tell us that foreign capital inflows will not be large enough to fundamentally change the capital availability in developing countries. So, relying on international capital flows to change the comparative advantage of developing countries is not feasible.

Paul Krugman's criticism about economic growth in East Asia

Before the East Asian financial crisis broke out, the breakneck growth of that region was arousing popular enthusiasm around the globe.[5] Paul Krugman, a Nobel laureate economist, pointed out in his 1994 article, "The Myth of Asia's Miracle,"[6] that the so-called "miracle" was no miracle at all. His argument was that the rapid growth in output in these economies was driven mainly by the rapid growth in inputs. In his regressions there was no TFP or technical progress as measured by the Solow residual. He concluded that East Asian growth was not sustainable.

Krugman's argument is based on the following theory. Output growth comes from growth in capital, growth in labor, and technological progress. Simply put, if the capital growth is 10, the labor growth is 10, and the output growth is 12, then the residual is 2. The residual is also called the growth in TFP, or technical progress, as generalized by many economists. Again, if the capital growth is 10, the labor growth is 10, and the output growth is also 10, then the residual is 0. That is how the growth data look for East Asian economies.

The United States, Western Europe, Japan, and other developed countries don't have much capital growth, and the growth in population and labor is rather slow. Indeed, TFP growth accounts for two-thirds of the output growth of those economies. It is believed that the growth is sustainable if it mainly relies on technological progress – and that it is not sustainable if it relies solely on capital growth, because the marginal return on capital will be diminishing. Based on this logic, Krugman argued in his 1994 article that the growth of East Asian economies was not sustainable, because there was no TFP growth or technological progress – and that the East Asian Miracle was achieved through growth in capital and labor.

When the East Asian financial crisis broke in 1998, many people thought that it confirmed Krugman's prediction. But the former Prime Minister of Singapore, Lee Kuan Yew, refuted Krugman's argument. The annual rate of capital accumulation in Singapore had exceeded 40 percent for four decades, yet the return on capital did not decline, impossible without technological progress. Lee, though not an economist, has amazing economic intuition and better understanding of economic phenomena than many economists.

Many economists have blind faith in TFP. As a residual, it cannot be obtained without paying some cost. Technological advance in developed countries relies on indigenous R&D, which is not counted in the input costs of the standard production function. So, it manifests itself as residual. By contrast, the reason that we see low or no residual in the growth of developing countries is that their technological progress relies on technology borrowings, mainly through imports of capital goods. In other words the cost of technological progress is counted as a capital input. So, there is no residual in the statistics. But this definitely does not mean there is no technological progress, because the import of better equipment also suggests improvement in technology.

In fact, even developed countries do not always have TFP growth. For example, the United States had little TFP between the 1880s and the early twentieth century.[7] Why? Because it imported most of the new technologies from Europe, the cost of technological advance was already paid in the purchase of the technologies. Consequently, during that period, the United States did not have much TFP despite rapid growth. Today, the United States is the most developed country, with all its technologies at the forefront. These technologies brought the United States high TFP, but the huge R&D costs are not included in the inputs, so the data show a large residual. By the same token, although the East Asian economies achieved rapid growth in a very short period, their overall economic level still lagged behind the most developed countries.

Nor was innovation their strong suit, so their TFP would not look good. But we cannot deny their technological progress.

The theory of competitive advantage

David Ricardo first put forward the theory of comparative advantage nearly two centuries ago. Generally it is believed that the more recent a theory is the better. A new theory seems always to replace an old one. In the 1990s Michael Porter, a management scholar at Harvard University, proposed the "theory of competitive advantage."[8] It aroused great attention in policy circles in the world, and its influence was far-reaching. Porter believes that the competitiveness of an industry is determined by four factors: the use of abundant, low-price domestic factors; the size of the domestic market; industrial clusters and specialized divisions of labor; and market competition.

What makes this theory especially appealing is its comprehensiveness: it seems that the theory has covered all the conditions needed for industrial development, and it seems to suggest that if all the conditions are satisfied, a bright future is around the corner. But economics is an interpretative discipline. When we do research, the most important thing is to find the causal relationship amid complicated phenomena, so that we can explain the reality and guide actions. That is why we should be wary of "perfect" theories, because they tend to mix causes with results and can be misleading.

So let us revisit Michael Porter's competitiveness theory. Among the four factors, only two stand alone; the other two are actually the results of one of the two independent factors. The first independent factor is comparative advantage. Factor prices reflect the relative abundance of factors, so the prices indicate the comparative advantage. The second independent factor is the size of the domestic market, also exogenous.

The third factor, industrial clusters, cannot stand alone. For example, a textile cluster is not likely to take shape in the United States, because it is highly labor-intensive; likewise, a capital-intensive industry cluster will not be seen in a developing country. Whether an industry and its related horizontal and vertical industries can develop into an industrial cluster in some area is determined by whether it conforms to the local comparative advantage. Defying the comparative advantage and blindly expanding the industry for its cluster effects goes nowhere. Even if the industry cluster were built up, it would not be competitive. On the contrary, firms in an industry will come together spontaneously in line with their comparative advantage for greater efficiency.

As for the fourth factor, market competition, firms that follow comparative advantage are viable and need no protection or subsidies from the government. And markets made up of those firms must also be competitive. By contrast, firms that defy comparative advantage are not viable and cannot survive without government protection or subsidies, which remove competition in that market.

To conclude, Porter's theory comes down to two factors: comparative advantage and the size of the domestic market. Of the two, the first is more important: because in an open market, if a firm develops in a CAF manner, it can have the whole world as a market. Take Finland-based Nokia. Even though the population of Finland is just slightly more than 5 million, Nokia is the most competitive mobile phone company in the world.

Some important issues of the CAF strategy and development economics

Based on the theory of comparative advantage, we can clearly interpret many issues of long-term concern in development economics from the perspective of the factor endowment structure, comparative advantage, and enterprise viability.

- *Capital accumulation and economic growth.* Solow's neoclassical economics holds that the rate of capital accumulation determines the rate of economic growth. We now understand that the CAF strategy can speed up the pace of capital accumulation, upgrade the factor endowment structure, and therefore accelerate economic growth. On the flipside, although the CAD strategy can mobilize funds for investment at amazing speed in a very short period, the accumulated capital always goes to industries with no comparative advantage. So the economy is inefficient and therefore likely to stagnate in the long term.

- *Technological innovation and economic growth.* The CAD strategy focuses on the most advanced and capital-intensive products. The technologies are costly, and some of the core technologies not accessible. Indigenous R&D costs are even higher. So technological progress under this strategy will be very slow. As for developing countries, due to their weak technological basis, they don't even have many low-end technologies, and the trial and error cost will be immense. By contrast, under the CAF strategy the cost of technological change is relatively low, and technological progress will stimulate economic growth more effectively.

- *The degree of openness.* The definition of comparative advantage itself indicates an open economy. The CAF strategy brings about more openness than the CAD strategy.

- *Financial liberalization.* Professor Ronald McKinnon, a financial economist at Stanford University who proposed the financial repression theory in the 1970s, advocates financial liberalization.[9] According to his theory the poor economic performance of many developing countries is caused by financial repression. But countries that liberalize their financial systems have ended up in financial crises. The problem is that those who study finance see only finance and nothing else. So, they tend to intervene in financial arrangements, the endogenous variables, as if they were exogenous conditions. In fact, the CAD strategy will inevitably entail financial repression by setting up non-viable and capital-intensive firms through artificially low capital costs. Financial liberalization based on non-viable firms will ultimately lead to bankruptcy, social unrest, and multiple crises.

- *Macroeconomic stability.* Empirical evidence shows that an economy with macro stability will develop smoothly. In fact, if an economy develops in a CAF manner, prioritizing its competitive industries, it will see rapid capital accumulation and steady development. But if it develops in a CAD manner, or implements a CAD strategy, channeling capital to non-competitive industries through various means by the state, the economy will suffer inefficiency and stagnation. The accumulated capital may turn into debt and fiscal deficits. As there is no adequate surplus created to pay for it, a financial crisis is likely, reducing macro stability. In sum, macro stability and steady economic development are the results rather than causes of an appropriate national development strategy.

- *Employment structure and urbanization.* One of the outcomes of prioritizing heavy industries in China is high industrialization but low urbanization. On the surface, this makes no sense, but the apparent conflict is easy to explain. A higher level of industrialization is the direct outcome of the strategy of prioritizing heavy industries. But since heavy industries do not create many jobs in cities, either urbanization is very low when the government controls migration to avoid high urban unemployment or we will see a large number of slums as in many cities of developing countries. If instead, a CAF strategy is implemented, labor-intensive industries will be encouraged, and more jobs can be created not only for urban residents but also for rural migrant laborers. So the degree of urbanization will be increased.

- *Income distribution.* The East Asian Miracle brought not only rapid economic growth but also significant improvements in income distribution. A CAF strategy can upgrade the factor endowment structure, and thus change the relative prices of capital and labor. Because capital is usually owned by the rich, and labor by less rich laborers, with declining capital price and improving labor price, in relative terms, the assets of the rich will be depreciated and those of the poor move north. So, the distribution of income improves. If a CAD strategy is in place instead, the government will have to mobilize funds to support capital-intensive industries, collecting taxes from the poor to subsidize the rich. So, implementing the CAD strategy in a market economy will result in a less equitable income distribution.

References

Hayami, Yujiro, and Y. Oshinisa Goto. 2005. *Development Economics: From Poverty to the Wealth of Nations*, 3rd edn. Oxford: Oxford University Press.

Krugman, Paul. 1994. "The Myth of Asia's Miracle." *Foreign Affairs* 73(6): 62–78.

1999. *The Return of Depression Economics*. London: Allen Lane, The Penguin Press.

Lewis, Arthur. 1955. *Theory of Economic Growth*. London: Allen & Unwin.

Lin, Justin Y. 2003. "Development Strategy, Viability and Economic Convergence." *Economic Development and Cultural Change* 53(2): 278–309.

2009. *Economic Development and Transition: Thought, Strategy, and Viability*. Cambridge: Cambridge University Press.

2011. "New Structural Economics: A Framework for Rethinking Development." *World Bank Research Observer* 26(2): 193–221.

Lin, Justin Y., and Peilin Liu. 2001. "Viability and State-owned Enterprise Reform." *Jingji Yanjiu* [Economic Research] 9: 60–70.

Lin, Justin Y., Fang Cai, and Zhou Li. 1999. "Bijiao Youshi yu Fazhan Zhanlue: Dui Dongya Qiji de Zaijieshi" [Comparative Advantage and Development Strategy: A Reinterpretation of the East Asian Miracle]. Peking University CCER *Working Paper* No. C1999006, Beijing.

2003. *The China Miracle: Development Strategy and Economic Reform*, revised edn. Hong Kong: Chinese University Press.

Maddison, Angus. 1995. *Monitoring the World Economy, 1820–1992*. Paris: Organisation for Economic Co-operation and Development.

2006. *The World Economy*. Paris: Organisation for Economic Co-operation and Development.

McKinnon, Ronald I. 1973. *Money and Capital in Economic Development*. Washington, DC: Brookings Institution.

Porter, Michael E. 1990. *The Competitive Advantage of Nations*. New York: Free Press.

World Bank. 1993. *The East Asian Miracle: Economic Growth and Public Policy*. New York: Oxford University Press.

Notes

1. This chapter draws on Lin (2003, 2009).
2. Lin (2011).
3. Maddison (2006).
4. Hyundai is viable and competitive globally, and does not rely on government subsidies and protections anymore because Korea's level of development and endowment structure have upgraded.
5. Including World Bank (1993).
6. Krugman (1994).
7. Hayami and Goto (2005).
8. Porter published a series of works on national competitive advantage; *The Competitive Advantage of Nations* is a classic (Porter 1990).
9. McKinnon (1973).

SEVEN

Rural reform and the three rural issues

China's economy went on a long detour under the traditional planned economy. Around the world, except for the silver lining of several East Asian economies, many developing countries shared the same woes as China. So, it is no surprise that when China started its reform and opening in the late 1970s, many other socialist countries and developing countries also embarked on reforming their economic systems. Different reform ideas and approaches produced disparate results. Countries guided by the then-mainstream economic theories failed to achieve their desired results. But China, based on its own exploration, achieved unprecedented success with its gradual dual-track reform, once ridiculed as the worst reform model.

Starting with this chapter, I will introduce China's reforms in different fields and the remaining issues. Solutions will also be proposed, based on the theoretical framework in Chapters 5 and 6.

The process of reform

Consider the pre-reform institutional arrangements for agriculture. The land reform was implemented between 1949 and 1952. The Agricultural Cooperative Movement was launched in 1953. After a three-year agricultural crisis in 1959–61, a new system of coopera-tion based on the production team as the business unit was initiated in 1962, remaining in place until 1978.

Before 1962 the government wished to improve productivity without increasing inputs, so it constantly expanded the scale of cooperatives to boost output through economies of scale. After 1962 the focus shifted from economies of scale to developing and using modern agricultural technologies such as fertilizer and improved seed varieties. Hence the 1970s slogan: "Mechanization is the answer to agricultural development."

The average crop growth rate from 1952 to 1978 was 2.5 percent a year and that for grain (food) 2.4 percent. In the same period the average growth of the population was about 2 percent a year, so the growth of grain was only 0.4 percentage points faster than that of population. Per capita food production grew only 10 percent in total from 1952 to 1978.

The need for reform

The reform program that China embarked on at the end of 1978 was the earliest and most effective among socialist and developing countries. And in retrospect it may even have been inadvert. After the downfall of the Gang of Four[1] in 1976, the second genera-tion of leadership headed by Deng Xiaoping took office. Because any new leadership must have legitimacy, Deng's administration felt it necessary to develop policies that not only differed from those of the Gang of Four but also, and more important, benefited the people – to win popular support. The Gang of Four had advocated an ultra-leftist line, extremely detrimental to economic development.

As shown in Table 7.1, in 1950 when the People's Republic of China was newly founded, there was not much of a per capita income gap between the Chinese mainland and Japan, South Korea, or Taiwan, China. But by 1978 Japan had basically caught up with the United States, and South Korea and Taiwan, China,

TABLE 7.1 *China and other emerging industrial economies in efficiency of growth (1990 international dollar, purchasing power parity)*

Economy	1950	1978
United States	9,573	18,168
Japan	1,873	12,186
South Korea	876	4,124
Taiwan, China	922	5,044
Mainland China	614	1,352

Source: Maddison (1995).

had narrowed the income gap with developed countries. China, although boasting a complete industrial system, an atomic bomb, and a man-made satellite, had a standard of living a far cry from that of the developed world. The new leadership had to improve national economic performance and make its people as rich as their neighbors, or it might lose support and its legitimacy for rule.

China initiated its reform in late 1978, emphasizing gradualism and a dual-track approach. It fared much better than the former Soviet Union and Eastern European countries that went through the shock therapy proposed by mainstream theories. The prevailing view of many foreign scholars was that the market economy was best, the planned economy was bad, and the dual system combining the market and planned economy was worst.[2] Mainstream theory urged socialist countries to make the leap from a planned to a market economy in a single bound.[3]

Why did Chinese leaders ignore the mainstream theories and opt instead for a gradual dual-track approach to reform? It has something to do with the working style of Chinese leaders represented by Deng Xiaoping: "Emancipating the mind; seeking truth from facts; keeping up with the times." They were not, by any means, dogmatic – and they would not blindly follow any established model. Those in the second generation of leadership were also in the first generation of revolutionaries. They had taken part in (and some had even led) China's Socialist Revolution and the establishment of the planned economy after the foundation of the People's Republic of China. It was natural that they would not totally scrap the system they had built, but they were willing to fine-tune it without compromising its rationale.

The measures and results of the reform

When the government reviewed the problems in agricultural development, it arrived at four conclusions.[4] First, artificially low state procurement prices dampened farmers' enthusiasm for work. Second, after the abolition of the farm produce market, rural areas regressed to an autarkic economy. Third, oversize production teams killed incentives. And fourth, agriculture was very inefficient due to the lack of specialization.

To address these issues the government proposed three resolutions at the Third Plenary Session of the 11th Central Committee of the Communist Party of China in 1978, which started the reform and opening program:

- *Scaling down production teams.* The team-based output-quota contract system and responsibility system were allowed. But that was as far as the collective production system went, for a household-based system was prohibited. Then something unexpected happened: the household responsibility system emerged to score an overwhelming success.
- *Price reform.* Quota prices were raised 17.1%, and above-quota prices were raised 30–50%, so the weighted average increase was 22.1%.
- *Market reform.* The farm produce market and long-distance transport of goods for sale, or arbitrage, were reinstated.

The household responsibility system was not designed by any leader – it was a product of villagers in Xiaogang village in Fengyang county,

TABLE 7.2 *Agricultural growth, slow before 1978 (%)*

Item	1952–78	1978–84	1984–87
Agriculture	2.9	7.7	4.1
Crop	2.5	5.9	1.4
Grain	2.4	4.8	−0.2
Population	2.0	1.3	1.5

Source: National Bureau of Statistics of China (1992).

Anhui province. Driven by bad weather and low production in 1978, they took responsibility for their own gains and losses, with a proviso that if any of them were to go to jail for secretly embarking on this illegal system, the others would take care of their children. Seeing the incredible results, the Central Rural Work Conference at the end of 1979 decided that the poorest residents in rural areas would be allowed to engage in this system. At the end of 1980, 14% of the production teams around the country followed the system, yet the poorest population accounted for only 10%. All production teams under the household responsibility system had remarkable results that year. So in 1981 the government started to promote the system across the country. By the end of the year, 45% of production teams were in the system, in 1982, 80%, and in 1984, 99%.

The expansion of the system produced an unexpected result. During the first years, from 1978 to 1984, the agricultural growth rate more than doubled, jumping from 2.9% to 7.7%; the food growth rate also doubled (Table 7.2). Meanwhile, thanks to the family planning policy, population growth declined from 2% to 1.3%, so per capita food production grew even faster. Since then, China has been basically self-sufficient in grain, even enjoying a surplus in a good year. True, after promoting the household responsibility system, the growth of agriculture was remarkable. But there was a heated debate in the 1980s about the system's contribution to agricultural growth.

The debate on the household responsibility system

There were two sides in the debate. One held that the system is good, because the result was positive at both the village and the national level. The other believed that the household-based production model is not consistent with socialism. Since "mechanization is the answer to agricultural development," and mechanization requires economies of scale, how can household-based production be the right move? People holding the second view regard it as regression rather than reform. They believe that other reforms produced the growth in 1978–84, including those for fertilizer, scientific research, and mechanization, as well as the price and market reform. They argue that the benefit of those measures outweighed and thus concealed the damage done by the household responsibility system, and that the big slump in production after 1984 clearly exposed the problems in that system (see Table 7.2).

Overseas economic pundits had a similar debate. Orthodox theory concludes that collective production creates higher incentives than individual production and that its resource allocation is just as efficient. In short, collective production system is superior, and the household responsibility system is not desirable. The theory, although supported by mathematical models, cannot explain why farmers in Xiaogang village took such huge risks to engage in the household responsibility system and why many production teams that did not fall into the state's "poorest" category followed suit against state policy. A premise of economics is that everyone is rational. Then why should these rational farmers take great risks to follow a supposedly bad system? *When the theory is not consistent with reality, we can only say that the theory is flawed.*

Traditional economic theory uses two models to prove the superiority of collective production.[5] The first is based on the production function, with inputs of labor, land, and capital. It assumes that, under any system, one laborer provides one unit of labor input. So, based on economies of scale, collective production is more efficient than individual production. Theoretically, the argument is fine, but it is not applicable to agricultural production. Why? Because it equates every laborer as a unit of labor input – or, put another way, it treats laborers as tractors. The theory's problem is that laborers have subjective initiative. One laborer plus one laborer does not necessarily equal two units of labor input. The answer depends on the individual's effort in production.

For incentives to work, the traditional economic model also attempts to offer a plausible explanation. According to the theory, China's old distribution system – according to "work points" at the end of the year and need at other times of the year – is excellent. Distribution solely according to work would create an excess incentive, and thus lead to declining well-being for farmers. But combined with distribution according to need, the mechanism can dampen farmers' production enthusiasm only a little bit and achieve an appropriate level of well-being.

The second model is based on the system of distribution according to work in China's agricultural production cooperatives. According to this model, when someone increases his labor input, his work points as well as his share in the final distribution will increase accordingly. So, under the production-team system, farmers should have more incentives than under a household-based system. But this model is based on a direct link between work and work points. To ensure that the direct link is in place, complete supervision is essential.

But the supervision of agricultural production is rather ineffective. Usually there are two types of supervision, for processes and for results. Unlike industrial production, which usually takes place under a roof in a limited space, agricultural production extends over a vast area, making process supervision impractical. Nor is there a uniform standard for agricultural production. Most production behavior, like that for planting, weeding, fertilizing, and harvesting, is based on personal judgment and experience.

Supervising results is just as difficult. Agricultural production is a biological process, which can take months or even a year to get to harvest. This long period makes supervising results impractical. In addition, agricultural production is susceptible to external factors such as climate. In a bad year, no matter how hard farmers work, they cannot get a good harvest, but in a good year, with average effort, there can be a bumper harvest. So, the work points, which are supposed to base distribution on the amount of work done, are actually based on the amount of time spent. A day's work equals eight hours of work points, but it has nothing to do with the quality of the work. So it is no surprise that the incentive is so weak in agricultural production teams.

To realize economies of scale in collective production, supervision is essential. But it is prohibitively expensive and impractical. A telling example: Fengyang county once sent seventeen cadres to Xiaogang village to supervise eighteen households. These cadres boarded with local farmers, placing a heavy burden on these households. It turned out the output that year was even worse. Under the household output-quota contract, the supervision cost could have been spared. All in all, the household-based system, though it does not have economies of scale, should still be more efficient than the flawed collective production system, because it does not have high supervision costs.

Regression analysis of the data also shows the contribution of the household responsibility system to agricultural growth.[6] For a base of total growth from 1978 to 1984 of 100, it is found that the increase in factor inputs (such as land, fertilizer, machines, and labor) contributes 46 to output growth and that the household responsibility system (institutional changes) contributes 47, with an unexplained residual of 7 (46 + 47 + 7 = 100). With agriculture growing by 42 percent during those seven years, the contribution from the household responsibility system would be about 20 percentage points. But institutional changes to output growth are a one-off boost, different from a sustained push to economic growth. For example, the boost from switching to the household responsibility system is a one-off boost to farmers' enthusiasm. While the productive work hours per day can be increased from four to twelve, they cannot be increased further to sixteen hours, because people have to eat and sleep. That explains why the agricultural growth rate declined after 1984: the household responsibility system had been implemented nationwide, and its 47-point (institutional) contribution ceased.

The decline in grain production was actually a positive result of the household responsibility system. In 1978 the government reformed procurement prices of grain and cotton to improve farmers' income; it also promised to take all of the farmers' produce. But due to continuous output growth for many years in a row, its grain reserves were piling up. In some locales even classrooms were borrowed to store grain. Both the burden and the waste were huge.

So, starting in 1985 the government replaced the monopolized procurement practice with contracts placed directly with each household. The contract price was based on a 30–70 principle: 30 percent was based on the original quota price, and 70 percent on the above-quota price, with the above-quota part not fixed but based on the market price. So, the new price was lower than the original above-quota price.

The change helped the government ease the fiscal burden. But due to the diminishing marginal price of grain, farmers' enthusiasm to produce grain fell accordingly. Meanwhile, the markets for vegetables, fruits, livestock, and other farm produce were liberalized, increasing their prices. That is why some farmers shifted to other non-staple foods, reducing grain output during 1984–87.

The household responsibility system was the most remarkable achievement of the rural reform, but it also created some problems, notably in food security and the "Three Rural Issues" (*San Nong Wen Ti* in Mandarin).

Issues in post-household responsibility system reform

Food security and policy choices

Food security affects people's subsistence, so it is always a political issue. No country would like to put its rice bowl in the hands of others, and most countries have a policy of self-sufficiency in food production. For China, with more than 1 billion people to feed, food security is especially important. But with the breakneck economic growth after the reform, food security began to face challenges.

- With industrialization and urbanization, a lot of rural land has been taken by new factories, roads, and houses.
- Although population growth has come down, the net increase is still high, pushing up the demand for food.
- Although grain consumption is falling with rising living standards, the consumption of meat, eggs, and other non-staple foods is increasing. And many non-staples are converted from grains, so the consumption of grain increases.

With shrinking arable land, and rising demand, food security in China looks gloomy. Lester Brown, the founder and former president of the World Watch Institute, published a book in 1995, predicting that by 2020 China's grain imports would reach 200–300 million tons, exceeding the total volume to be traded globally. In other words even if all the grain exports of other countries were shipped to China in 2020, some Chinese would still be starving. Meanwhile, many other countries around the world are hungry.[7] In the 1990s China's food needs were a major argument in the then-prevailing China Threat theory.

The rising demand has to be met, but to offset for shrinking arable land, unit output must be enhanced – in two ways. One is to increase factor inputs, the other to improve technology. Both require policy support.

Market liberalization and the pricing mechanism. Farmers are the major players in agriculture production. Production-related decisions – whether to buy more chemical fertilizer, invest in tools, apply more effort, or adopt new technology – have to be made by farmers. If rational farmers increase their inputs, they hope to see more returns. So, part of the returns generated from the increased inputs has to go back to the farmers. Otherwise, no farmer would produce more than his family needs. But if the food price goes up with increasing demand, farmers will be more than happy to increase inputs and adopt new technologies so that they can sell more food for more cash.

R & D. Because land is limited, and excessive development of arable land will degrade the environment, progress in science and technology is the best way to increase unit grain output, because increasing factor inputs, like chemical fertilizer, will eventually lead to diminishing marginal output.

Even in market-based economies, agricultural research is financed mainly by the government for two reasons. First, agricultural research generally is costly and requires a very long period to get results. Even for hybrid rice, whose research period is relatively short, it usually takes Professor Yuan Longping, the father of hybrid rice in China, four to five years to develop a new hybrid variety. For developing a new conventional rice variety it takes ten years, and for a new animal breed, say a lean pig, it may take two to three decades, or even longer.

Second, R&D results are not always suitable for commercialization. For example, except for hybrid rice and hybrid corn, farmers don't have to buy most of the seeds of the improved varieties year after year, because they can usually save seeds for future use.[8] More importantly, consumers rather than farmers are the ultimate beneficiaries of agricultural research. With the improvement and dissemination of agricultural technologies, the price of farm produce will decline. A basic principle of economics is, "He who benefits, pays." But average consumers will not voluntarily support agricultural research, so the government has to step in to support it through fiscal transfers using tax revenues collected from consumers – only to overcome the long period, high risk, and low commercial value.

A modest amount of food imports. Farm production is either land-intensive or labor-intensive. Grain is land-intensive, and vegetables are labor-intensive. In China it takes 7 to 8 labor days to grow one mu of wheat or corn, 15 to 16 labor days for one mu of paddy rice, and around 200 labor days for one mu of vegetable (one mu = one-fifteenth hectare).

Because China has so little arable land per capita, it does not have a comparative advantage in land-intensive products. The United States, by contrast, has a lot of arable land per capita, giving it a comparative advantage in land-intensive products, so its grain prices are relatively low. The trade friction for several years after 2000 among China, Japan, and South Korea was caused by the latter two countries' attempt to impose protective tariffs on Chinese garlic, mushrooms, and bamboo shoots – all labor-intensive.

Clearly, China enjoys a comparative advantage in those products. If it can import a modest amount of grain products in which it has no comparative advantage, it can use more land to grow labor-intensive products for which it does have a comparative advantage. That way, exports will increase, and so will the farmer's income. That improves resource allocation. If grain imports also increase gradually, overseas grain exporters will have time to increase their output. And if the imports are modest, food security will not be jeopardized.

The Three Rural Issues and their solutions

Issues related to rural areas, farmers, and agriculture. Inspired by the success of its rural reforms, the government began in 1985 to introduce market-oriented reforms to cities. Ever since, China has witnessed sustained and rapid growth nationwide. But at the end of the 1990s the Three Rural Issues began to concern scholars at home and abroad – and the government as well in the early 2000s: rural areas are poor indeed, farmers are miserable indeed, and agriculture is in real jeopardy. The three issues boil down to one problem: the sluggish growth of farmer income.

Agricultural production is not the major problem. In the twenty-five years between 1978 and 2003 the average annual growth of agricultural production was 6.2 percent – high, whether looking across countries or over time. A simple theoretical rule: sustained agricultural growth of 3 percent a year is an achievement. Normally the population growth rate will not exceed 2 percent. As long as the growth of agricultural production is 1 percentage point higher than that of population, home demand will basically be met, because the income elasticity of demand for farm produce is very small, sometimes even close to 0. In China, even between 1998 and 2003, when the Three Rural Issues were seen at their most serious, agricultural growth was 4.3 percent a year. Meanwhile, the population growth rate was only 1 percent, so the difference of 3.3 points was way above the 1 point standard. So, the alarm, "agriculture is in real jeopardy," was false.

For "rural areas are poor indeed" and "farmers are miserable indeed," both are manifestations of the sluggish growth of farmer income. From 1978 to 1984 the average annual growth of farmer income was 13.9 percent, quite impressive at twice that of urban residents. But after 1984, although farm income continued to grow, its growth was slower than that in cities. Starting in 1985 the focus of reform shifted from rural to urban areas. As a result, the income growth in urban areas caught up with rural areas, and the gap has been widening ever since. The government adopted some measures to increase rural income after the mid-2000s and obtained some results, but the trend of a widening gap between rural and urban income has not been reversed (see Table 7.3). There is an old saying in China, "Inequity is worse than scarcity." When the income of a certain group of people grows phenomenally, others, even if their

TABLE 7.3 *Urban and rural income growth in China, 1978–2004 (%)*

Area	1978–84	1984–88	1988–95	1995–2000	2000–04	2004–09	1979–2009
Rural	13.9	2.1	3.8	2.9	4.0	7.9	7.2
Urban	7.1	5.2	6.3	5.6	7.6	10.1	7.3
	1978	1985	1993	1995	2000	2004	2009
Urban/rural income ratio	2.4:1	1.7:1	2.5:1	2.5:1	2.8:1	3.2:1	3.3:1

Source: National Bureau of Statistics of China.

income still grows, will look poor by comparison. So, the country-side is "poor" compared with cities, but not with the past.

In addition, "miserable" does not mean that farmers are slave labor. Thanks to mechanization and the use of chemical fertilizer, the labor input, no matter its quantity or intensity, is greatly reduced. But health, education, and social services are rather backward in the rural areas. Before the reforms, college was free for all, and healthcare in rural areas was also publicly funded, with "barefoot doctors" (farmers who received basic medical and paramedical training and worked in rural villages).

Although the services were underdeveloped, they could meet some farmers' demand. But when the reform program kicked off, education and social services became commercialized, and prices were liberalized. So, many farmers found education and healthcare not only expensive but hardly accessible. If some family member had a severe illness, the family would become instantly impoverished. In sum, it was the meager and far from sufficient income that made farmers' lives so miserable.

Traditional solutions and their limits. Different approaches have emerged to address rural problems and increase farm incomes. In the 1950s and 1960s the emphasis was on infrastructure and irrigation, as land and water were seen as the most important elements for agricultural production. With better irrigation the capacity to fight drought and flood should be enhanced, and output should be increased as well. But despite the increased output, infrastructure improvements had limited impacts on farm incomes.

In the 1970s and 1980s a new approach was advocated – to improve human capital by promoting science, technology, and education. A decade later it turned out that those who first adopted some new technologies did see increased yields and incomes, but once the technology was disseminated widely, farmers could not improve their income further despite better yields. In the 1980s and 1990s structural restructuring became the buzz word – this time, to promote higher value-added agricultural products. But history repeated itself. Pioneering farmers did earn more, but the followers did not. Again higher output practices failed to produce higher income.

The sluggish farm income despite higher output is caused by the two basic features of farm produce: its low income elasticity of demand, and its low price elasticity of demand. In plain words, when people's income increases, their demand for farm produce increases only marginally; yet when the supply increases, the price of those products will decline by a large margin. Infrastructure improvement, technological advance, and structural restructuring did increase total agricultural output. But when output surged, prices would quickly slump, exactly what the saying depicts, "Low grain prices hurt farmers." All in all, farm income improved at a relatively slow pace.

Transferring rural labor to cities. If the major reason for the sluggish growth of farm incomes is a combination of low income elasticity of demand and low price elasticity of demand, a long-term and effective solution is to reduce the number of farmers by, say, transferring them to cities.

First, a direct result of some farmers migrating to cities is that they turn from suppliers to consumers of farm produce. With declining supply and increasing demand, the price is bound to rise. Farmers who stay will then benefit from the increased price.

Second, when farmers migrate to cities, their land stays in the countryside, and those who stay can thus increase their scale of production and their output and supply per farm – and so increase their revenue.

Third, with a growing population and higher living standards, the demand for farm produce will keep increasing as well, whereas the arable land is shrinking and more rural workers are migrating to cities. Farmers will have greater interest in new technologies to increase output because the higher yields will boost their incomes under such circumstances.

Fourth, when migrant workers broaden their horizons in cities with exposure to new knowledge and technology, they can bring back some useful information and resources to stimulate rural development in their hometowns.

Dingxi, once a poverty-stricken county in Gansu province, has a good climate for planting potatoes. When some Dingxi farmers working on construction projects in cities noticed that city dwellers were very fond of potatoes, they started businesses selling potatoes produced in their hometown. Dingxi thus developed into a major potato production base.

Later, a graduate from the Department of Biology at Lanzhou University came to work at the Dingxi Agricultural Bureau and used some biological techniques to breed potatoes with specific ratios of protein and sugar. These new products attracted fast-food companies that have specific requirement for potatoes, such as McDonald's and Kentucky Fried Chicken. Dingxi has thus grown into a city famous for potatoes, all attributable to the entrepreneurship of farmers who migrated to cities and the facilitating role of the local government.

International experience tells a similar story. In the United States the income gap between urban and rural dwellers is rather narrow.

A major reason is that there are very small numbers of farmers. In 1870, 51% of the US labor force was in the countryside; today the figure is a mere 2%.[9] When most farmers have been transferred to non-agricultural sectors, those who stay can boost both the output and their income. Similarly in Japan, 70% of its labor force was in the countryside in 1870, 48% in 1950, 10.5% in 1980, and only 3.9% in 2000. Because a large number of surplus rural laborers moved to non-agricultural sectors, the incomes of Japanese farmers could stay close to those of their urban peers.

The same thing happened in China after its reform and opening. Between 1978 and 1984 "extraordinary growth" in agriculture resulted from the unleashed enthusiasm generated by the household responsibility system. But after 1985 that driving force did not work anymore. The new driving force was the township and village enterprise (TVE), located in rural areas but engaged in non-agricultural business. That is why the number of workers directly engaged in agricultural production was smaller than before.

By the late 1980s and early 1990s the driving force changed again: the farmers who migrated to cities. Their role in boosting farm income was even more obvious. Unlike those working in TVEs, migrant workers worked in industries in cities, divorced from agricultural production. This changed the supply and demand for farm produce – and injected a new vitality into the rural economy.

So, the migration of rural workers to cities is necessary to address rural issues, with one precondition – that cities should create enough jobs for migrant workers. In Chapter 4 I mentioned that whether a city can create enough jobs hinges mainly on the development model the government chooses. The CAD strategy in the pre-reform era was mainly to blame for China's lower urbanization among countries at the same per capita income. Some capital-intensive industries, like heavy industries, were set up and prioritized. Not consistent with China's comparative advantage, they created just a handful of jobs, insufficient to meet the needs of the growing number of urban workers.

To ensure full employment in the cities under the CAD strategy, workers in cities had to be sent to the countryside – the "Down to the Countryside Movement." So, for rural workers to flow freely to cities without imposing a burden on the economy, the national development strategy had to be adjusted toward labor-intensive industries consistent with the country's comparative advantage.

Building a unified national market to bridge regional gaps. Given the properties of farm produce (low income elasticity of demand and low price elasticity of demand), it seems that the only way to make sure farm income improves in the long run is to reduce the number of farmers. But in China's case there is another way to bridge the income gap between urban and rural areas and between different regions – to build a unified market across the country.

China is vast, and comparative advantage differs from region to region. The eastern area has convenient transportation and easy access to domestic and foreign markets. Generally speaking, it is good for manufacturing. And with enormous physical and human capital, it has enjoyed a higher level of development throughout history. Central and western areas, by contrast, boast better natural conditions than the east. The central area has higher rainfall and more arable land, so it is good for agricultural production. The western area enjoys abundant natural resources. If each area prioritizes the industries consistent with its comparative advantage, a unified market can be set up across the country to facilitate free trade of all those products.

In reality the eastern area still produces a large amount of farm produce, no longer consistent with its comparative advantage. Worse, it takes up resources from manufacturing, which does enjoy a comparative advantage. If a unified national market of agricultural products were in place, the eastern area could gradually reduce its agricultural production and instead purchase food from the central area. That way, the eastern area could focus on its comparative advantage – manufacturing – and the agricultural producers in the central area could benefit from rising prices driven by rising demand. In this sense the development of manufacturing in the eastern area could also stimulate the agricultural development and farm incomes in the central area.

By the same token, the faster the east develops, the more resources it will buy from the west. The higher the prices of resources, the higher the incomes of western residents. The rapid development of Inner Mongolia and the big boost of its people's income in recent years are attributed to higher prices for the province's substantial mineral resources.

There was no stimulus from the east to the central and western areas in the days of the planned economy. Resources were also allocated from this region to that, but to prioritize heavy industries the government artificially lowered the prices of staple food and mineral products. So, the faster the eastern region developed and the more agricultural and mineral products it got from the central and western areas, the more were its de facto subsidies from the less advanced central and western parts of the country. Historically, the eastern region has always been more advanced, and its per capita income has also been higher. So, the subsidies from the central and western regions were worsening the regional income disparity.

After the reform and opening, prices for most products were liberalized, but the government retained some control over the prices of staple food and mineral products. The central and western regions found that processing their own raw materials was more profitable than selling them to the east. That is how "Big and complete; small and complete" emerged. (The pattern refers to the situation that provinces in China all have a complete industrial system and enterprises have a complete system of production, supply, and marketing. This situation resulted from defying their respective comparative advantage and blindly pursuing completeness.)

Due to distorted prices, the western region's advantage in factor endowments cannot be translated into an economic advantage. Such a thing would not happen in full market economies. For example, Australia's major export, until this day, is iron ore (instead of iron and steel) and wool (instead of wool sweaters), because Australia is extremely rich in natural resources. If it exported processed iron ore and wool, the added profit would not cover the increased cost of processing.

A theorem in international trade models is Factor Price Equalization.[10] In an ideal model without transaction or transportation costs, or costs of wear and tear, the prices of factors of production in different countries are driven toward equality in the absence of barriers to trade. According to this theorem, if products could be traded freely in the domestic market in China, the price of factors of production in different regions will eventually be equalized, and the income gap will gradually be bridged.

So, China has to build a unified national market to narrow the urban–rural gap and regional gap by correcting distorted prices and giving full play to the comparative advantage of each region. Meanwhile, the physical infrastructure must be improved – communications, transportation, telecommunications, and so on – so that transaction costs can be reduced, efficiency improved, and the prices of production factors gradually equalized.

References

Brown, Lester R. 1995. *Who Will Feed China? Wake-up Call for a Small Planet.* New York: Norton.

Kuznets, Simon, and Dorothy S. Thomas. 1964. *Population Redistribution and Economic Growth: United States, 1870–1950.* Philadelphia: American Philosophical Society.

Lin, Justin Y. 1988. "The Household Responsibility System in China's Agricultural Reform: A Theoretical and Empirical Study." *Economic Development and Cultural Change* **36** (April): S199–S224.

1992. "Rural Reform and Agricultural Growth in China." *American Economic Review* **82**(1) (March): 34–51.

2004. *Fa Zhan Zhan Lue Yu Jing Ji Fa Zhan* [Development Strategy and Economic Development]. Beijing: Peking University Press.

Maddison, Angus. 1995. *Monitoring the World Economy, 1820–1992*. Paris: Organisation for Economic Co-operation and Development.

Murphy, K.M., A. Shleifer, and R.W. Vishny. 1989. "Industrialization and the Big Push." *Journal of Political Economy* **97**(5): 1003–26.

National Bureau of Statistics of China. 1992. *China Statistical Yearbook*. Beijing: China Statistics Press.

Sachs, J.D. 1992. "Privatization in Russia: Some Lessons from Eastern Europe." *American Economic Review* **82**(2): 43–48.

1993. *Poland's Jump to the Market Economy*. Cambridge, MA: MIT Press.

Sachs, J.D., and D. Lipton. 1990. "Poland's Economic Reform." *Foreign Affairs* **69**(3): 47–66.

Samuelson, P.A. 1948. "International Trade and the Equalisation of Factor Prices." *Economic Journal* **58** (June): 163–84.

Notes

1. The Gang of Four was the name given to a group led by Jiang Qing, the late wife of Mao Zedong, which effectively controlled the power organs of the Communist Party of China through the latter stages of the Cultural Revolution (1966–76) and was purged in a *coup d'état* one month after the death of Mao in October 1976.
2. Murphy, Shleifer, and Vishny (1989); Sachs (1992).
3. Sachs (1992); Sachs and Lipton (1990).
4. See Lin (1992).
5. See the review in Lin (1988).
6. Lin (1992).
7. Brown (1995).
8. Some foreign seed companies introduced a gene called "terminator" so that their seeds cannot be used for future cultivation, a highly controversial practice.
9. Kuznets and Thomas (1964).
10. Samuelson (1948).

EIGHT

Urban reform and the remaining issues

The development strategy oriented toward heavy industry was pursued through a trinity of the traditional economic system: micro incentives, resource allocation, and macro policies (Chapter 4). The focus of industrial reform was on the cities. So, in this chapter I elaborate on the different approaches and impacts of the urban reforms before and after 1978 to identify the main problems – and their solutions.[1]

Reform of the urban industrial sectors

China's urban industrial sectors had three major problems at the outset of reform and opening: structural imbalances, poor coordination, and weak incentives. Structural imbalances were manifest in the simultaneous existence of shortages and surpluses. Products in short supply continued to suffer from even more severe shortages, while some other products were overproduced. There was a popular saying: "Oversupplied products were always in excess supply, and products in shortage were always in short supply." Oversupplied products were those produced by heavy industries, especially the finished products. But even in heavy industries, some products were in short supply, such as energy and raw materials. Products in short supply usually referred to household products and other light industrial products. The coexistence of shortage and excess, leading to structural imbalances in resource allocation, was economically inefficient.

Second was poor coordination. Under the old system all resources were allocated by a central planning organ. A telling story: An Steel is in northeast China, and Wu Steel is in central China. Both areas have heavy industries. The demand for steel in the northeast was supposed to be met by An Steel, and the demand in central China by Wu steel. But under the old system before 1978, mismatches were common, increasing transportation costs and reducing efficiency.

Third were weak incentives. The incentive mechanism in the SOEs rewarded hard workers and shirkers equally. So, worker enthusiasm declined, and enterprise efficiency was low.

Pre-reform solutions

Before 1978 the state developed several solutions to address those problems.

First, the structural imbalance was adjusted by the central government. But the efficiency of adjusting the ratio of different industries was usually very low. Only when some products – such as agricultural products – were in such extreme shortage as to hamper the sustainability of the society would the central government allocate more funds to the sector. But as soon as the situation got any better, the inertia of the old system would kick in, and funds would revert to heavy industries as before.

Second, coordination was improved by delegating administrative power. The old system was based on vertical management, with the production activities of factories managed by the corresponding ministries under the State Council, compromising coordination. The Ministry of Iron and Steel paid attention only to production links, and often ignored geographical location when allocating resources. A division in the State Planning Commissions in charge of the use of iron and steel seldom produced cost-effective transportation arrangements.

To improve coordination, the central government replaced vertical management with horizontal, decentralizing administrative power at the provincial level, so that each province was in charge of its own resource allocation and production. For example, An Steel and other steel-related enterprises in Liaoning province were managed by the provincial government. This ensured that An Steel products went to enterprises in Liaoning province, improving coordination.

But under the old planned economy, there was a bizarre and repeated cycle. Decentralization led to dynamism. Dynamism led to disorder. Disorder led to retrenchment. Retrenchment led to stagnation. It is easy to understand why. Under the original pricing system, investment costs were suppressed. When economic decision-making power was devolved to the provinces, every province was eager to invest and develop its economy, especially heavy industries. The investment spree stimulated rapid economic growth in each province and thus the country.

But on the supply side, factor inputs like energy, iron and steel, mineral resources, and transportation cannot be increased in the short term, because their supply is limited by production capacity, whose expansion takes years. So, when investment grew at breakneck speed across the country, raw materials, transportation, and other factor inputs were instantly in short supply. In response, every province jumped at every possible opportunity to seize the resources, inevitably producing economic disorder. So, economic decision-making was again centralized, and the old problems of poor coordination and limited enthusiasm for work soon resurfaced, and the economy stagnated.

Third were the incentives from political mobilization. With worker incomes basically the same no matter how hard one worked, the enthusiasm for work was naturally low. To solve this, the government called on everyone to learn from Lei Feng (a soldier recognized for his volunteerism) and asked every workplace to reward model workers, who would receive social and political honors. But such political mobilization had its limits. The model workers selected would be admired and even obtain some political benefits (for example, they could be selected as members of the Chinese People's Political Consultative Conference or representatives of the National People's Congress). But the awards went to the few, certainly not to everyone. If everyone was recognized as a model worker, the award would make no difference and would thus lose its incentive magic. True, everyone had a spiritual pursuit, but the spiritual reward for work cannot be granted to everyone either. So, its boost to enthusiasm was rather limited.

Post-reform solutions

In 1978, at the Third Plenary Session of the 11th Central Committee of the Communist Party of China, the central government examined the inefficient industrial sector and spotted problems in structural balance, coordination, and incentives. The first post-reform solutions were not much different from the earlier ones.

First, for restructuring, the reform still relied on investments from the central government to adjust the ratios of primary, secondary, and tertiary industries. Investment in agriculture was 11 percent of the total in 1978. Resolutions at the Third Plenary Session raised this to 18 percent. This kind of adjusting was no different from before, so the results were similar. After the household responsibility system was introduced, agricultural output increased by a large margin. In the following years the ratio of the investment in agriculture never hit 18 percent as promised – indeed, it fell.

Second, for coordination, when administrative power was delegated to the provincial level and management changed from vertical to horizontal, there was a massive surge of investment in every locality. With breakneck economic development, shortages of materials occurred everywhere. With gradually liberalized prices, inflation was high. Ever since the hyperinflation of the Kuomintang administration during the civil war era, the communist government has always been sensitive to inflation.[2] So, when inflation surfaced, the central government immediately started to rectify it by cutting investment projects. But when inflation slowed, so did economic growth. So, to boost growth, administrative power was again delegated to stimulate incentives. From 1978 to 1996 there were three cycles of decentralization–inflation–retrenchment–stagnation–decentralization, just as before 1978.

Third, for the incentives, material rewards were acknowledged – a major departure from the earlier solutions. Deng Xiaoping recognized that businesses with good performance should be distinguished from those with poor performance, and that productive workers should also have higher wages than less productive workers. The previous wage standard was based on academic qualifications, seniority, gender, type of work, and the cost of living in different cities. This measure, seemingly making a small difference, hit a crucial problem and thus made a big difference.

The process of reform

Material rewards were recognized as boosting worker enthusiasm, and workers' wages began to be aligned with their effort. In the era of the planned economy, managers had no autonomy to determine workers' wages according to their effort. So, a precondition for the recognition of material rewards was to grant some autonomy to managers; that is, to allow the enterprises to retain part of their profits, so that the managers could allocate them at their discretion. This was a breakthrough in the trinity of the traditional economic system.

When autonomy was granted to the micro units, pricing and resource allocation naturally became more market-oriented. If enterprises could retain part of their profit, they should be able to use it, otherwise it would be meaningless. But because the old quota system did not cover this part of newly generated demand, outside-the-plan supply was needed, and that is how market-based resource allocation developed.

Before the reform there was a single track of the planned economy. The reform initiated a dual track of plan and market. The planned economy track was controlled by the state, and the other was decided by supply and demand in the market. At first the market track was small, but it gained momentum as the reforms deepened. Over time the defects and problems of the planned economy were fully exposed, and the state gradually decided to give up the planned track. The dual track eventually developed into a single market track.

In sum, China's urban reform started by devolving management to the SOEs and moved to resource allocation and price formation. It evolved from a single-track planned economy to a dual track of both planned and market economy and finally to the single-track market economy.

Management reform

The post-1978 reform started with devolving management to enterprises to build incentives in order to boost worker enthusiasm and ultimately to improve productivity – in a power-and profit-sharing phase and in a property rights-clarifying phase.

The system of profit retention

Introduced as a trial in 4,000 SOEs in Sichuan province in 1978, the system allowed enterprises to retain 12 percent of their increased profits. They could apply the retained profits to a bonus fund to reward model workers, to a welfare fund to build dormitories, hospitals, kindergartens, and the like, or to a development fund to invest in expanding production. Similarly, loss-making enterprises could retain 12 percent of their reduced losses. This trial reform achieved great results. The more profits an SOE made, the more it could retain. Naturally a discrepancy emerged between the profit-making and loss-making SOEs. But the state was the ultimate beneficiary, for it claimed 88 percent of the higher profits and lower losses.

When the profit-retention system was promoted nationwide in 1979, the results were mixed. At the micro level, both the enthusiasm of the SOEs and their efficiency were dramatically improved, but the state's profits and taxes actually fell. Not only did the state not obtain the supposed 88 percent, but in some cases it received even less than before. A major reason for this was the problem of supervision.

Before the reform, managers were deprived of decision-making power precisely because it was hard to supervise them. Now, the SOEs could present false information about their operations. For example, if their profit increased by 100%, the company should retain 12%. But if the manager lied and reported only a 50% profit increase, the company could retain the legitimate 6% and the concealed 50%, or much more than the supposed 12%.

The SOEs could also cook the books. If they used the retained profit to build dormitories, they could allocate the expense to production costs instead. It was not easy for the state to audit all accounts. The State Planning Commission dispatched supervisors to monitor SOEs, but they could be bought off. So, in the game with SOEs the state failed to obtain its due share from the increased profits the reform generated.

The contract system

To address the problems in the system of profit retention, the state – inspired by the positive results from the household responsibility system – decided in 1985 to promote the contract system among all SOEs. The state made a contract with the director/manager of each SOE. The enterprise had to turn over a fixed contract fee to the state each year; and if the profit exceeded the contract fee, the difference had to be allocated between the state and the enterprise according to a certain ratio. Sometimes the state got the lion's share, other times the enterprises got it. The state's interest should in theory have been better protected under the contract system, because it received not only an annual contract fee but also a share in the additional profit. In reality, however, the results were very much the same as before.

In trials the results were quite positive. Yet when the model went nationwide, more often than not the interest of the state was diminished. First, the contract system did not consider inflation, which would shrink the purchasing power of the contract fee. Before 1986 China experienced little inflation, but the retail price index jumped 18.5 percent in 1988 and 17.8 percent in 1989. Even though the face value of the contract fee remained unchanged, its purchasing power declined.

Second, the rights and obligations of the contract were imbalanced. If the company was well managed, a certain share of its profit was turned in according to the contract. But if it suffered a loss, the state could not punish the director/manager responsible. The imbalance induced some directors/managers to pursue private interests by seemingly legitimate means. For example, they could purchase raw materials at inflated prices from companies owned by their relatives and friends or even by themselves. Or they could also sell products at suppressed prices to those companies. This way, part or even all of the profit of the SOEs was transferred to the companies closely related to the directors and managers. It was difficult for the state to spot and investigate such cases.

Clarifying property rights

In the late 1980s there was a debate over the losses to the national interest from the profit retention and contract systems. The general consensus was that the losses came from the state ownership and an ambiguous definition of property rights. So, no one bothered to concern themselves with the maintenance and value of national assets. The SOEs were run by directors/managers, but the state – the owner on behalf of all the people – had no representative in the enterprises to protect its interest. The solution proposed in the academic literature was to clarify the property rights.

Two approaches were suggested, based on the company's size. One was to privatize small and medium SOEs. The other was to introduce the commercialized large SOEs, with a board of directors representing the interest of all owners, and a board of supervisors monitoring the decision-making and operations of the enterprise. The shareholding system was introduced to some enterprises, which were allowed to issue shares on the stock market, but the holders had to be natural persons – living human beings, not a group acting as a legal person. It was believed that natural persons would concern themselves with the maintenance and appreciation of the stocks they bought. Therefore, they would supervise the directors/managers; and their supervision would improve the management of the enterprises. Stocks that increased in value benefited not only the individual investors, but also the state, the major shareholder.

The result was much the same as before: the productivity of the enterprises increased, but the interest of the state was not protected. Even worse, in clarifying property rights and privatizing smaller SOEs, considerable national assets were lost. And even now, except for monopoly industries, most large SOEs still have difficulty making a decent profit, despite the many reforms and the greater incentives (see Chapter 9).

The pilot projects succeeded because they received close attention not only from related state departments but also from the media. In the spotlight it was difficult for the enterprises to encroach on the state's interest. But when the model was promoted among hundreds of thousands of SOEs and attention was diluted, effective supervision was impossible. Inevitably the state lost out to the SOEs.

The reform in resource allocation and the pricing mechanism

The emergence of the market and the coexistence of the planned and market economic systems

When autonomy was granted to the SOEs, it became necessary to reform the resource allocation and pricing mechanisms. Before the reform, materials were allocated according to the state's plan. Because enterprises could retain 12 percent of the additional profit, to turn the profit into tangible benefits, enterprises and workers should be allowed to buy what they wanted, including goods outside the plan. They should also be allowed to sell their extra products outside the plan to realize their value. This way, enterprises would be motivated to produce more. Market-based allocation and pricing thus emerged on both the demand and the supply sides.

The transition from the planned economy to the market economy

With products outside the plan generally priced higher than those in the plan, enterprises had more incentive to invest in and produce products with market-based prices. As a result, the output of those products grew rapidly while products within the plan gradually shrank. The mix of products in and outside the plan changed dramatically.

When the market price was higher than the planned price of the same commodity (economists call the difference between the two "rent"), there would be rampant rent-seeking behavior.[3] Corruption would be rife, and social tensions would be intense. To alleviate the tension, the best approach would be to scrap the planned allocation of resources and let the market play its due role.

The reform process

Materials

From 1979 to 1984 many materials, including reinforced concrete and steel, could be produced and sold outside the plan. After 1984 the state's mandatory part was shrinking, and production was more market-based. In the end the planned system was scrapped completely.

In the 1980s the dual track brought out a large number of profiteers (nicknamed *Daoye* in Mandarin), who, through their connections, could get materials at the lower quota prices and sell them at the higher market prices, amassing great fortunes. The best way to eliminate such "rents" was to transform the dual track to a market-based single track. In the early 1990s the market was finally liberalized, and all prices were based on the market. As a result, the rents disappeared, as did the *Daoye*.

Foreign exchange management

Before the reform only eight companies were allowed to engage in foreign trade, each with a monopoly on the commodities they specialized in. All exports at that time had to go through them. Funded by the state, they purchased goods from various enterprises in various locales and handed all their foreign exchange earnings to the state.

The reform of 1978 granted local autonomy in foreign trade, allowing provinces, municipalities, and autonomous regions to establish their own foreign trade companies. But specialized trading companies gave way to comprehensive ones, and the mandatory plan of the state was replaced by the guiding plan.

Similarly, 12 percent of the additional forex earnings could be retained by the companies and used at their discretion. Initially there was a time limit on the retained forex. Because some foreign trade companies had more than enough forex, and others were in need of it, a sort of foreign exchange swap market was established in 1983, so that companies could trade forex at their discretion.

The adjustment price of forex in the swap market was basically the market price, usually 30–60 percent higher than the stipulated price. Meanwhile, the official exchange rate was adjusted in accord with the swap price. The reform in the foreign trade and foreign exchange management system promoted China's export growth. The total value of foreign trade in 1978 was $20.6 billion, and the export value about $10 billion, completely under state control. Exports grew to $100 billion in 1993, only 20 percent of them under state control. In relative terms the state's control fell from 100 percent to 20 percent, but in absolute terms the amount under the state's control doubled.

At the beginning of the reforms in 1978 the official exchange rate was RMB 1.5 to the dollar. In 1983 the swap price was RMB 3 to the dollar. After then, the official exchange rate was adjusted in accord with the swap price. In 1993 the swap price was about RMB 8.7 to the dollar, and the official exchange rate about RMB 5.7. The RMB 3 difference meant a rent of RMB 3 for every dollar. So, for the $20 billion under state control, the rent was RMB 60 billion. To eliminate the rent-seeking, the state scrapped the dual track of foreign exchange in 1994 and introduced a managed floating system.

The financial sector

Before the reform the financial system had unified revenue and appropriation – all the surplus in the national economy was collected and allocated by the Ministry of Finance. The state budgets also covered the budget of SOEs. In addition, there was only one bank – the People's Bank of China, a bureau under the Ministry of Finance. It had branches in the center and in every province, city, and county. More than an ordinary bank, it also provided an accounting and cashier service for the SOEs. Because the funds allocated for projects by the State Planning Commission could not be used all at once, the balance had to be deposited in the People's Bank of China.

The state hoped that the reformed banks in China could evaluate projects and monitor capital use as effectively as foreign financial institutions did. Starting in 1979 the four major state-owned commercial banks – the Industrial and Commercial Bank, Construction Bank, Agricultural Bank, and Bank of China – were reopened. And some non-bank financial institutions – including insurance companies, trust investment companies, and leasing companies – were established as well. Meanwhile, to improve incentives, regulations were gradually relaxed. Banks could lend more if they had more deposits. In addition, a capital market was created in 1990 with the establishment of the Shanghai and Shenzhen stock exchanges. The four state-owned commercial banks have been turned into stock-holding banks and listed in Hong Kong stock exchanges and Shanghai stock exchanges.

But China's financial system was still on a dual track, instead of being completely based on the market. The government kept administrative controls on the entry to the banking sector, the interest rates of savings and loans, and the listings of companies on the stock markets. The role of the market was restricted.

The emergence of the TVEs and other non-SOEs

The reform doubtlessly improved the allocation of resources, and gave more play to the market, thus stimulating economic growth. A big part of the growth can be attributed to the emergence of TVEs, private businesses, and foreign-funded enterprises, including joint ventures and solely owned enterprises.

TVEs were actually created before 1978. Thanks to the promotion of agriculture mechanization, each commune had its own maintenance shop, the earliest TVE. Later, they expanded their business operation to produce some parts and components, as well as some daily necessities. But before 1978 they could not obtain equipment and raw materials from the relevant state departments, and their products were excluded from the country's commercial system, so they had to produce and sell locally.

After the household responsibility system was introduced at the end of 1978, farmer enthusiasm for production increased significantly, as did output. Because farmers could retain the remaining produce after they had fulfilled the state quota, they began to have some capital for investment. They could now buy equipment and raw materials from the market for production and sell their products to other provinces.

These profit-driven TVEs would not, of course, invest in industries that had no comparative advantage. Nor would the non-SOEs (including private businesses and foreign-funded enterprises). As a result, the private sector developed at an amazing speed. In 1978 the output of TVEs was only 9.3% of the industry's total, but in 1994 more than 42%. TVE exports were only 11% of the total in 1987, but 35% in 1994. The rapid growth of TVEs has everything to do with taking full advantage of China's comparative advantage. The emergent market mechanism unexpectedly stimulated the development of TVEs and other non-SOEs – and improved the allocation of resources.

The achievements and problems of the reform

China's reform took a gradual approach, aptly described by Deng Xiaoping as "Crossing the river by groping the stones." At the beginning of the reform, there was no blueprint or clear orientation. The initial goal was more planned-economy-based than market-based. But the gradual reform brought China closer and closer to the market economy – in some ways closer even than some market economy countries.

How is this so? Behind every economic issue, there is economic logic. During the reform, problems cropping up along the way were dealt with in accord with the principles of "emancipating the mind," "seeking the truth from facts," and "keeping up with the times." So the gradual reform proceeded in accord with a certain logic. The traditional planned economic system was created because a capital-strapped country was desperate to build capital-intensive heavy industries. The inherent conflict was the root cause of the trinity of distorted prices, highly centralized allocations, and zero autonomy at the micro level.

The starting point of the reform was to recognize that managers and workers needed a material interest in their enterprises. To respect the material interest of enterprises and individuals, the enterprises at the micro level of management needed a degree of autonomy. Then, to realize the interests of enterprises and individuals, reforms in resource allocation and price formation became essential. Under the dual-track system, if enterprises and individuals could control a certain amount of resources, they would certainly invest their resources in profitable sectors in accord with the comparative advantage. (Those sectors had been suppressed by the government under the CAD strategy.) So, resource allocation improved. Meanwhile, to eliminate rent-seeking and corruption, the dual track was gradually trans-formed to a single market track. Despite the original design, reform in China moved step by step toward the market economy.

This gradual reform scored tremendous achievements. First, the productivity of SOEs was enhanced considerably. Before 1978 their productivity was terribly low. After the reform the TFP of the state-owned sector (2.4%) was still very low compared with the non-state sector (5.6%). But compared with its previous performance – 0.5% or even as low as –1.0% – the improvement was quite impressive.[4]

Second, the output share of SOEs in the industry declined rapidly. In 1978 it was more than three-quarters, but in 2000 it was down to one-quarter, so most of the products in the market were produced by private businesses.[5]

Third, the economy became more open. In 1978 foreign trade was only 9.9% of GDP, but in 2009 it was 44.7%. Among countries with a population over 100 million, China has the greatest dependence on foreign trade. It is also the world's fastest growing economy, with average annual growth of 9.9% from 1979 to 2009.[6]

Impressive as the reform has been, it has many vulnerabilities. First, the banking system is rather fragile. The proportion of non-performing loans is very high, and some scholars believe it was as high as 40 percent at the end of the 1990s.[7] The stock market bubble and speculation are also serious. When the stock market was established in 1991, only individual investors were allowed to buy stocks. It was believed then that investors would concern themselves with the value of the stocks they bought. It turned out that those investors cared very little about the operation of enterprises. Their only concern was to speculate on the rise and fall of stocks, so the turnover of stocks was very high. In 1998 investment funds were introduced so that China could learn from foreign experience. The result was even worse. Some fund managers attempted not only to speculate but even to manipulate stock prices.

Second, corruption is rampant. The widespread corruption in the 1980s was mainly caused by a spread of rent-seeking behaviors resulting from the difference between the plan prices and the market prices. Later, although the plan price system was scrapped, the government continued to intervene in the market, and price distortions have not been completely eliminated. For example, it takes about RMB 20 million ($3 million) for a company to be listed. Because the interest rate of the state-owned banks is lower than the market rate, the spread leads to rent-seeking. Rent-seeking also exists in the lucrative real estate and mining industries, because the land price is artificially low and totally controlled by the government. And although the prices of mineral resources have been liberalized, the royalty is very low. So, as long as the government intervenes in market access and price distortions persist, corruption will continue.

Third, the SOEs have yet to be reformed. They have been the focus of reforms since 1978. Now almost all small and medium SOEs have been privatized, but most large SOEs, except for those in the monopoly industries, still depend on government protection and subsidy.

One of the causes of these problems is the mismatching of institutions. Because China's reform took a gradual approach rather than shock therapy, it did not eliminate all the distortions in one go. Instead, it has taken baby steps. To boost worker and farmer incentives, the reform initiated a power- and profit-sharing system, resulting in a dual-track system of both plan and market. It then gradually moved to the single market track. But not all sectors are market-based: as just seen, land, finance, and natural resources are still subject to direct interference and allocation by the state.

Naturally, there is some friction between the planned system and the market system, and its manifestation is the rent-seeking from the price disparity. This explains the rent-seeking behavior of the profit-driven enterprises, especially private and foreign-funded ones, but also some SOEs. The best way to eliminate rent-seeking is to scrap the dual-track system and rely on a single one, planned or market. But there is no turning back.

So why does China not lift controls over the prices of land, capital, and natural resources all at once? To protect the SOEs. If the poorly operated SOEs are incapable of paying off the loans they have received from the banks, those loans will turn bad. When the listed SOEs cannot pay dividends due to their poor management, stock buyers have to speculate to profit, crippling the financial sector. The state had also subsidized inefficient SOEs by suppressing interest rates and the prices of land and resources.

The other reason the state supports and protects SOEs is their indispensable role in the country. What they produce is usually closely related to people's livelihood or to national security. And if a major SOE went bankrupt, a large number of workers would be laid off, creating social tensions. So the government cannot leave the SOEs to go bankrupt.

To conclude, if we cannot find a way out for the SOE reform, institutional distortions will remain. If the state does not allow the non-viable SOEs to go bankrupt, it has to offer them some protection. Usually the protection takes the form of the administrative methods inherent in the planned economy, methods that obviously conflict with the market system.

References

Krueger, A.O. 1974. "The Political Economy of Rent-seeking Society." *American Economic Review* 64(3): 291–303.

Lardy, N. 1998. *China's Unfinished Economic Revolution*. Washington, DC: Brookings Institution.

Lin, Justin Y. 2004. *Fa Zhan Zhan Lue Yu Jing Ji Fa Zhan* [Development Strategy and Economic Development]. Beijing: Peking University Press.

Lin, Justin Y., Fang Cai, and Zhou Li. 2003. *The China Miracle: Development Strategy and Economic Reform*, revised edn. Hong Kong: Chinese University Press.

National Bureau of Statistics of China 2010. *China Statistical Yearbook 2010*. Beijing: China Statistics Press.

Notes

1. This chapter draws on Lin, Cai, and Li (2003).
2. Hyperinflation was attributed as a main reason for Kuomintang's loss of popular support and defeat in the civil war.
3. Krueger (1974).
4. Lin (2004).
5. Lin (2004).
6. National Bureau of Statistics of China (2010).
7. Lardy (1998). After recapitalization and listing in the stock markets, the proportion of non-performing loans in the four commercial banks has improved substantially, estimated at less than 5%.

NINE

Reforming the state-owned enterprises

China's reform has produced some tremendous achievements in the last thirty years, but also some problems, most of them related to the gradual manner of reform. A gradual reform implies that, when new arrangements of the market system emerge, some elements of the old system still linger on. The conflict between the two systems is the root cause of many problems. In fact, both systems have their strict underlying logic and both are made up of correlated and interacting institutional arrangements. Likewise, while some new institutional arrangements have emerged, others are denied due to the persistence of some old arrangements. In such circumstances friction and conflict are inevitable.

In theory a solution to the dual system is either a complete transition to the market system or a complete restoration of the original planned system. But in practice neither option is easy. True, the original system could get rid of the problems of the financial system – corruption and loss-making state-owned enterprises (SOEs). But it simply is no longer possible to go back. Even if it were possible, after tasting the sweetness of the reform, people would not be willing to do so. And if the old system were reinstated, the incentives to work would be even weaker. So, China's economic reform has to forge ahead with full momentum.

Although the reform started over three decades ago, China has not yet completely transformed to a market economy. The major reason is that the reform of its SOEs has yet to be accomplished, imposing great inertia on the transition. Because the reform of SOEs is closely related to the reform in other areas, only when the reform of SOEs has been completed will the transition to a market economy be complete.

In this chapter I first discuss the problems in the SOE reform and analyze how best to reform the SOEs.[1] The chapter will then compare the "shock therapy" in the Soviet Union and Eastern Europe with the gradual approach in China, analyzing their respective pros and cons.

Problems in the banking system

As I mentioned in Chapter 8, there was a bizarre and repeated cycle in the national economy: decentralization led to dynamism; dynamism led to disorder; disorder led to retrenchment; retrenchment led to stagnation. A major reason behind this cycle was the adjustment of bank interest rates. When the interest rate was artificially low, businesses rushed to borrow for investment, resulting in capital shortages. To maintain a balance, the banks had to apply tight controls over loans, reducing efficiency. When the controls were relaxed again, the investment spree and loan rush resurfaced, stimulating investment-driven rapid economic growth for a while.

With the same interest rate, deposits did not increase, but loans increased a lot, opening a gap between the two. To bridge this gap, the state had to issue more currency, producing inflation. And when investment grew rapidly, the demand for construction materials and iron and steel would surge. But the construction period of a steel plant is very long, so the supply elasticity is very low in the short term. When demand suddenly surged, prices would go straight up. Similarly, the surge in the investment and production activities would increase the demand for transportation. But the supply elasticity of transportation is also very low, producing bottlenecks.

Inflation and shortage are the "chaos" phase in the cycle. There are two ways to get rid of the "chaos." One is to liberalize the interest rate. But that is not an option for the state, for a low interest rate is necessary for many SOEs to survive. The other is to cut back investment projects to artificially reduce loans and investments. But when investment falls, the economy would stagnate, slowing employment growth, which requires more investment and less regulation. So, the cycle would repeat itself.

There is an easy way to break the cycle: give the banks the final say in which projects to invest in. That is exactly what the 1994 resolution did – commercialize the banks and liberalize the interest rate.

The original idea was that, when investment demand increased, adjusting the interest rate could balance the supply and demand for capital. When the interest rate went up, investment and consumption would contract, and deposits would increase. That way the economy would not overheat. But it did not work out that way.

Starting in 1983 the state stopped fiscal appropriations for the SOEs; instead, the SOEs began to rely on the low interest rate for survival. That is why 70 percent of bank loans have gone to the SOEs. These were de facto policy loans. When the SOEs could not pay back the loans due to poor performance, the loans became non-performing, eroding the balance sheets of banks. If the banks could have had a say in which enterprises could get the loans, based on their balance sheets, the non-performing loan ratio would have fallen sharply, but many SOEs would have had to shut down. That is why liberalizing the interest rate could not be put on the agenda until the SOEs improved their efficiency.

Problems in the stock market

The original reason for establishing the stock market was to serve the needs of SOEs. The consensus was that the stock market would sort out the issues of corporate governance and ownership structure. But most listed SOEs were not competitive in the market. They went public with a view to "enclosing money." Because they made hardly any profit, they could not pay dividends. Shares that pay no dividend are like casino chips. The only good way to profit is to gamble trading stocks. That is why the stock market in China was perceived by many as a casino in its early years; people bought stocks for speculation. That is also why the turnover rate of the stocks was so high – and the dramatic ups and downs of stocks so commonplace. The root cause of China's speculative stock market is that the problems of SOEs cannot be solved as long as listed companies make no profit and shareholders receive no dividend.

Corruption

Corruption is also intertwined with the SOEs. Corruption here refers to government officials taking bribes. As long as the government has too much power, all kinds of corruption will be in play. Corruption was rampant during the transition period because the government was too powerful. First, the government regulated market access, creating monopoly profits and inevitably leading to rent-seeking and corruption. Second, the government artificially suppressed the prices of some goods well below market prices, also leading to rent-seeking and corruption.

Take the financial market. Total loans in 1993 were RMB 2.6 billion. The official interest rate was 11 percent, and the market rate was about 25 percent, so there was a more than 10 point spread. Quite a few people had a say in the allocation of the RMB 2.6 billion, including the presidents of the four major state-owned banks at the central, provincial, and city levels and the administrators and even some assistants in the credit divisions. In the 1990s if a person could get a loan from the banks at the official interest rate, he or she could earn at least 10 percent immediately by relending at the higher rate. So, if one had connections with the right people in the banking system, one could earn handsome rents, a source of corruption.

In sum, both the distorted banking system and the regulation of market access were born out of the non-viability of the SOEs. The state has to protect the SOEs by overt or covert means, and in the end the same problems remained unsolved. To eliminate the distortions, the problems of the SOEs would have to be tackled first. Otherwise, a large number of SOEs would go bankrupt, leading to serious social disorder.

Solving the problems of SOEs

The SOEs can be classified as large, medium, or small. Privatization can solve the problems of the small and medium SOEs capable of exploiting their comparative advantage. Even if they have a historical burden of too many staff, bad assets, and social responsibilities, as long as their assets are in good hands, that burden can be lifted. For example, the small and medium SOEs are usually in the downtown area. With economic growth, the supply elasticity of land is very low, hence the upsurge of the land prices. After 1978 China's annual growth was 9.9 percent, and the growth of land prices was even greater. So, if the enterprises can exploit their land, they could have room to lift their historical burden.

The real headache is the reform of large SOEs. Today there are some 4,000–5,000 large SOEs. They face the same principal-agent problem as large enterprises anywhere. The owner and manager of a small business can be the same person, but for large businesses, they usually are not. Separating the owner and the manager can create two problems. First is the incentive disparity between the owner and manager: the owner pursues returns on investment while the manager focuses on wages and benefits. Second is the asymmetric information between the owner and the manager. Because owners are usually not directly involved in the operation, they do not have a clear picture of the costs and benefits of the enterprises. What's more, it is difficult for owners to see which expenses are necessary. So managers can encroach on the owner's interests by taking advantage of their exclusive information, giving rise to a moral hazard.

For any large enterprise, only proper management can protect the interests of its investors, thereby attracting more investment. So, the reform in large SOEs must start with tackling the asymmetric information and incompatible incentives between the owners and managers.

Some theories suggest that privatization is the only way out for large SOEs. But the premise is that the owners are also the managers of the enterprises. Generally neither the president nor the general manager of a large SOE is the owner, and no shareholder is willing to manage the enterprise alone, because he or she can get only a small proportion of the higher profits from improving efficiency through his or her management.

In addition, a large SOE may have a big number of shareholders but a limited number of executives. If the enterprise is managed by a major shareholder, the rights and interests of the minor shareholders could be violated. For example, a major shareholder could transfer the profits of the enterprise he or she is managing to another enterprise that he or she owns, by selling low and buying high (or price-fixing). That way the shareholder can personally obtain the lion's share of the profits, and the rights and interests of the minor shareholders who are not directly involved in the management are cut out of the benefits.

Another suggestion is to hire internal or external auditors to supervise the SOE, but that is not a solution either. Whether internal or external, the auditors are hired by the general manager. If an auditing company produces false information, the minor shareholders cannot find out the real situation. The Enron scandal is a telling example. Even if the auditor is not fraudulent, it will be difficult to discern the need for every expenditure. For example, it is hardly possible for the auditors to discover the on-the-job consumption and distribution of the manager. Even if discovered later, the manager may have already left the company.

Adam Smith discussed such a case in *The Wealth of Nations*.[2] Back then, international trade was already well developed, but it had high risks. To reduce the risks, trading companies would try to find many investors, prepare several ships, and hire all the captains – a precursor to the modern corporate system. In the 1930s Adolf Berle and Gardiner Means, two lawyers who studied listed companies in the United States, found that most were run by professional managers.[3] They argued that due to asymmetric information, the companies run by managers were not as efficient as those run by owners.

The reality is that professionally managed listed companies have since mushroomed, so there must be some rationality in the modern corporate system. Theoretically, the issue of information asymmetry has to be solved first to address the issue of incentive incompatibility. The most effective solution is to create full competition in the market. If the profit of a company equals the average profit for the industry in a fully competitive market, the manager's performance is average. If the profit is below average, either the capacity or integrity of the manager is questionable. If the profit is above average, both the capacity and integrity of the manager should be recognized. Therefore, if the assessment of the manager's performance is based on the difference in profit between the company and the industry average, information asymmetry and incentive incompatibility can be solved.[4]

Here's how. Competition must be introduced to the selection of managers. Capable managers – those who can bring a high return on investment – should be rewarded with better wages and benefits. And those who have made their company suffer losses should be punished with reduced wages and benefits, or even fired. This way, the incentives for the managers become compatible with those for the owners, and an incentive mechanism links the payment of managers to their performance.

For this, the market must be fully competitive, otherwise information asymmetries will remain. Whether in capitalist or socialist countries, monopolies are generally inefficient. A consensus in the literature is that a fully competitive market is necessary but not sufficient for solving information asymmetries. In a fully competitive market each corporate governance arrangement has its pros and cons: no single arrangement fits all.[5]

In the traditional planned economic system there was no competition, so there was no way to solve the problems of asymmetric information. In such circumstances, to keep managers from abusing their power and encroaching on the state's interest, they were completely deprived of power. That explains why the pilot programs of reform could succeed – be it the "power and profit-sharing" reform or the "clarifying the property rights" reform. But without exception the reforms were futile once they were promoted nationwide. The pilot programs succeeded because the pilot enterprises were under the spotlight of the whole nation: not only the government but also the media. In these circumstances it was hardly possible for the enterprises to encroach on the national interest, so both the efficiency of the enterprises and the revenue of the country improved. But when the program was disseminated nationwide, national attention was diluted. And with asymmetric information, managers could abuse their power and exploit the government.

Removing the policy burden

Before the reform and opening, there was little competition in the domestic market, and the government applied restrictions over imports and exports. After the reform and opening, more and more non-SOEs and foreign-funded enterprises began to enter the market, so market competition intensified. In fact, except for the monopolistic industries, such as telecommunications and oil, other industries were liberalized.

But the competitive market did not bring in enough information to enable the SOEs to design a mechanism to solve incentive incompatibility. Most important, the root cause of the inefficiency of the SOEs was not addressed: that they are not viable. Before the reform the SOEs, set up for the state's CAD strategy, were overly capital-intensive and not in line with China's comparative advantage. Their problems could be called the "strategic burden."

Another burden is also related to the national development strategy. Before the reform production and investment were concentrated in the capital-intensive industries, which did not create enough jobs. But because the government wanted to guarantee full employment in the urban areas, it overstaffed the SOEs. These redundant workers were not regarded as a burden, because all the investment and expenditures of the SOEs were covered by financial appropriations. But after the reform the burden of these redundant workers was shifted to the SOEs, thus creating a "social burden." The payment of the retirees' pension was also shifted to the SOEs, so the longer the history of an enterprise, the heavier burden it had to bear.

Both the strategic burden and the social burden are policy burdens, resulting in policy-induced losses in a competitive market. Because the government is responsible for the losses, it grants enterprises policy subsidies (such as preferential treatment in market access, taxes, bank loans, and so on). Due to asymmetric information, the state cannot have a clear picture of the exact losses incurred because of the policy burden. The enterprises can thus take the opportunity to report operational losses as policy-induced losses. The state cannot tell which is which, so it has to bear all the losses of the enterprises, creating a "soft budget constraint."[6]

Enterprises have two ways to increase the wages and benefits of their managers: one is to honestly improve productivity, the other is to ask for more subsidies from the state. The way to solve this problem is to remove the policy burdens; otherwise, any corporate-governance reform will be futile, and privatization will be worse instead of better for the government. Why? Because after privatization the owners could ask for state subsidies to cover policy burdens, but the subsidies could end up in their pockets, and would be totally legal.

Naturally, the enterprises will be all the more motivated to ask for subsidies, and corrupt government officials will decide which enterprises get what subsidies. So, if the policy burden remains, privatizing the SOEs will only encourage corruption. That is why a key to the SOE reform is to remove the policy burden of the SOEs, both the social burden and the strategic burden.

Removing the social burden

To remove the social burden on the SOEs, the state has to take care of the redundant employees and the pension funds. It can have the SOEs spin off their social burden by establishing and paying for an unemployment insurance system and a social security system. Otherwise, it will have to pay for the losses of the SOEs, because if the enterprises bear the social burden, they will have an excuse to ask for more subsidies by reporting their operational losses as policy-induced losses. So, if the social burden is spun off from the SOEs, the expenditure of the government will not increase, and there is a good chance that it will decline and that the efficiency of SOEs will improve as well.

Removing the strategic burden

The strategic burden of the SOEs also has to be spun off. Consider four categories of SOEs according to the features of their products:

- The products are critical for national security, and thus must be produced by SOEs, subsidized, and under the direct supervision of the state. Their number is very small.
- The products are very capital-intensive and enjoy a huge domestic market, but the domestic financial market cannot support their capital needs. Such enterprises should try to be listed overseas or to cooperate with foreign counterparts to use their capital and technology. The oil, automobile, and telecommunications industries have adopted this approach.
- The products do not have a huge market, but the enterprises enjoy abundant human capital. Such enterprises should produce in line with their comparative advantage. Sichuan Changhong, which produces household electronics, and Chongqing Jialing, which produced motorcycles, are cases in point. The precondition for changing the line of production is that they have advantages in engineering design and in management.
- The enterprises that have no advantage in their products, their human capital, or their markets have to be shut down. The number of such enterprises is very small.

After spinning off the social and strategic burden on the SOEs, if they still cannot survive in the competitive market, then the management should be held responsible. When the enterprises are free from the policy burden, an incentive mechanism can be designed to solve the incentive incompatibility.

The SOE reform and privatization

After spinning off the policy burden, the key to the reform shifts to corporate governance at the micro level. Some economists in China hold that the poor management of SOEs should be attributed entirely to the lack of professional managers. I beg to differ, because if the enterprises have to bear the policy burden, even professional managers cannot make much difference. If the policy burden is not removed, privatization will lead only to a huge loss of state assets, because the people in charge of the privatization are the managers. In a management buyout, managers could artificially suppress the prices for state assets, resulting in a huge loss for the state, which was what happened in Russia and many former socialist countries in Eastern Europe.[7]

To avoid such a loss, the policy burden must be spun off first. Then the profit flow is calculated in the absence of the policy burden. Statistics show that the profit margin of most SOEs around the world is less than that of private businesses. But this is because most of them have to bear a policy burden. In developed countries some public utilities cannot attract investment from the private sector, and so have to be run by publicly owned companies. The poor performance of these companies is not necessarily due to the ownership.

For large SOEs, eliminating the policy burden is key for performance improvement. For example, New Zealand redefined the responsibilities of its SOEs in the 1980s. Their original mission was to provide public services in remote rural areas at low prices, and they were operating at a loss. The redefined SOEs are profit-oriented, but do not enjoy a monopoly. Guided by the new principle of market orientation, prices were liberalized, and boards of directors and supervisors were introduced. After a series of reforms, the SOEs quickly turned a loss into a profit.[8]

Sweden has a similar story. The only difference is that the loss-making projects were originally subsidized by the profits from other projects in the same company. After the loss-making projects were spun off, other projects became market-based, so information asymmetry was no longer an issue. The Swedish SOEs account for 25 percent of the country's GDP, around the same proportion as Chinese SOEs.[9]

Because SOEs are the core of the reform, if their problems can be solved, other problems related to the reform can also be solved.

But the CAD strategy still appeals to some government officials and social elites. As long as the old strategy still has its influence, the CAF strategy cannot be fully implemented, and more non-viable enterprises with a strategic burden will be created. To protect these non-viable enterprises, the government has to distort the price signals and intervene in the banking system and in market access.

So, for the planned economy to be transformed to a market economy, the strategic thinking must be changed first. Because the old system was born of the CAD strategy, for a complete transition to the market economy, that old strategy must be abandoned, and a CAF strategy must replace it. Such a shift in strategic thinking is a prerequisite for economic success and a guarantee for smooth progress of the SOE reform.

Shock therapy or gradual reform?

The implicit assumption of shock therapy is that the enterprises are viable, and the core idea is to establish, in a very short period, a package of institutional arrangements necessary for a sound market economic system. Shock therapy has three major policy recommendations: liberalize prices, privatize enterprises, and achieve fiscal balance and macroeconomic stability.[10] It failed, however, to produce the expected J-shaped economic recovery. Instead, it led to an L-shaped recession – for three main reasons.[11]

- First, it is difficult to use the fixed assets of heavy industries in other industries, so a decline in GDP was inevitable. For example, it was difficult to use the machinery and equipment of heavy industries to produce light industrial products. For an extreme example, it is very difficult to use the machinery and equipment of nuclear weapons to produce refrigerators.

- Second, price liberalization did not necessarily lead to market competition. The initial capital outlay of large industries is usually enormous, so even in an open market the high barriers to entry would prevent full competition, producing a monopoly. Some enterprises would use their monopolistic position to raise prices, increasing the costs for all related enterprises. As a result, the economic links between the upstream and downstream enterprises would be interrupted and production would shrink.
- Third, the policy burden and soft budget constraint will inevitably lead to macroeconomic instability.

That is why the three policy recommendations of shock therapy are logically inconsistent when the enterprises are non-viable. The implicit assumption of shock therapy is that enterprises are viable in an open and competitive market. But enterprises in Eastern Europe and the former Soviet Union were not viable, and they had substantial policy burdens. After privatization the new private owners did not help the state bear the policy burden – on the contrary, they asked for more protection and subsidies.

For social stability, national security, and the modernization drive, the state could not afford large-scale bankruptcy of the advanced and capital-intensive enterprises, so it had to protect and subsidize those already privatized enterprises. The subsidy was likely to be even higher. And after privatization the state's tax revenue declined, resulting in budget deficits. So, the government had to issue more currency to make up for the budget deficits, producing hyperinflation.

A famous saying about shock therapy is: "You don't try to cross a chasm in two jumps." But if the chasm is too deep and too wide, to jump is tantamount to suicide.

By contrast, the gradual reform in China produced economic growth and thus made the chasm narrower and shallower. In the dual-track system the market prices were higher than the planned prices, which were constantly adjusted according to the market prices, so the gap between the two was getting smaller, and the proportion of market allocation was increasing. So when the chasm got narrow and shallow enough, it could be crossed (more safely) in just one jump.[12]

References

Barro, Robert J. 1998. *Determinants of Economic Growth: A Cross Country Empirical Study*. Cambridge, MA: MIT Press.

Berle, Adolf A., and Gardiner C. Means. 1932. *The Modern Corporation and Private Property*. New York: Harcourt, Brace & World.

Blanchard, Olivier, Rudiger Dornbusch, Paul Krugman, Richard Layard, and Lawrence Summers. 1991. *Reform in Eastern Europe*. Cambridge, MA: MIT Press.

Brada, Josef C. 1996. "Privatization is Transition, Or is It?" *Journal of Economic Perspectives* 10(2): 67–86.

Detter, Dag. 2006. "Valuable Companies Create Valuable Jobs: The Swedish Reforms of State-Owned Enterprises – A Case Study in Corporate Governance." Working Paper, June (www.detterco.com/docs/77_en.pdf).

Easterly, William R. 2001. "The Lost Decades: Explaining Developing Countries' Stagnation in Spite of Policy Reform 1980–1998." *Journal of Economic Growth* 6(2) (June): 135–57.

Freeland, Chrystia. 2005. *Sale of the Century: The Inside Story of the Second Russian Revolution*. New York: Little, Brown.

Hart, Oliver D. 1983. "The Market Mechanism as an Incentive Scheme." *Bell Journal of Economics* 14(2): 366–82.

Lin, Justin Y. 2004. *Fa Zhan Zhan Lue Yu Jing Ji Fa Zhan* [Development Strategy and Economic Development]. Beijing: Peking University Press.

2009. *Economic Development and Transition: Thought, Strategy, and Viability*. Cambridge: Cambridge University Press.

Lin, Justin Y., and Guofu Tan. 1999. "Policy Burdens, Accountability, and the Soft Budget Constraint." *American Economic Review: Papers and Proceedings* 89(2) (May): 426–31.

Lin, Justin Y., Fang Cai, and Zhou Li. 1998. "Competition, Policy Burdens, and State-owned Enterprise Reform." *American Economic Review: Papers and Proceedings*, 88(2) (May): 422–27.

2001. *State-owned Enterprise Reform in China*. Hong Kong: Chinese University Press.

2003. *The China Miracle: Development Strategy and Economic Reform*, revised edn. Hong Kong: Chinese University Press.

Premfors, Rune. 1998. "Reshaping the Democratic State: Swedish Experiences in a Comparative Perspective." *Public Administration* **76**(1) (Spring): 141–59.

Sachs, Jeffrey D. 1992. "Privatization in Russia: Some Lessons from Eastern Europe." *American Economic Review* **82**(2): 43–48.

1993. *Poland's Jump to the Market Economy*. Cambridge, MA: MIT Press.

Sachs, Jeffrey D., and David Lipton. 1990. "Poland's Economic Reform." *Foreign Affairs* **69**(3): 47–66.

Smith, Adam. [1776] 1976. *An Inquiry into the Nature and Causes of the Wealth of Nations*. Chicago: University of Chicago Press.

State Service Commission. 1998. *New Zealand's State Sector Reform: A Decade of Change* (www.ssc.govt.nz/publications-and-resources/964/all-pages).

Notes

1. This chapter draws on Lin, Cai, and Li (1998, 2001).
2. Smith ([1776] 1976).
3. Berle and Means (1932).
4. Lin, Cai, and Li (1998, 2001).
5. Hart (1983).
6. Lin and Tan (1999).
7. Freeland (2005).
8. State Service Commission (1998).
9. Detter (2006); Premfors (1998).
10. Blanchard *et al.* (1991); Sachs (1992, 1993); Sachs and Lipton (1990).
11. Barro (1998); Brada (1996); Easterly (2001).
12. Lin (2009); Lin, Cai, and Li (2003).

TEN

The financial reforms

The sustainability of a country's economic development hinges on its potential and capacity for continuous technological innovation. But technological innovation is not a free lunch, it needs capital.[1]

Developing economies have two ways to innovate. One is R&D, costly and risky, with a slim chance of success. The other is technological adoption, but the new technology is usually embodied in new machinery and equipment, which has to be purchased. So additional capital is needed. In short, both R&D and technological adoption need a lot of capital.

In the modern economy the financial sector is important for financing and for risk-sharing. If the financial sector is inefficient, technological innovation suffers, and the economy is bound to stagnate or even encounter crisis. That is why, without a modern financial sector, there will be no modern national economy.

In Chapter 9 I mentioned that the financial sector is fraught with problems, especially a high ratio of non-performing loans and the speculation and "bubbles" in the stock market. These problems can be alleviated when the innate problems of SOEs are addressed. But the financial sector still has an irrational structure. The ratio of direct financing to indirect financing is low. Direct financing refers to financing through the stock market and indirect financing refers to financing through banks and other financial intermediaries. And the ratio of large banks to small and medium banks in the indirect financing is high.

The status of the financial sector

The current financial structure is based mainly on the four major state-owned banks, a legacy of the planned economy but still the core of the financial system. Starting in 1978, to improve incentives, the government gradually relaxed its regulation of the economy – that is what the power-and-profit-sharing reform was about. As the state's control over resource allocation weakened, TVEs and other private enterprises began to thrive, and non-governmental sectors controlled more and more surplus. Meanwhile, the reform of the SOEs was deepening, and their autonomy increasing. Their need for financial services became obvious. So the state restored the four major commercial banks, which were not functioning during the Cultural Revolution, and abandoned the original capital allocation system. As a result, enterprises got financing from bank loans instead of government appropriations.

In the early 1990s the stock market was introduced, and the regulation of foreign exchange was gradually relaxed, so the renminbi depreciated. But because the SOEs are not completely market-based, liberalizing the financial market would have greatly increased their capital costs, something policy-burdened SOEs could not afford. To protect them, the state could not allow the financial sector to be completely market-based, instead requiring it to serve some policy functions. That is why 80 percent of bank loans have gone to the SOEs, making it difficult for private enterprises to acquire financing. Other financing channels, such as the stock market, are also out of the private sector's reach. True, the private sector is a big part of China's rapid economic growth since the reform and opening, but its continuing development has been crippled due to the lack of a normal financing channel, with the official system either too costly or too inaccessible.

The state also gradually restored or created financial institutions like insurance, trust, securities, and others, but they have far less capital than the four major state-owned banks. And like the stock market and the trust and investment companies, they face problems. With the reform of the SOEs yet to be finished, they still have to bear the policy burden so that the state can continue to take care of them. Starting in 1983 the state stopped fiscal appropriations for SOEs, so the SOEs began to rely on the financial market for subsidies. To conclude, all the bizarre phenomena in the financial market are related, directly or indirectly, to the absence of fair competition and a sound legal system, because the financial market still has to subsidize the SOEs for their policy burden.[2]

The characteristics of direct and indirect financing

It's hard to say which arrangement is better – direct financing (the stock market) or indirect financing (the banks). A capital holder can either invest capital in the stock market or deposit it in a bank. In the stock market, with its serious information asymmetries between the suppliers of capital and the businesses that require it, and because of difficulty in supervision, capital suppliers, especially small investors, have virtually no control over how their capital is used. So, their investments face high risks.

By contrast, indirect financing (bank deposits) presents few risks for investors (depositors), because the commercial banks are supervised by the central bank and the investors are protected by the reinsurance mechanism. In addition, the enterprises that apply for loans must undergo the banks' strict scrutiny. From loan application, to use and to repayment, every link is subject to rigorous supervision by the banks. In indirect financing the depositors can get a relatively stable return on deposits, usually less than that from direct financing. Because the banks have to take risks and are responsible for capital management, they are entitled to part of the return on loans. Experience from elsewhere suggests that in the long term, the returns in the stock market are, on average, 7 percentage points higher than those for a bank deposit.[3]

Direct investors have to face considerable investment risks: investment failures cost them not only the interest but also the principal. The stock market may bring high yields, accompanied by high risks, while the bank produces lower yields but the risk is also considerably lower. So, an investor's decision should be based on his or her attitude toward risk and investment purposes. To persuade capital suppliers to buy their stocks or bonds, the enterprises need to do a lot of work, hiring investment banks to prepare an initial public offering and engaging credible accounting firms to audit their financial reports regularly. And to compensate for risk, they have to pay a relatively high return to the investors. So the cost of direct financing is high. Indirect financing, by contrast, costs much less, because the capital suppliers are the banks (and their depositors), and the transaction cost is relatively low.

Those raising capital through direct financing can allocate the capital freely, as there is little or even no supervision from the suppliers. They can choose to pay – or not to pay – dividends to investors based on their profit. Even if they fail, they are not required to repay the investors, so the risk for them is very small. Enterprises borrowing from banks do not have that freedom. When a loan matures, if they cannot repay the principal and interest, they will be forced to liquidate.

In sum, for capital-raisers, direct financing (the stock market) presents low risk but the cost is higher, whereas indirect financing (banks) costs less but is accompanied by a higher risk (Table 10.1).

TABLE 10.1 *The risk, cost, and return of direct and indirect financing*

	Stock market		Bank	
For investors	High return	High risk	Low return	Low risk
For enterprises	High cost	Low risk	Low cost	High risk

It's hard to say which is better. Both have pros and cons, and these features alone cannot indicate what the best financial structure might be.[4]

The stage of development and its corresponding optimal financial structure

The basic functions of the financial system

To understand the optimal financial structure for each stage of development, we must understand the three basic functions of the financial system. The first is to raise capital. The surplus in the economy is scattered among individuals, and a good financial system can collect the surplus. The second is to allocate the capital raised to all sectors of the economy efficiently – to achieve the maximum productive efficiency. The third is to minimize risk. In the economic and financial systems, both capital-raisers and suppliers face various risks. A good financial system reduces the risks facing individuals, thus avoiding financial crisis.

Which of the three functions is most fundamental? The answer is capital allocation, which is also the most important criterion for measuring the efficiency of a financial system. If the allocative efficiency of the financial system is high, the efficiency of the production using the capital allocated will also be high. In addition, the resulting surplus will be abundant, and there will be more capital to be raised for the next period. Moreover, the return on capital and the willingness to save will also be higher. Therefore, the capital-raising capacity of a financial system depends on its efficiency in allocating capital.

If the financial sector can allocate the capital raised to the industrial sector that enjoys the highest rate of return and to the most capable entrepreneurs, the risks facing the financial system and the economic system at large will be greatly reduced – as long as moral hazard can be prevented. At different stages of development the most competitive industrial sectors and enterprises have different requirements for the size of capital and the nature of the risk.

A financial system has a variety of financial institutions, such as big banks, small banks, the stock market, and so on. The system must avoid entrepreneur-related risk by ensuring that the entrepreneurs are capable and do not take excessive risks or hide their profits. The entrepreneur problems are called moral hazard. From the demand side the system may face two other risks: technical risks associated with technological innovation and market risk. Even if a new technology is developed or introduced, there is no guarantee that it can be transformed into marketable products.

The capacity of different financial institutions to avoid these risks varies, as do the costs for different financial institutions to raise and allocate capital. The optimal financial structure for a certain development stage is one that matches the capital demands and risk of enterprises in the most productive sectors.

The factor endowment structure, optimal industrial structure, and optimal financial structure

An efficient financial system must be able to allocate limited financial resources to the most dynamic industrial sectors in the economy and to the most capable entrepreneurs in those sectors. What are the most dynamic industrial sectors in the economy? Who are the most capable entrepreneurs in those sectors? What are the characteristics of those industries and entrepreneurs? At different stages of economic development the characteristics of the most dynamic industrial sectors and the best-performing companies in those sectors are different.[5] So, the financial arrangements must evolve to match the changing characteristics of the industrial sectors and companies, to maximize the efficiency of capital allocation.

At China's current stage the factor endowment structure is distinguished by an abundant labor force and relatively scarce and expensive capital. So, for the moment, the most dynamic industrial sectors that enjoy a comparative advantage are labor-intensive industries – or the labor-intensive sectors in the capital-intensive industries. Compared with their counterparts in the developed countries, both the technologies and products of China's enterprises in the labor-intensive industries are quite mature.

The technologies adopted in the capital-intensive industries in developed countries are already the best in the world, so further technological upgrading and innovation has to rely on R&D. As a result, the enterprises face considerable technical risks. Even if the R&D part is successful, the products developed will not necessarily be accepted by the market.

For enterprises in developing countries it makes much more sense to import technologies from their counterparts in developed countries to avoid the technological and marketing risks, because the imported technologies and the products are proven, as argued in Chapter 5. In addition, enterprises in labor-intensive sectors demand less capital because the capital inputs are smaller. Meanwhile, most enterprises in these sectors are small and medium size. They require less capital, and their technological and marketing risks are also smaller.

The major risks for enterprises in the labor-intensive sectors in the developing countries are thus entrepreneur-related risks, specifically the capability and honesty of entrepreneurs.

Therefore, to improve the efficiency of China's financial system at its current stage of development, capital should be allocated to the labor-intensive industries that enjoy a comparative advantage, the small and medium enterprises (SMEs) whose capital demands are smaller, and the entrepreneurs who are talented and pose no moral hazard. But China's current financial system is based on big banks and the stock market, so how can it meet these criteria?

First, it is difficult for SMEs to get listed on the stock market. Today, the cost for an enterprise to be listed is about RMB 20 million ($3 million), including the cost of accounting and auditing, the vetting of applications, assessing of prices, getting approval from the listing qualifications panel, hiring an investment bank to issue stocks, and so on. Few SMEs can afford such high costs. And after being listed, the enterprise still has to engage a credible accounting firm to prepare its financial statements regularly, something even fewer SMEs can afford.

Second, it is also difficult for SMEs to get loans from the big banks, which are naturally inclined to serve large enterprises, because no matter how large the loan is, the information cost and other transaction costs are almost the same. So, the average lending cost is much lower for large loans than for small ones. And because labor-intensive SMEs are usually scattered across the nation, distant from big banks and other large financial institutions, the cost of obtaining their operating and credit information will be considerably higher. Moreover, large enterprises have considerable fixed assets to put up as collateral, while SMEs don't have many. That is why the four major banks are still reluctant to lend to SMEs despite the fact that the government has repeatedly asked them to do so, even asking them to set up SME loan divisions.

Third, even a second-board stock market (the Growth Enterprise Market) could not satisfy the capital needs of the labor-intensive SMEs. It had been suggested that a second board should be established to help finance the SMEs, because of their difficulty in obtaining loans from the four major banks. But the costs of being listed in a second-board market in Shenzhen would also be very high. And the risks for investors are higher than on the main board (the Shanghai Stock Exchange), so the cost of capital is higher.

The second-board market usually finances enterprises with cutting-edge technologies in developed countries. This type of enterprise faces enormous risks in the innovation of technologies and products, and very few succeed. The patents held by these enterprises are protected throughout the world, and once the products are accepted in the market, the return can be tens, even hundreds, of times the investment. For SMEs in China the technologies and products are quite mature, and most of the technologies are imported. If one enterprise succeeds, others will follow, and market competition will be intense. So the pioneers cannot get high monopoly profits. That is why the high-cost second-board market is not that promising as a source of finance for most SMEs in China.[6]

In general, the most appropriate financing channel for SMEs is through regional small and medium banks. They are incapable of handling large projects, so SMEs are natural clients. Scattered across the country, they have a good understanding of the credit and operation conditions of the local SMEs. Information costs are not that high, and they are in a better position to monitor the SMEs and their entrepreneurs.

Big banks also have regional branches, but the vetting and approval process is still cumbersome, many loan decisions need approval from headquarters, and the information of the local SMEs is difficult to present accurately in reports. Moreover, the managers of the regional branches are usually chosen by headquarters. If the manager is well informed and discerning, he may indeed deliver excellent performance in allocating loans to the right SMEs. But his excellence will land him with a higher position in the head office or a larger branch, so what he knows about the local SMEs will go with him. If a manager is incapable or unwilling to glean information about local SMEs, he will not have a clear picture of the local SMEs. So, the small and medium banks are in a better position than the big banks to avoid entrepreneur-related risks.

China still has many major projects that need finance from big banks, and some enterprises are large enough to get listed on the stock market, so the big banks and stock market provide a service in the current financial structure. But SMEs account for the largest proportion of businesses in the economy, so the optimal financial structure for China's current stage of development should center on small and medium banks, supplemented by big banks and the stock market.

The government's policy for the small and medium banks

Starting in 1979 the state stopped fiscal appropriations for SOEs and has gradually moved to financial markets to meet the financing needs of the large SOEs by developing big banks and the stock market. Both decision-makers and the public then believed that the institutions of developed countries were more advanced. Since their financial structure mainly comprised big banks and stock markets, it was assumed that China should follow their "advanced" examples. But what they failed to see is that the comparative advantage of the developed countries lay in the capital-intensive industries and cutting-edge technologies, determined by their factor endowment structure. The capital demands for the investments and operations of these businesses are huge, and the risks associated with the industry and technological innovation are also very high. But if the innovation is successful, the technology will enjoy patent protection and its products could conquer the world market, so the returns could be handsome.

For a long time the Chinese government did not support small and medium financial institutions, including small and medium banks. But with labor-intensive SMEs burgeoning throughout the country, their total demand for capital is huge. To facilitate local economic development, local governments are motivated to support the development of small and medium financial institutions and regional banks, including credit cooperatives and rural cooperative funds. Since the reform and opening started, the government's control over the small and medium financial institutions from time to time has swung from tight to loose. When control was loose, these institutions mushroomed with the support of the local governments.

In 1993 more than 5,000 urban credit cooperatives were set up, and a variety of cooperation funds also appeared in rural areas. The cooperation funds worked like banks: farmers deposited their money in the funds, and the funds granted loans to SMEs. But the banking industry requires sound supervision by the government to avoid moral hazard, non-performing loans, and other risks. Besides incentive incompatibility and information asymmetry, financial enterprises also have symmetry of accountability: one party of the financial transaction gives cash but in return gets a piece of paper promising debt service or dividends in the future. The banker might try to embezzle the funds, or even abscond with the money.

In addition, the depositors have no idea how the banks are going to manage the money (information asymmetry). The high risks associated with the stock market also originate from information asymmetry and responsibility imbalance. It is difficult for shareholders to monitor the operation of the enterprises and find out about the malpractices of the managers. Moreover, shareholders get nothing if the enterprise does not profit. Even worse, they can lose everything if the enterprise goes bankrupt, since the creditors will get repaid first. Therefore, without sound regulation and supervision from the government, the financial system will be fraught with problems, including fraud.

Because the government generally does not support the development of small and medium financial institutions, it showed little interest in supervising them, and even less in formulating related policies and regulations. So, when the government relaxed its control during the reform, a large number of small and medium financial institutions mushroomed across the country, causing much trouble. In 1993 the non-performing loan ratio of the 5,000+ urban credit cooperatives exceeded 50 percent, much higher than for the major banks. Seeing this, the government reacted by applying tighter controls. The 5,000+ cooperatives were reorganized, and their numbers fell to a little over 100. The rural cooperative funds were also facing bad debts and fraud. In response the government shut them all down.[7]

Principles for promoting small and medium banks

The small and medium banks should play the most important role in China's economic development.[8] But the government has to oversee them to overcome financial abuses from the three attributes of financial institutions: incentive incompatibilities, information asymmetry, and accountability asymmetry. If China is to replace the big banks with small and medium banks as the core of its financial structure, the government must change its attitude toward them and, more important, establish an appropriate regulatory system so that small and medium banks and financial institutions have a healthy climate in which to develop. At the third National Financial Work Conference in 2007, after years of discussion and exploration, the government finally put small and medium financial institutions high on its agenda.

A few points should be noted.[9]

First, the small and medium banks should "make up for lost time." Even today's developed countries, at an early stage of their development, had their financial structures revolve around small and medium banks. As they developed, the enterprises scaled up, and their demand for capital increased accordingly. And with constant technological advances, their need for independent R&D projects increased, and the capital demand for – and the risk associated with – each project grew. That is why large banks and a stock market that could handle large loans and reduce risks were born.

From this we can see that the change in financial structure is the result of economic development rather than the cause. The financial institutions scaled up because they had to meet the growing capital needs of the expanding enterprises. Before 1979 China did not have any formal financial institutions. Later, when financial institutions were restored, their purpose was primarily to finance large SOEs, so large banks and the securities market received a lot of support while the small and medium size ones were suppressed. At the current stage the most dynamic sector in the economy is the labor-intensive SMEs, which badly need to be financed from small and medium regional banks and financial institutions. That is why these regional institutions need to "make up for lost time," because due to the government's intervention, they missed their opportunity to develop in the early stage of the reform.

Second, the small- and medium-size regional banks, important as they may be, also suffer from the vulnerabilities of incentive incompatibilities, information asymmetry, and accountability asymmetry, vulnerabilities that can spawn more problems. Some bank managers might take advantage of information asymmetries, and some banks are set up for the sole purpose of running away with the deposits they took. Some other banks have been set up not for all businesses but for some particular businesses of the banker, in what is called "relation lending." If a bank is set up by a business for the purpose of exclusively supporting the development of that business, the risks will be huge. Such cases, though not always malicious, can also fleece depositors.

Bankers might also act like compulsive gamblers. A capable banker can attract as much in deposits as possible and allocate the capital raised to the most efficient sectors and enterprises. But even if the banker is well intentioned, the bank is not necessarily successful. Several bad loans may make a bank insolvent. It stands to reason that an insolvent bank should be closed and liquidated, and the depositors refunded what's left of their capital. But in the hope of avoiding bankruptcy the bank may choose to offer a higher interest rate to attract more deposits. With the cost of capital higher, the bank has to lend to projects that aim for higher returns, with higher risks. If these loans are not repaid, the bank has to offer even higher interest rates to attract even more deposits, with even greater risks.

That vicious circle is driven by a compulsive gambling mind-set. Once the news is out, it can lead to a run on the bank and even trigger a financial crisis. So, although it is important to develop small- and medium-size banks, the watchdog should be alert to fleecing and compulsive gambling. And policy-makers should take full account of incentive incompatibilities, information asymmetry, and accountability asymmetry.

For policy design, the government should place some restrictions on bank entry. As long as there is an entry restriction, existing banks can enjoy monopoly profits, which may make the bankers more cautious about their operations to safeguard their edge and interests. The institutional arrangement for an appropriate amount of monopoly profit can thus induce banks to discipline themselves.[10] Another institutional arrangement is to set the bar high for entry – for example, in the requirements for equity capital. If part of each loan is funded by the bankers' own capital, they will be more cautious about their operation and reputation.

As important as small- and medium-size banks are, their development should never be rushed. Only qualified bankers can win the trust of depositors and grant loans to the most dynamic enterprises. So, rather than blindly pursue the quantity of small- and medium-size banks, the government should ensure that bank entry restrictions are appropriate and that persons employed in the industry are qualified.

Last, strict regulations should be introduced for deposit–loan ratios, asset–liability ratios, and so on. Only by stringent regulation and monitoring can compulsive gambling and dishonest behavior be avoided.

References

Ju, Jiandong, Justin Y. Lin, and Yong Wang. 2009. "Endowment Structures, Industrial Dynamics, and Economic Growth." Policy Research Working Paper No. 5055. Washington, DC: World Bank.

Levine, Ross. 2003. "Bank-Based or Market-Based Financial Systems: Which is Better?" *Journal of Financial Intermediation* 11: 398–428.

Lin, Justin Y. 1999. "What is the Direction of China's Financial Reform?" Peking University CCER Working Paper No. 20.

    2001. "Four Issues on China's Stock Market." *Jin Rong Xin Xi Can Kao* [Financial Information Reference] 4.

    2002. "How to Develop Small and Medium-sized Banks." Peking University *CCER Newsletter* 48.

Lin, Justin Y., and Zhou Li. 2003. "China's SOE and Financial Reforms." Peking University CCER Working Paper, October.

Lin, Justin Y., Xifang Sun, and Ye Jiang. 2009. "Toward a Theory of Optimal Financial Structure." *Policy Research Working Paper* No. 5038. Washington, DC: World Bank.

Stiglitz, Joseph E. 1985. "Credit Markets and the Control of Capital." *Journal of Money, Credit and Banking* 17: 133–52.

Notes

1. This chapter draws on Lin, Sun, and Jiang (2009).
2. Lin and Li (2003).
3. Lin, Sun, and Jiang (2009).
4. Levine (2003).
5. Ju, Lin, and Wang (2009).
6. Of course, China also has some high-tech enterprises that need to be financed on the second-board market, but the number is too small to create a complete market. Even in developed countries only NASDAQ in the United States is successful. Second-board markets in Japan and Europe are not in good shape, because the number of relevant enterprises in those areas is not big enough. The few Chinese enterprises that enjoy homegrown intellectual property rights can choose to get listed on NASDAQ, as the internet company, Sina, and on-line game company, Shanda Interactive Entertainment, did – both achieving remarkable success.
7. Lin, Sun, and Jian (2009).
8. Lin (1999).
9. Lin (2001, 2002).
10. Stiglitz (1985).

ELEVEN

Deflationary expansion and building a new socialist countryside

China experienced deflation, an economic phenomenon distinguished by constant falling prices because of excessive supply, from 1998 to 2002 (Figure 11.1). Deflation is generally accompanied by zero or negative growth, but in China it was accompanied by average annual growth of 7.8 percent, then the fastest in the world (Figure 11.2). Such growth is supposed to be accompanied by higher energy consumption, because industrial production, transportation, and other aspects of economic activities consume energy. But in China it was declining from 1997 to 1999 (Figure 11.3). In many other countries energy consumption is positively correlated with economic growth.

Is China's growth real?

Around 2000 a number of foreign scholars doubted the truth of China's economic growth.[1] According to their research, 2–3 percent growth would have been extremely remarkable, and China's official statistics, they implied, were simply too good to be true.

Were they correct about China's statistics? To answer requires first understanding the causes of deflation. Is it true, as many

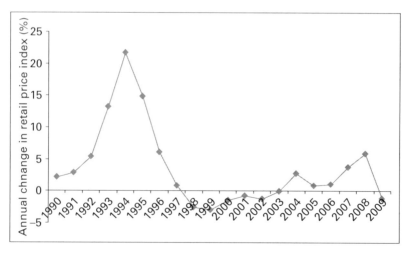

Figure 11.1 Deflation from 1998 to 2002
Source: National Bureau of Statistics of China.

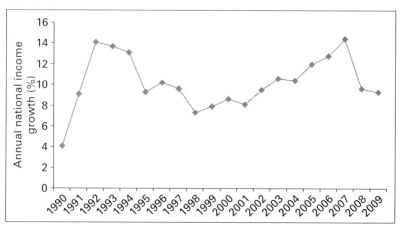

Figure 11.2 But growth continued at 7.8% a year
Source: National Bureau of Statistics of China.

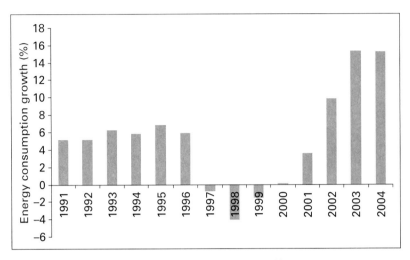

Figure 11.3 Yet energy consumption fell in 1997–99
Source: National Bureau of Statistics of China (2005).

foreign scholars believe, that deflation is inevitably accompanied by economic stagnation? No.

The cause and mechanism of deflation

Deflation has two possible causes: one is a sudden drop in demand, the other a sudden increase in supply. According to foreign experiences, deflation is generally caused by a sudden drop in demand, primarily related to economic bubbles. Residents of developed economies put a small portion of their wealth in banks, and instead buy stocks or invest in real estate. When the stock market or real estate market has a big bubble, people generally feel rich, producing a wealth effect and increasing spending, as observed before the financial crisis in 2008.[2]

In most economies domestic production is usually to meet domestic demand. For example, in the United States exports account for about 10–12% of GDP, and Japan's foreign trade accounts for 16–17% of its GDP (imports for 8% and exports for 9%).[3] So, for both countries more than 80% of domestic production is to meet

TABLE 11.1 *Average annual growth rate of fixed asset investment*

	%
1981–85	19.5
1986–90	16.5
1991–95	36.9
1996–2000	11.2
2001–05	20.2

Source: National Bureau of Statistics of China.

domestic demand. When demand increases suddenly, investment increases accordingly, and so does the production capacity. But when a bubble bursts, many people's wealth suddenly disappears. The negative wealth effect leads to a slump in spending. So, the production capacity that expanded to meet demand during the boom years becomes an excess capacity, and investment declines as well. The simultaneous reduction of consumption and investment leads to lower demand, declining prices, and an overall weak national economy – hence zero or negative growth.[4]

By contrast, in China, starting in 1998 when deflation began, there was neither a bursting property bubble nor a bursting stock market bubble. Under such circumstances deflation can be caused only by a sudden increase in supply. After the reform and opening China's investment growth was quite fast, especially from 1991 to 1995, when the average annual growth of fixed asset investment jumped from 16.5 percent to 36.9 percent (Table 11.1). Continued overheated investment led to an overall expansion of productive capacity at a pace far faster than the growth in consumption. That is why in the mid-1990s when China finally overcame shortages, it was immediately caught with excessive production capacity and deflation.

Although the phenomenon of deflation is the same for China as for other countries – that is, continuing price declines – the cause and mechanism are completely different. To understand why

China's economy could sustain rapid growth despite deflation, first analyze China's basic conditions.

China's deflation and rapid growth

Investment growth in the five years before the 1998 deflation started with Deng Xiaoping's Southern Tour in 1992.[5] On that tour he stated that "Poverty is not socialism, and development is the last word," and development must be driven by investment. In the following five years domestic and foreign companies, inspired by Deng's speech, rapidly increased their investment in the country. Before 1992 the proportion of foreign investment in China's fixed production assets never exceeded 5 percent, but after 1992 the figure rose to 12 percent, and even to more than 20 percent in some years.[6] Within a few years the economy underwent great structural changes as it transformed from a shortage economy into a surplus economy.

Because deflation in China was caused by excessive supply, not a collapse in demand, there was no wealth effect, and consumption was barely affected. The average annual growth of consumption was around 7 percent, just as before deflation. Private investment did fall due to overproduction, but overall it maintained annual growth of 11.2 percent in 1996–2000 and 20.2 percent in 2001–05.[7] Such rates were possible because China was still in the early stage of industrialization. There was plenty of room for technological and industrial upgrading, and the government adopted an expansionary fiscal policy, investing heavily in the construction of public infra-structure. So, given the annual growth of consumption and invest-ment in China, it is not surprising that it maintained annual growth of 7–8 percent during the deflation period. Once the deflationary period was over by 2003, China's growth rate jumped to more than 10 percent. China's economic growth was real, not illusory.

Nor can other countries' experience explain the decline in energy consumption for three consecutive years after 1997. Before the early 1990s China was a shortage economy, with demand across the nation far exceeding supply. That is why the town and village enterprises (TVEs) – despite backward technology, high energy consumption, and poor product quality – still developed at a fast pace. After 1998 supply began to exceed demand, and the overcapacity became obvious. Due to fierce competition, enterprises churning out shoddy goods were the first to be eliminated by the market, and later many enterprises using backward technology with high energy consumption were shut down as well. 1998 and 1999 witnessed the bankruptcy of many TVEs and massive debt in the rural areas. The failed enterprises were replaced by new ones with better technology, lower energy consumption, and higher quality products. As a result total energy consumption declined despite rapid economic growth. But with output continuously increasing, energy consumption eventually increased, and starting in 2000 it returned to normal growth.

The consequences of deflation

Although deflation in China did not lead to stagnation, it produced many adverse consequences. Overcapacity meant a general decline in prices, and shrinking profits or expanding losses for enterprises as suppliers. Meanwhile, inventories increased, and operations across the nation were seriously under capacity, so less labor was needed, and unemployment became an issue. In addition, many loss-making businesses were not paying back their loans.

A government has two means to address deflation: monetary policy and fiscal policy. Monetary policy influences the market interest rate by changing the supply of money. For example, in a time of deflation the government can increase the money supply to lower the interest rate. This will stimulate investment, because a lower interest rate means a lower cost for investment. But it will also reduce savings, because the price of future consumption increases. Normally, lower interest rates stimulate demand, but during deflation such monetary policy is ineffective. Even if the interest rate were zero, the principal would still have to be repaid. When overcapacity is obvious, there is little enthusiasm to invest. Because the economy is operating below capacity, the income of workers cannot be guaranteed. As a result, even if higher consumption can be encouraged, as it generally is when the interest rate is low, the capacity to consume declines considerably as a result of shrinking purchasing power. So, in the case of deflation a lower interest rate can neither stimulate investment nor increase consumption, so monetary policy is basically ineffective.

Fiscal policy has a more direct effect than monetary policy. Unlike monetary policy, which influences investment and consumer behavior by adjusting interest rates, expansionary fiscal policy encourages consumption through direct government-led investment and construction or through transfer payments to increase people's income.

The Japanese government, in response to the deflation starting in 1991, issued a "Japan Revitalization Coupon" to people over 65 years old and elementary students in hopes of stimulating consumption. But because demand was stimulated by increasing the budget deficit, the national debt grew very fast. Before the 1991 deflation the accumulated deficit accounted for 60 percent of its GDP, a fairly low ratio for a developed Organisation for Economic Co-operation and Development (OECD) country, so Japan's fiscal status then was very sound. But ten years after implementing the expansionary fiscal policy, the accumulated fiscal deficit in Japan jumped to 140 percent of GDP and now 220 percent, the worst among OECD countries.

So, increasing the fiscal deficit is effective but not sustainable. It seems that both monetary and fiscal measures are essentially ineffective. That is why economists are basically helpless when it comes to tackling deflation, though they have many tricks to tackle inflation.

Take the United States in 1929 as another example. When the stock bubble in New York suddenly burst, wealth evaporated, and many became poor. Consumption plummeted, leading to over-capacity, continuously falling prices, and shrinking investment. Consumer confidence continued to decline, leading to a vicious circle of declining consumption and falling investment. Although Roosevelt's "New Deal" adopted an expansionary fiscal policy to build some infrastructure, scholars generally believe that the impact of New Deal on the economy was rather limited. What really helped the United States out of the deflation in 1941 were the massive budget deficits during World War II.

Overcapacity and its solution

In combating deflation various policies have proved ineffective. Most countries have no choice but to wait for some companies to go bankrupt so that production capacity declines naturally. But they also want production to increase to absorb excessive capacity. They are thus helpless.

A closer look at the concept of excess capacity reveals that it is by its nature equivalent to a stock.

Assume that there are one hundred machines. When the supply is excessive, fifty machines may suffice for production; the remaining fifty machines become idle and turn into "a stock of unused production capacity." The best way to solve the problem is to find "a stock of unsatisfied demand" equal to the stock of unused capacity. Demand may come from investment or consumption. "Unsatisfied demand" is the demand that cannot be realized due to the imbalance between demand and supply or to the constraint of government policies, even though the agent has both the desire and ability to pay for the demand. In a market economy such demand does not exist, because if people want to buy something and can afford it, their demand will generally be satisfied. But in China, as a transition economy, a big portion of its demand could not be satisfied due to institutional, policy, or structural constraints.

There were mainly four types of unsatisfied demand in China: two related to consumption and two to investment. If all the constraints were removed, the long-term unsatisfied demand would be released like water in a reservoir when the floodgate is opened. All the stock of unused capacity will be consumed in no time.

The first unsatisfied demand was for foreign direct investment (FDI). Over two decades of sustained and rapid growth, China developed a huge market, which is very attractive to foreign enterprises, but the Chinese government imposed a lot of restrictions on the entry of foreign capital. Before China's accession to the World Trade Organization, FDI was channeled mainly to export-oriented production, with China serving as a processing and manufacturing base. Products were sold in overseas markets and not allowed to enter the domestic market. As a result, many otherwise attractive foreign investments were discouraged by policy constraints. But after its accession China scrapped all the policy restrictions and started to grant national treatment to foreign enterprises, allowing them to sell in China's market. As a result, the inflow of foreign capital began to surge, and China has since become the largest or second largest recipient of FDI in the world, a telling example of releasing unsatisfied demand.

The second unsatisfied demand was for investment by the private sector. Private businesses did not emerge in China until the start of the reform and opening, and after two decades of rapid growth many of them have since become sizable. Due to the planned-economy mentality, however, some parts of the national economy were out of bounds. After China acceded to the World Trade Organization, it granted the national treatment not only to foreign companies but also to domestic private companies.

The third unsatisfied demand was for urban consumption. Since the reform and opening, the consumption demand and capacity of urban families has been growing continuously. At the beginning of the 1980s the "three major items" for urban families in China were a watch, a sewing machine, and a bicycle, which cost around RMB 100. To buy the three items, a family not only had to save RMB 100 but also needed some special coupons. By the end of the 1980s the "three major items" changed to a fridge, a washing machine, and a TV set, which cost around RMB 5,000, again requiring family savings. By the beginning of the 1990s the "three major items" became an air conditioner, a stereo set, and a cell phone, which cost around RMB 10,000.

By the end of the 1990s the list of "major items" changed again to cars and apartments, which cost around RMB 250,000 (about $30,000) and RMB 500,000 (about $60,000), respectively. Such high-priced consumer goods are usually bought in installments even in countries like the United States, because consumers would be too old to enjoy such goods if they could buy them only when they had saved enough money.

Consumer loans are usually granted on the basis of the borrower's future income. As long as one has a job, and one's future income is big enough to pay off the principal and interest, one can get a mortgage or a loan from a bank to buy apartments or cars. In the three decades after the reform and opening, the cities are now home to a large number of white-collar workers perfectly capable of affording mortgages. But most bank credit served enterprises, especially state-owned enterprises. As a result, due to policy constraints, white-collar workers could not get loans for consumption before 2000. The solution was to develop consumer loan services.

The fourth unsatisfied demand was also the most important – for consumption in rural areas, with nearly three-fifths of the population. The first three stock demands were basically satisfied in 2002 when China joined the World Trade Organization and when consumer loans were liberalized. But consumption in rural areas still lagged far behind that in cities.

Take home appliances. In 2002 cities had 120 color TV sets for every 100 households, but for rural areas only 60 (Table 11.2). For refrigerators the figures were 82 for urban households and 15 for rural households (18 percent of the urban). For washing machines they were 93 for urban households and 32 for rural households (34 percent of the urban). So the urban market for home appliances was already saturated, yet the rural market still had much room for expansion.[8]

TABLE 11.2 *Penetration rates for home appliances in China's urban and rural areas*

	1991 Urban households	1998 Urban households	1998 Rural households	2002 Urban households	2002 Rural households
Color TV (%)	68.4	105.4	32.6	120.0	60.0
Refrigerator (%)	48.7	76.1	9.3	81.9	14.8
Washing machine (%)	48.7	90.6	22.8	92.9	31.8
Per capita net income (RMB)	2,025	5,425	2,162	7,702	2,475

Source: National Bureau of Statistics of China.

Some argued that the low consumption in rural areas was mainly due to farmers' meager income. In 2002 the per capita income of urban dwellers was RMB 7,702 while that of farmers was RMB 2,475 (32 percent of the urban). But income is not the main reason for the low consumption in rural areas. The rural per capita net income in 2002 (2,475) was 22 percent higher than the urban level in 1991 (2,025). But in 1991 every 100 households in cities had 68 color TV sets, while in 2002 the figure for rural households was only 89 percent of the urban in 1991, when every 100 households in cities had 49 refrigerators. In 2002 the figure for rural households was only 30 percent of the urban in 1991. Similarly, in 1991 every 100 households in cities had 81 washing machines, while in 2002 the figure for rural households was only 39 percent of the urban in 1991.[9]

Prices make the comparisons even more stark. A 25-inch color TV with a remote control cost almost RMB 6,000 in 1991, but only about RMB 1,200 (a fifth of the earlier price) in 2002. The 2002 prices for refrigerators and washing machines were half those in 1991.[10] Yet rural consumption in 2002 was far below urban consumption in 1991. So, income is not the only constraint on rural consumption. There must be other restrictive factors.

Many rural areas had no TV signals in the early 2000s. To watch TV programs, a satellite TV receiver had to be installed, but it cost about RMB 4,000–5,000. So, although farmers could afford the TV sets, they could not afford the receivers. Farmers joked that all the TV sets in the rural areas were the "snowflake" brand, because they showed nothing but white dots on the screen due to weak signals. TVs also need power, but many areas in rural China had no electricity back then, or if they did, the voltage was not stable enough for home appliances. Due to power shortages, outages were frequent, especially at peak hours during the evening when many people were watching TV. Naturally, farmers were turned off by power shortages and poor signals.

The stories for other home appliances are similar. Running water is necessary for washing machines, but few rural households had it. Refrigerators consume one kilowatt a day on average, which costs half a renminbi in cities, but one to two in rural areas. So if a refrigerator costs two renminbi for power per day, that would be RMB 60 a month and RMB 720 a year. Compare that with the annual income of a farmer of RMB 2253 in 2000.[11] So, although the farmers could afford the horse, they could not afford the saddle.

To boost rural consumption, the infrastructure and supporting facilities had to be improved. That is why, in 1999 I called for a "new village movement" to improve rural infrastructure. The state put the building of a new socialist countryside high on its agenda in 2005, with detailed planning and guidance to rural development.

Building a new socialist countryside

The construction of a new socialist countryside was officially put forward as a national policy in the "Proposal for the Eleventh Five-Year Plan," passed at the Fifth Plenary Session of the 16th Central Committee of the Communist Party of China in October 2005. According to the proposal the main contents of a new socialist countryside are summarized as "advanced production, improved livelihood, a civilized social atmosphere, clean and tidy villages, and democratic administration."

At the end of 2005 the Central Rural Work Conference released the no. 1 document of 2006, "Opinions on the construction of a new socialist countryside," explicitly stating that rural development is the most important task in the eleventh Five-Year Plan. During the People's Congress and Chinese People's Political Consultation Conference in March 2006 the revised Plan and the "Government Work Report" both reiterated it as the priority. The campaign to build a new socialist countryside is of great significance to solve the "Three Rural Issues," discussed in Chapter 8, and to absorb the current and future excess capacity in the cities.

Deflation and the "Three Rural Issues"

In Chapter 8 on rural reform I mentioned that the migration of rural workers to cities is an ideal solution to increase farmers' income in the long run and in a sustainable manner, because it can overcome the restrictive factors of low income elasticity of demand and low price elasticity of demand. Unfortunately the deflation in the late 1990s hugely affected the manufacturing sector. Cities could not absorb more rural labor, and workers were trapped in the countryside. In addition, due to the underuse of capacity in enterprises, many workers lost their jobs, with the rural migrant workers suffering the brunt. What's more, in the last round of investment rush before the deflation a large number of private and foreign-funded enterprises emerged, which boasted more advanced technology and higher quality products, crowding out the TVEs.

The intensified competition forced many TVEs, which had absorbed a massive non-agricultural labor force in the rural areas, into bankruptcy. And with a growing rural labor force, farmers' income was actually falling (see Figures 11.4 and 11.5). There were two factors behind the shrinking income: the rural labor force could

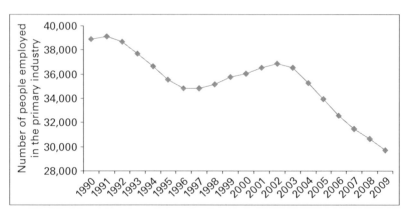

Figure 11.4 More employed in primary industry in the later 1990s
Note: Primary industry includes farming, forestry, animal
husbandry, and fishing.
Source: National Bureau of Statistics of China.

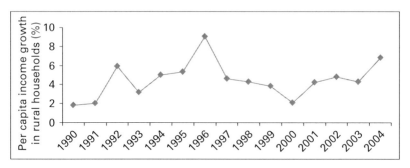

Figure 11.5 Slower growth of per capita incomes in rural households
Source: National Bureau of Statistics of China.

not migrate to cities, and the migrant workers originally in cities
had to return to their home villages. This explains the drop of
income growth in rural area to 2.9 percent only in 1995–2000 (see
Table 7.3) and why the "Three Rural Issues" were particularly acute
in the late 1990s.

Judging from the overall price level, deflation seemed to have
ended in China in 2003. But the overall price rise was brought
about by a new round of investment, which quickly boosted prices

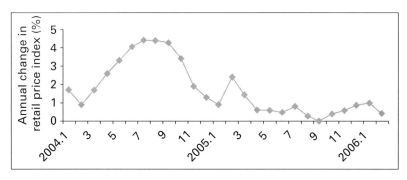

Figure 11.6 Prices generally falling in 2004–05
Source: National Bureau of Statistics of China.

for energy and building materials. The prices for other products were generally falling (Figure 11.6). As the overheated investment between 2003 and 2005 led to excess capacity in building materials, once the investment rush ended, prices fell, inventories increased, and so deflationary pressures re-emerged.

To avoid deflation and keep the "Three Rural Issues" in check, the unsatisfied demand has to be met to consume the excess capacity. With the largest stock of unsatisfied demand in rural areas, improving rural infrastructure is essential not only for improving the living and production environment and bridging the urban–rural gap, but also for stimulating rural demand, consuming excess capacity, facilitating rural labor mobility, and ultimately increasing farm incomes.

Building a new socialist countryside and meeting unsatisfied demand

According to one of my studies and based on the 1999 data, if the power price is cut by 10 fen (1 renminbi = 100 fen), its stimulative effect on the demand for a color TV is equivalent to a boost to farmers' income of RMB 370; the effect on the demand for a refrigerator and washing machine is equivalent to RMB 607 and 909, respectively.[12] In short, a cut in power prices can effectively stimulate rural demand for home appliances. Therefore, the key to activate the massive unsatisfied rural demand is to significantly improve the consumption-related infrastructure.

After I proposed the "new village movement" in 1999, a reporter from *Hunan Daily*, seconded to a village in Hunan province, tried out those ideas. The result was marvelous. When he first arrived, there were no TVs in the village, so the reporter mobilized all the local villagers to chip in to buy a satellite receiver (he also donated a certain sum). The price of a receiver was RMB 5,000, and with all the cables needed, the whole set cost nearly RMB 10,000. A single household certainly could not afford it, but if 200 households chipped in, it would cost only on average RMB 50 per household. This approach quickly increased the TV ownership rate from zero to 100 percent.

We usually assume that farmers are poor, but we also find that they always try to keep up with the Joneses. For example, since 1978 many houses in rural areas have been regularly renovated and rebuilt. At first everyone lived in thatched cottages, but when one family built a brick house, others would quickly follow suit for fear of being looked down on. Then when someone built a two-story home, other families would start to demolish their old brick houses and build two stories too. When the two-story home became the norm, the richer families decided to distinguish themselves by three stories. Renovation of this kind usually cost tens of thousands of renminbi. So, farmers were not really poor; they just did not spend their money in the right place.

In sum, improving consumption-related infrastructure can unlock rural potential and consume the excess capacity of the cities. As a result, the fortunate enterprises in cities improve, and they can once again absorb rural migrant workers, improving farmers' incomes. In fact, stimulating rural consumption is just a byproduct of the investment in rural infrastructure because the investment can also generate demand. The raw materials used for infrastructure construction are usually locally produced, and so can stimulate growth for the local TVEs. Workers employed are also mostly local, creating more jobs and increasing incomes for local farmers. This is a virtuous circle. That is why at the press conference at the conclusion of the People's Congress and People's Political Consultation Conference in March 2006, Premier Wen Jiabao described the construction of a new socialist countryside as a key link to put economic development on an even more solid footing – if successful, it can boost both domestic demand and consumption.

Some issues in building a new socialist countryside

The timetable

Building a new socialist countryside is an integral part of China's modernization drive.[13] Every development stage poses a new objective for the next stage, so building a new socialist countryside is a long-term task. As mentioned, the major objectives of building a new socialist countryside are advanced production, improved livelihood, a civilized social atmosphere, clean and tidy villages, and democratic administration – all definitely long-term goals.

For the shorter term targets, such as the improvement in rural infrastructure I called for in 1999, it would be best if they can be met by 2020. The 16th Party Congress established the goal of building a moderately well-off society in an "all-around" manner; but if the development and living standards in rural areas are perpetually lagging behind those in the cities, China will fall short of the all-around standard. With a large part of China's population staying in the rural areas, and without the modernization of the countryside, modernization of the whole nation is impossible. And unless farmers are getting richer, China will never fulfill its goal of building a moderately well-off society in an all-around manner.

The construction of a new socialist countryside is also an essential part of a harmonious society. The current urban and rural income ratio is 3.3:1 (see Table 7.3). Based on the average growth after 1998

(4.5 percent for rural and 8–9 percent for urban), the disparity would grow to 4.9:1 by 2020, with the income of urban dwellers almost five times that of their rural fellows.[14] The current 3.3:1 ratio is already among the highest in the world, so a five-to-one gap is unimaginable. Social tensions will be so acute that a harmonious society will be out of the question. So improving the rural infrastructure nationwide by 2020 is not just what the government should do for its people – it is what it has to do.

Where to implement the drive?

Economies of scale apply to infrastructure construction, so the cost will be much higher in the rural areas where residents are much more scattered than in urban areas. To overcome this, some people propose that new towns be built on the fringe of cities to accommodate all the nearby farmers and save on the cost of infrastructure construction. But since the infrastructure is built for the farmers, their convenience should be duly considered.

Because farmers have to start their work in the early hours and work until the sun sets, they always live on the farms or nearby. An unnecessary commute to work would make their work even tougher. So, except for the non-agricultural development areas near the city suburbs and the areas suitable neither for human habitat nor for development, the new socialist countryside drive should be based on the existing natural villages. In fact, as a result of a series of collectivization movements, rural households have already become quite concentrated, except for some remote mountainous or river areas. In short, farmers should stay in their villages.

Another caveat is that unlike infrastructure, a public good, farmers' houses are private property. Asking farmers to live in a concentrated manner means demolishing their old houses, tantamount to encroaching on their private goods. Such a practice should never be allowed. Especially when land prices are surging, some people are tempted to destroy villages to seize the land under the pretext of building a new socialist countryside. Such practices must be prevented by all means.

How to fund the drive?

The total budget for rural infrastructure investment is estimated at around RMB 4 trillion, which means an average annual budget of about RMB 270 billion from 2006 to 2020.[15] Because infrastructure is a public good, this astronomical budget should be mainly funded by the government. In reality, however, the government's budget for this purpose was only RMB 44.1 billion in 2005. In 2006 the Government Work Report committed to an increase of RMB 27.3 billion, for a total of RMB 71.4 billion. But that package still had to cover healthcare, education, and other soft infrastructure. So, the drive is underfunded. To fill the gap, all social sectors must be mobilized.

First, government finance can be further tapped. Previous investment focused on cities, but as urban development has gradually taken shape, the focus should shift to rural areas. The 2006 Government Work Report also indicates the change: "In order to build a new socialist countryside, we must accelerate development of rural infrastructure. We need to resolutely work to reorient investment by shifting the government's priority in infrastructure investment to the countryside."

Second, the government can lead in mobilizing all social forces. Different locales have different demands for infrastructure. If the central government had to fund all the projects, local governments would tend to ask for more subsidies than they actually need, increasing the financial burden on the central government. A basic principle of economics is, "He who benefits, pays." So, after some massive infrastructure has been accomplished, the government can charge the beneficiaries – toll-houses along highways are an example. Rural infrastructure can learn from this example: the projects that can generate returns can be funded by the private sector or by bank loans. In addition, the government can also encourage better-off farmers to give something back to their home villages – helping to build schools, roads, and so on.

Third, projects that fit into the category of private goods should be funded and staffed mainly by farmers themselves, subsidized appropriately by the government. For example, the biogas digester is a private good. Whether it is large, built by the government, and used by the whole village, or smaller, built by each household, and used separately, the villagers are the ultimate beneficiaries. One problem: without the biogas digester, villagers would not have sufficient fuel, and so would probably fell trees on mountains. In this sense the biogas digester is not a totally private good. Therefore, the government should subsidize a small part of the project, while villagers fund the major part. Projects involving satellite TV receivers and toilets are similar, to be dealt with through a similar approach.

If these three funding sources can be used to the full, the RMB 270 billion package is no problem. Private funding is also good for monitoring the construction and quality of the rural projects, usually small and scattered. It can facilitate "democratic management," as villagers become the stakeholders through their inputs of capital and labor.

Matters meriting attention

Building a new socialist countryside and urbanization
The major approach to solving the rural issues, including increasing farmers' income, is urbanization – transferring rural labor to light manufacturing and services in cities. Rural development may seem to contradict the idea of urbanization, but it does not. Urbanization will be a rather long process for China. It is estimated that by 2020 at least 40 percent of the population (about 600 million people) will still live in the countryside. By 2030 when China's per capita income will be above the world's average, its rural population will

still account for at least 15 percent.[16] By then if the rural infrastructure has been considerably improved, and the urban–rural income gap has been significantly narrowed, living standards will not differ much between the cities and the rural areas. Some people may even prefer to live in the countryside. Also by 2050 big cities may already be saturated, so there could be more than 30 percent of the population living in the rural areas, or about 400 million people. That is why urbanization and the construction of a new countryside are not mutually exclusive.

Solving rural issues and non-agricultural development

The precondition for transferring rural labor to non-agricultural industries is that more jobs are created in those industries; otherwise, it would transfer rural problems to cities, causing massive unemployment. In rural areas farmers can rely on natural resources to feed themselves, while in cities, if one cannot find a job, one may not be able to survive. To create more jobs in cities, China needs to promote labor-intensive SMEs, in line with China's comparative advantage. So far SMEs in China have been making good progress, but the lack of appropriate financial services is a major bottleneck. As mentioned in Chapter 10, an effective way to create more jobs is to promote the development of SMEs by facilitating the development of small- and medium-size local banks.

Modern agriculture is the material foundation for the new socialist countryside

As economic development and urbanization progress, the rural labor force will gradually shrink. To increase agricultural production, meet domestic demand, and improve farmers' incomes, the key is to constantly enhance productivity. The government should thus increase investment in agricultural infrastructure and modern agricultural-related science and technology and promote the dissemination of science and technology. It should also support leading enterprises, cooperative businesses, and a modern logistics system to expand the agricultural market. And it should support the development of specialized financial institutions to serve agriculture production, such as microfinance, rural banks, and agricultural insurance.

Farmers are the most critical factor in the success of a new socialist countryside

As the program of building a new socialist countryside proceeds, the focus will shift to soft infrastructure in rural areas, including medical services, health, and education. Soft infrastructure is a make-or-break factor for farmers. To fit in cities, rural migrant workers have to acquire certain knowledge and skills. Increasing employment opportunities is just one precondition to ensure a successful transfer of rural labor – the other is improving the education and vocational skills of these farmers. And because fewer farmers will stay in the countryside, to feed more people, they also need to be equipped with new technologies and to know how to use them. Moreover, with higher urban and rural incomes, people will demand agricultural products of higher quality and greater variety. So farmers who produce these products have to learn new technologies to meet the new needs. Basic and vocational education in rural areas thus have to be strengthened, an intellectual guarantee for boosting farmers' income.

Some remaining problems

Building the new socialist countryside, now on the right track, has produced remarkable results. But some problems have emerged in the process.

First, for optimal development the construction drive should upgrade the existing natural villages rather than destroy old villages for new ones. But the new countryside construction should not be carried out on environmentally fragile, banned development zones. Relocation is the solution for farmers in those zones.

244 • Deflationary expansion and building a new socialist countryside

Second, the new socialist countryside construction drive can be a sort of "affirmative action," because for a long time cities have been the focus of national construction. It's time to readjust the government's investment orientation and give more attention to rural construction. Farmers' interests should be protected throughout the process. It is a good idea to mobilize the private sector and farmers themselves to invest in and work for the drive. It is not a good idea to set up some obligatory targets regardless of the current stage of development, particularly if they put additional burdens on farmers.

Third, the government should not set a one-size-fits-all standard throughout the country, because different locales have different conditions. What the government should do is to make a long-term plan, ensuring that projects are adapted to local conditions and capacities. Most important, the urgent needs of farmers should be addressed first. Building a new socialist countryside should be a part of the village autonomy reform. Local farmers should take part in the discussion, decision-making, and supervision of the drive, not be passive recipients. This will reduce corruption and "tofu" projects (of terrible quality) and nurture a democratic atmosphere.

References

Gong, Gang, and Justin Y. Lin. 2008. "Deflationary Expansion: An Overshooting Perspective to the Recent Business Cycle in China." *China Economic Review* 19(1): 1–17.

Lin, Justin Y. 2004. *Fa Zhan Zhan Lue Yu Jing Ji Fa Zhan* [Development Strategy and Economic Development]. Beijing: Peking University Press.

2007. *Juedu Zhongguo Wenti Meiyou Xiancheng Moshi* [There is No Textbook Paradigm for Understanding the Chinese Economy]. Beijing: China's Social Sciences Literature Press.

2009. "Beyond Keynesianism: The Necessity of a Globally Coordinated Solution." *Harvard International Review* 31(2) (Summer): 14–17.

2010. "Shocks, Crises and Their Determinants." *Middle East Development Journal* 2(2) (December): 159–76.

National Bureau of Statistics of China. 2004. *China Statistical Yearbook*. Beijing: China Statistics Press.

2010. *China Compendium of Statistics 1949–2008*. Beijing: China Statistics Press.

2011. *China Statistical Yearbook*. Beijing: China Statistics Press.

Rawski, Thomas G. 2001. "What's Happening to China's GDP Statistics?" *China Economic Review* 12(1) (December): 298–302.

World Bank. "Data: Indicators." data.worldbank.org/indicator.

Notes

1. Rawski, representative of these scholars, wrote a paper questioning the truth of China's economic growth (2001). In addition, the *Quarterly Journal of Economics* 2(1) (October 2002) published five papers on China's GDP statistics (one by Rawski).
2. Lin (2010).
3. World Bank data.
4. This is exactly what has happened in the current global financial crisis (Lin 2009).
5. This section draws on Gong and Lin (2008).
6. National Bureau of Statistics of China (2010).
7. *Ibid.*
8. *Ibid.*
9. *Ibid.*
10. *Ibid.*
11. *Ibid.*
12. Lin (2004).
13. This section draws on Lin (2007).
14. *Ibid.*
15. *Ibid.*
16. *Ibid.Source:* Maddison (2006)

TWELVE

Improving the market system and promoting fairness and efficiency for harmonious development

Since 1978 China has maintained rapid economic growth for thirty-three consecutive years. The average annual GDP growth is 9.9% and the average annual growth of foreign trade 16.3%. Between 2003 and 2010 annual GDP growth exceeded 10%, and foreign trade 21.5%. Even during the current global crisis, the most serious since the Great Depression, China's growth rate reached 9.6% in 2008, 9.1% in 2009, and 10.1% in 2010.[1] But with the deepening reform and opening, various socioeconomic issues keep surfacing in the transition, and new tensions have emerged.

In the late 1980s and early 1990s the SOE reform was the topic of the day. Back then the SOEs were described as "one-third making apparent loss, one-third making hidden loss, and another third making profit." After the reform roughly along the lines discussed in Chapter 9, profitability is no longer an issue. Many small SOEs have been privatized, and many large ones make handsome profits, especially those in the monopoly sectors. The new focus for the SOE reform is improving their competitiveness. The fragile banking system witnessed by non-performing loans in the four major state-owned banks has also been improving substantially after recapitalization and listing in the stock exchanges in Hong Kong, China, and

Shanghai: the non-performing loan ratio has been reduced from 40% to less than 5%.

New problems replacing the old

But as old problems disappeared, new ones appeared, with minor ones escalating into major ones. The major problems in the macroeconomy since 2003 are the "three excessives." First is excessive investment and insufficient consumption. Second is excessive money supply and credit. Third is the excessive trade surplus. The root of these problems lies in excessive investment growth, which produces excessive production capacity. When the domestic market fails to digest the production capacity, the products are exported to foreign countries, thus leading to excessive trade surplus. The long-term trade surplus has earned astronomical foreign exchange, but to buy the foreign currency, the state has to issue more currency, leading to excessive money supply and credit and other related problems.[2]

Since 2003 the Chinese government has been using macro controls to cool the economy, but it has not worked. Why? For a simple reason: the government failed to take radical action to tackle the cause, the increasingly inequitable distribution of income in recent years. Personal income is used either for consumption or investment. The low-income group tends to spend more income on consumption than on investment, but they don't have much to consume. The high-income group spends a minor part of income on consumption, with the rest channeled into investment.

Pre-reform China was egalitarian. With the deepening reform and opening, some regions and some people got rich ahead of others, and the income gap between the urban and rural areas grew wider. Now the gap in China is the world's largest. Even in the cities the income gap had been widening, with the unemployed and retired left behind. China's Gini coefficient – a common measure of inequality where a value of 0 is complete equality and a value of 1 is complete inequality – has exceeded 0.42, higher than the internationally recognized warning line.[3] In addition, health and education services have become inaccessible and unaffordable for the vulnerable.

True, with rapid economic growth, living standards have improved considerably, and even in poor areas subsisting is no longer a problem. But due to these social problems, discontentment and grievances have begun to simmer in the community. Some people are even nostalgic about the "good old days." They believe that being poor was not so bad when others around them were just as poor. But now, even if they get richer than before, when others around them are so much richer, they appear even poorer.

In all, a fairer distribution of income bears not only on the health of China's macroeconomy but also on social harmony. So, it has become a common concern, with many calling for redistribution of income. For example, in 2005 and 2006 when income tax was discussed, it was suggested that the rich should pay a higher rate and that part of the revenue could be used as a transfer payment to subsidize the poor. But the income tax rate for the highest bracket is already 45 percent, one of the highest in the world.

I argued in a public speech that what needs to be addressed is the collection of taxes rather than the rate. This point of view caused a public outcry among the "netizens," who believed I was speaking for the rich. Even so, the outcry reflected a general sentiment in China that the rich were perceived as too rich. In fact, the pockets of Chinese rich are not as big as their overseas counterparts. It would be best if they can be motivated to create even more wealth. Although the income gap is a pressing issue, Robin Hood redistributions are not the answer.

Based on the different features of different stages of economic and social development, the Chinese Communist Party established an important principle: keep up with the times. In 2002 the 16th Party Congress adopted a scientific outlook on development. According to this outlook China will keep economic development as its top priority, adhering to the principle that development is the last word. What's more, China is aiming at a comprehensive development, which requires keeping five balances in five dimensions:

- Between urban and rural development.
- Between social and economic development.
- Between regional development.
- Between man and nature.
- Between domestic and international markets.

In 2007 the 17th Party Congress advocated building a harmonious society for better living standards for the people. And both the 2007 and 2008 reports on the Work of the Government rolled out many specific policies.

Comparative advantage and achieving unity between efficiency and equity in income

What is the best way to put the scientific concept of development in place and build a harmonious society? The general view in academic and policy circles in China is that the functional distribution of income (to capital, labor, and land) should focus on efficiency and that redistribution should focus on fairness.[4] Efficiency is defined by the technology level. The more capital-intensive or technology-intensive the industry is, the more efficient it is. According to this view the government should play an active role to make sure that redistribution (through tax policy, fiscal policy, and fiscal transfers) can correct inequality generated by functional distribution so as to achieve harmony and the betterment of society. While it is necessary to redress inequity, it would be much better if unity between efficiency and equality can be achieved from the start.

I am not opposed to redistribution. But implicit in this view is that equity can be sacrificed in the functional distribution and then use redistribution to redressing inequity. Sadly, the results in reality are neither efficient nor fair. It is better to achieve, from the very beginning, unity of efficiency and equity at the functional distribution and to use redistribution only as a supplementary means to address outstanding problems.

Is it a fantasy to achieve unity of efficiency and equity?

The objective of "unity of equity and efficiency in the functional distribution of income" should have at least two aspects. First, national income should be constantly improved through rapid economic growth. This is essential. After thirty-three years of sustained and rapid growth, China's per capita income in 2009 reached $3,744, but it is still very low, only about 43 percent of the world average and 8 percent of that in the United States.[5] So, efficiency and rapid growth will always remain priorities. Second, to achieve equity, the income growth of the poor must be faster than that of the rich. In sum, unity between efficiency and equity means constantly improving the income distribution in the context of rapid economic growth while taking into account the five dimensions of balance in the scientific development outlook. The key to achieving unity between efficiency and equity is to choose appropriate industries/products/technologies based on a CAF strategy at every stage of economic development.

Generally speaking, China's comparative advantage still lies in labor-intensive industries – manufacturing and service industries, and also the labor-intensive sections in some capital-intensive industries. These industries and sectors can create many job opportunities. As we all know, the major difference between the poor and the rich is that the rich mainly increase their income by making use of their capital, meaning they can hire others to make money, while the poor have nothing to rely on except their labor. If China adopts a CAF strategy, abundant jobs can be created for the poor, and they can thus share in the fruits of economic development. A CAF strategy can also help China boost its competitiveness and increase its share in the global market. That way, as argued in Chapter 5, China can maximize its profit and surplus, and its capital will accumulate quickly. In the meantime population growth is rather limited.

Against that backdrop, the factor endowment structure will constantly evolve from relatively abundant labor and scarce capital to scarce labor and abundant capital. That is exactly the process developed countries have gone through. When capital is more abundant and labor scarce, their relative prices change, too: salaries go north and the returns on capital go south. In other words the assets of the poor will appreciate while those of the rich will depreciate, and so the income distribution is adjusted and improved. Postwar Japan, South Korea, Singapore, and Taiwan, China, were together branded an East Asian Miracle, because the economies maintained fast yet sustained economic growth and improved income distribution simultaneously in the process.[6] The income distribution is also more equal in provinces that follow more closely the CAF strategy.[7]

A CAD strategy?

Several years ago I proposed a "trotting ahead" strategy for China, suggesting that industrial and technological upgrading did not require major changes, but the pace had to be quick enough so that within a generation or two, China would catch up with developed countries.[8] But most people were aware only of the industrial and technological gap between developed countries and developing countries and the obvious negative impact that the underdeveloped industries and technologies have on national strength and income. They thus wished to bridge the gap as soon as possible, so that China could catch up with the advanced economies without delay.

Actually, what they proposed was a CAD strategy, as Chapter 4 analyzed. Developing countries and developed countries have different endowment structures and thus different comparative advantages. If a backward country tries to adopt a CAD strategy by setting up some large-scale capital-intensive industries, not only will those industries have no comparative advantage at all, but the efficiency of resource allocation and economic development will also suffer. A CAD strategy will thus create more trouble. For instance, capital-intensive industries cannot create sufficient jobs, so many low-income laborers cannot find employment and thus cannot share in the fruits of economic development. In addition, hidden unemployment soars, and those lucky enough to have jobs begin to earn less when too many people are competing for too few vacancies.

Even worse, the struggling capital-intensive industries need protection and subsidies from the state to survive. Under the planned economy the government funded the investment in capital-intensive industries, but in a market economy it has to be funded by the rich businessmen in the private sector. So where does the subsidy come from? Directly or indirectly it eventually comes from the pockets of the poor, who have little to do with these industries. As a result, the poor who have nothing to offer but their labor end up not only underpaid but also having to subsidize the rich with their meager wages through repressed wage rates, low returns to their savings, and even taxes. So, the already very wide income gap inevitably becomes even wider.

In some developing countries without a household registration system, a large number of jobless rural laborers flood into cities, but with no access to the formal job market, they end up in slums. Of course, developing countries can establish several high-end industries and create conglomerates and big brands. But the profits from those industries are basically sustained by protection and subsidy, so in fact it is a transfer of wealth, not a real creation of surplus. Besides, many people who could have engaged in labor-intensive industries that enjoy comparative advantage do not have enough capital to produce capacity, let alone create a surplus. Inevitably, the surplus created across society is very limited, and the pace of capital accumulation and structural upgrading is really slow.

Developing countries that pursued a CAD strategy have a common pattern. At the very beginning their rapid economic development is fueled by protection and subsidies from the government. Later, with a shrinking surplus and weak domestic investment, they begin to look for foreign investment, which can prolong rapid economic growth for a certain period. Finally, when the day of reckoning comes, the newly established industries turn out to be unable to create enough profits to pay the foreign creditors and investors. So they suffer a financial meltdown and social crisis. And a "bad market economy" may ensue, with businesses more motivated to ask for more subsidies from the government than to improve their corporate performance. Rent-seeking becomes rampant.

After World War II many Latin American countries carried out the "secondary import substitution" strategy to develop some capital-intensive industries, which is also a CAD strategy. Not surprisingly, it resulted in inadequate employment, an unfair distribution of wealth, and a mushrooming of slums. Under the pressure of unemployment and social tension, those countries resorted to so-called democratic politics. The politicians offered very tempting social welfare policies to the electorate. But it produced the Latin American middle-income trap, featuring stagnation, failure to narrow the income gap with advanced countries, periodic financial turmoil, and economic crises.[9]

The current distribution system in China claims to seek efficiency in the functional income distribution, but the efficiency we are talking about here is not a market-based one free from any government protection and subsidies. Enterprises, sheltered under the government's umbrella, can enjoy handsome profits. But the profits are actually generated from protection and subsidies, so they are no more than a transfer of wealth. And they will inevitably trigger myriad social problems. If China attempts to address these social problems with redistribution, it may easily be caught in a situation like the Latin American trap. That is why I am against the idea that "functional income distribution should focus on efficiency, and redistribution on equity." I suggest that unity between equity and efficiency should basically be achieved through functional income distribution, and that redistribution should only be a supplementary method.

Or a CAF strategy?

This goal can be attained as long as China continues with a CAF strategy. So the next question is: Which industries in China enjoy comparative advantage? There is no simple answer. The factor endowment structure is constantly changing and upgrading; labor-intensive and capital-intensive are used only in a relative sense. Besides, China is a vast country, with different regions having very different comparative advantages. For example, coastal cities like Guangzhou, Shanghai, and Shenzhen are different from inland provinces like Anhui, Jiangxi, Hubei, and Hunan, which again are different from western provinces like Gansu, Ningxia, and Xinjiang. How, then, should a CAF strategy be implemented in China?

Entrepreneurs care little about comparative advantage. What they care about is profit, determined by the prices of the products and factors. So, to answer the question about how best to implement a CAF strategy in China, as argued in Chapter 5, what is needed is a sound pricing system. If the pricing system can fully and promptly reflect the relative scarcity of all the factors in the endowment structure, a relatively abundant factor will have a relatively low price and vice versa. If such a price system works, profit-driven entrepreneurs will naturally make the most of the cheaper factors of production to reduce their costs. The government's facilitating role is limited to coordination of various investments in hard and soft infrastructure and compensation for the externality generated by the first movers.

The key is to establish a highly competitive market domestically. Based on such a market, if a CAF strategy is followed in each locality, capital accumulation will speed up, and capital will gradually grow from being relatively scarce to become relatively abundant. Then with adequate capital, the production and industrial structure will be upgraded from labor-intensive to capital- and technology-intensive. Meanwhile, the distribution of income will increasingly favor labor.

The purpose of China's economic reform is to set up a sound socialist market economy, and it is exactly the CAF strategy that drives China's rapid economic growth since its reform and opening. In the planned economy period the government, defying comparative advantage, established a batch of capital- and technology-intensive industries by artificially suppressing the prices of all productive factors and by using administrative measures to allocate scarce capital to those industries.

Since 1978 China has adopted a gradual reform, giving the industries with no comparative advantage protection and subsidy while setting free the industries with comparative advantage. As a result, China has achieved not only social stability but also robust economic growth. As the world's third biggest trading nation, China exports mainly labor-intensive products. But as its economy continues to soar and its capital accumulates, the share of capital- and technology-intensive products in the export mix will increase, the natural result of a CAF strategy.

Yet distortions remain

China still does not have a fully competitive market system, and the government from time to time still intervenes in resource allocation to protect and subsidize the industries with no comparative advantage. These long-standing problems are caused mainly by the following distortions.

Financial distortions

First are distortions in the financial structure. In the pre-reform era the government used fiscal policies instead of financial institutions to allocate capital, so China had neither banks nor a stock market. Soon after the reform and opening, the government started to improve its financial system. In 1983 the fiscal appropriation was replaced by bank loans: SOEs were no longer directly funded by the government but financed by low-interest loans from the banks. It is fair to say that the major purpose of the financial system then was to serve large SOEs. For this purpose, the government continued to suppress interest rates and established large state-owned banks to subsidize large SOEs.

The current financial system is basically a legacy of that time, and its backbone is still the four national banks, controlling 70% of the capital in the system, mainly serving the needs of large SOEs. During this period the stock market also emerged, but again only large companies could be listed.

So, under such a highly centralized financial system, most financial services are out of reach for SMEs that have a comparative advantage in labor-intensive industries. As a result, their development has been hampered. The distortions in the financial system caused four problems.

- The SMEs that typically concentrated in labor-intensive manufacturing and service industries could not get the financial support they so urgently needed. The most conspicuous consequence is that the service industry, the mainstay of SMEs, is underdeveloped. In recent years the government has paid a lot of lip service to the development of services, but in 2009 it contributed only

42.6% to GDP, far behind the average of 53% in the countries at the same level of development.[10]

- Most farmers have no access to bank loans, either. Agriculture modernization certainly needs capital. For example, a plastic greenhouse costs RMB 10,000–20,000, and a modern chicken coop costs more than RMB 100,000. As a result, despite the huge capital surplus in the country, because the efficiency of capital allocation is rather low, industries with comparative advantage cannot obtain the financial support they deserve.

- Job opportunities are inadequate. The ever-widening income gap appears not only between urban and rural areas but also within the cities.

- Some industries are excessively capital-intensive. Because only large enterprises had access to loans, whether a SOE or a private one emerging from the reform and opening, and because they were able to get capital at a cost far below the market rate, they naturally invested in capital-intensive industries. As a result, some industries became overly capital-intensive.

Furthermore, the income distribution becomes even more uneven because many people cannot find jobs in the capital-intensive industries and those who have access to loans can also enjoy a discounted interest rate.

Resource price distortions

Second are distortions in the resource prices. In the era of the planned economy, prices of capital and resources were artificially suppressed; since the reform and opening began, the government has kept correcting the price distortions, but the results are rather patchy. For example, in the early 1990s, to protect the state-owned mining enterprises, the royalty paid to the government constituted only 1.8 percent of the resource price. What's more, both the royalty and the fees were collected based on the quantity of goods to be sold rather than on the prices. Since the 1990s the government has started to relax its control over resource prices, so that now the prices of coal, petroleum, copper, and iron ore are in line with the prices in the global market. In other words the prices are much higher today than in the 1990s. So the royalty for mineral resources now accounts for only 0.5 percent of their current prices.

Since the mid-1980s private and foreign-funded enterprises were allowed to enter industries once reserved for SOEs. High resource prices combined with low royalties can easily turn anyone in this industry into a billionaire. According to my field studies in 2006, for a mine worth billions of renminbi or even tens of billions of renminbi, the cost to obtain a mining license is only tens of millions of renminbi, and the royalty to the government is less than 1 percent of the resource price. Under such circumstances an annual revenue of around RMB 100 million for a mine owner would not be at all surprising.

The staggering profit from the mining industry not only aggravates the uneven income distribution – it also leads to rampant rent-seeking. Even worse, if unqualified people are licensed to engage in this industry, mine accidents become more likely.

Administrative distortions

Third is the persistence of administrative monopolies. Most beneficiaries are SOEs in industries like electric power and telecommunications. But the profits generated from these industries are distributed within the enterprises not collected as national revenue – another cause of the uneven income distribution.

Why focus on distortions?

Due to these distortions, during the transition to a market economy, the functional distribution can hardly eradicate inequality, while redistribution is just as incapable. The uneven income distribution is a result of a patchy reform where the distortions from a CAD strategy have yet to be eliminated. If China can further its reform by eliminating those distortions, giving full play to market forces and continuing with a CAF strategy, laborers will have ample job opportunities and share in the fruits of economic development. Hopefully the functional distribution can achieve unity between equity and efficiency. Then all the government has to do is to attend to the vulnerable groups through redistribution and social safety net. Issues related to this group are not complex and easier to work out.

Deepening the reform and improving the market system

How best to carry out a reform to achieve unity between equity and efficiency through the functional distribution of income? The following measures are called for.

Solution no. 1: The key to deepening the market-oriented reform is to improve the financial structure

In a market economy productivity comes from the combination of capital and labor. Today, China's comparative advantage still lies in labor-intensive industries, including agriculture, manufacturing, and services. But the players in these industries are mainly SMEs and farms, and they cannot fulfill their potential due to their limited access to financial services.

Banking systems in other countries evolved from small to big. In the first stage of economic development, when labor-intensive industries led the economy, small- and medium-size banks served the needs of local SMEs and farms. With big banks and stock markets emerging as the economy grew, firms got larger and capital requirements increased. But in China the reform was top-down: from the very beginning the government set up massive SOEs together with large-scale state-controlled banks to serve their demands.

So we need to "make up for lost time," as discussed in Chapter 10. China should spare no effort to facilitate the development of small- and medium-size financial institutions. China's government began to give the green light to small rural banks to meet the financial needs of farmers after the Third National Financial Work Conference in 2007. This is a move in the right direction.

But there are some flaws in the policy design. First, the threshold of RMB 500,000 is too low. Second, the requirement that "the rural bank must be funded with an existing commercial bank whose share should be no less than 20 percent" is unrealistic, although understandable, because banking is a risky and special sector. But don't forget that the very reason farmers cannot get loans from commercial banks is that the banks are not interested in rural businesses. Although only owning one-fifth of the total shares, the large banks need to bear all the risks due to the concern for their reputation. It is hard to imagine that the large commercial banks will show serious interest in investing in the small rural banks. As mentioned in Chapter 10, instead of mandating that the large commercial banks be strategic investors, it is better to raise the bar of entry, so that any would-be banker should have an equity capital of at least RMB 10 million or even RMB 50 million. The operation of rural banks must also be subject to strict supervision.

Solution no. 2: The government must raise the resource royalty

The current resource royalty is only 1.8 percent of the price, but in other countries, taking oil as an example, the royalty is 12 percent for inland oil and 16 percent for offshore oil in the United States. In addition, China should introduce an *ad valorem* tax and scrap the current quantity-based practice. China should also impose a windfall profits tax if the price hits a certain level. However, a big problem facing policy-makers is the social burden of the state-owned mineral enterprises as they need to cover the pensions of many retired unfunded workers. The low resource royalty is the government's way to compensate the SOEs for their social burden. But many private enterprises that have since engaged in this industry have no such social burden. So, the solution could be to spin off the social burden from the SOEs, and hand it over to the social security system and then price the resource royalty on a market basis.

Solution no. 3: Break monopolies or tighten regulation over the monopoly industries

Once a monopoly is broken, prices will decline, and so will profits. In the industries that allow no competition, like electricity, the government has to step up regulation on prices, costs, and distribution of profits.

If the three solutions can deepen reform, a sound market system will come into being. Guided by a CAF strategy, industries with comparative advantage should be encouraged to export, and industries with no comparative advantage should be encouraged to import, resulting in relative balance in both the domestic and global market. Under such circumstances the competitiveness of companies will improve, and the government will no longer need to give protection or subsidy, thus reducing rent-seeking and improving social equity. Eventually, the functional distribution of income can obtain unity between equity and efficiency, and the income gap between urban and rural areas and across the different regions will be narrowed. The income distribution will generally be fairer, thus boosting consumption and curtailing excessive investment at the same time. In the end the three "excessives" can be rooted out.

Summary

To conclude, I think the suggestion that "functional distribution income focuses on efficiency, and the redistribution of income through tax and fiscal policy aims at equity" is flawed. What is more, the definition of efficiency in the functional distribution should not be based on what happens in developed countries, because China has different comparative advantages from the developed world. So it would cause rising unemployment, widening income gaps, and so on. And trying to achieve equity through redistribution could end up with a situation like the Latin American middle-income trap.

So the way out is to achieve unity between equity and efficiency through functional distribution. If the economy can develop in a fast and sound manner, the income gap between rural and urban areas and across regions can be bridged through more job opportunities. When people have more money in their pockets, they will have greater purchasing power, solving the problem of the affordability and accessibility of medical care. Meanwhile the government can avoid the resource-intensive development that harms the natural environment. If all that happens, the "five balances" and "a harmonious society" will no longer be a dream.

References

Fei, John C. H., Gustav Ranis, and Shirley W. Y. Kuo. With the assistance of Y.-Y. Bian and J. Chang Collins. 1979. *Growth with Equity: The Taiwan Case*. New York: Oxford University Press.

Lin, Justin Y., 2004. *Fa Zhan Zhan Lue Yu Jing Ji Fa Zhan* [Development Strategy and Economic Development]. Beijing: Peking University Press.

Lin, Justin Y., 2008. "Rebalancing Equity and Efficiency for Sustained Growth." In Ligang Song and Wing-Thye Woo (eds.), *China's Dilemma: Economic Growth, Environment, and Climate Change*. Canberra: ANU Press, 90–109.

Lin, Justin Y., and Peilin Liu. 2008. "Achieving Equity and Efficiency Simultaneously in the Primary Distribution Stage in the People's Republic of China." *Asian Development Review* 25(1–2): 34–57.

Lin, Justin Y., Hinh T. Dinh, and Fernando Im. 2010. "US–China External Imbalance and the Global Financial Crisis." *Chinese Economic Journal* 3(1) (June): 1–24.

National Bureau of Statistics of China. 2010. *China Statistical Yearbook*. Beijing: China Statistics Press.

Paus, Eva, 2011. "Latin America's Middle Income Trap." *America Quarterly* (Winter) (http: www.americaquarterly.org/node/2142).

World Bank. 2011. *World Development Indicators 2011*. Washington, DC: World Bank.

Notes

1. National Bureau of Statistics of China (2010).
2. Lin and Liu (2008); Lin, Hinh, and Im (2010).
3. World Bank (2011).
4. Lin and Liu (2008).
5. World Bank (2011).
6. Fei, Ranis, and Kuo (1979).
7. Lin and Liu (2008).
8. Lin (2004).
9. Paus (2011).
10. National Bureau of Statistics of China (2010); World Bank (2011).

THIRTEEN

Reflections on neoclassical theories

In the thirty-three years since 1978, China's reform and opening has achieved remarkable progress, with its GDP growing 9.9 percent annually and trade volume growing at 16.3 percent.[1] China has grown into the world's second largest economy and the largest exporter, as mentioned in Chapter 1. During this period people's living standards and incomes increased significantly; 600 million people were lifted out of extreme poverty.

Opinions in the international economic research community

China's reform and achievements can be called a miracle in economic history. But in the late 1980s and early 1990s the international economic research community did not understand much about China's reform, and many economists were far from optimistic, believing that a market economy should be based on private property, a feature that the Chinese economy apparently lacked at that time. China's large SOEs were not privatized, and a dual-track system was prevalent, with state planning still very important. Many economists thought the dual-track system would soon lead to efficiency loss, rent-seeking, and institutionalized state opportunism – in short, an inferior institutional arrangement.[2] Some economists even claimed that China's transition would finally fail due to incomplete reform.[3]

At the same time most economists were optimistic about reform in the former Soviet Union and Eastern Europe – because these countries reformed their economies according to the fundamental principles of neoclassical economics. The most representative of these principles was the "shock therapy" in the Czech Republic, Poland, and Russia, with three main elements: price liberalization, rapid privatization, and macroeconomic stabilization by closing fiscal deficits.[4] These elements are considered the base of an efficient economic system in neoclassical economic theory.

Economists recommending shock therapy also knew that it takes time to make the transition from one economic system to another and that it is costly to cast aside previously vested interests. But they optimistically assumed that the national economy would grow after six months or a year following an initial downturn stemming from the shock therapy.[5] They believed the former Soviet Union and Eastern Europe would overtake China through their reforms, even though they started their reforms much later. And they believed China's difficulties would loom larger due to inconsistencies that incomplete reforms left in the economic system.

Twenty years have elapsed since the predictions of many renowned economists were put forth in the early 1990s. Contrary to these predictions, China's economy has grown while countries that implemented shock therapy experienced severe difficulties. Instead of a "J-shaped" growth pattern, they experienced an "L-shaped" pattern featuring an abrupt slump and long-term stagnation (Figure 13.1). Russia's inflation reached 8,414% in 1993, and Ukraine's 10,155%. In 1995 Russia's GDP was only half of what it had been in 1990, and Ukraine's 40%.[6]

With significant declines in per capita income and extreme income disparities, all social indicators slid – male life expectancy

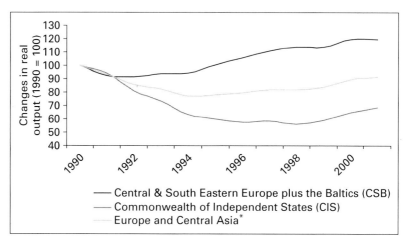

Figure 13.1 Falling output in the early 1990s in Eastern Europe and the former Soviet Union
Notes: * average of CSB and CIS. Aggregates are population-weighted.
Source: World Bank (2002).

in Russia fell from 64 years in 1990 to 58 in 1994.[7] In a survey of 23,000 households in twenty-three countries by the European Bank in 2006, 70 percent reported that their living standards were worse than fifteen years before the transition. Overall, the countries that implemented shock therapy experienced great difficulties in reform, in contrast to the optimistic expectation of most economists. Of the Eastern European countries, Poland scored best with only a 20 percent decline in its GDP. But it did not really implement shock therapy. Although prices in Poland were liberalized, many of its large SOEs were not privatized.[8]

The Chinese economy did suffer myriad problems in the 1990s and even up to now as discussed in Chapter 12. The SOE reforms initiated in the early 1980s had yet to be completed. Interregional and urban–rural disparities had widened. Many serious problems in the financial system awaited solution. The sustainability of the environment was a real concern. The surpluses from foreign trade and huge reserves of foreign exchange put mounting pressure on the currency. Even so, the economy grew 10.1% a year in the 1990s, and 10.4% in the 2000s, 1.1 percentage points and 1.4% higher than in 1978–90.[9] Moreover, people's living standards improved rapidly, especially in urban areas. Economic development in China not only promoted the welfare of the Chinese people – it also contributed greatly to the world economy. During the Asian financial crisis the Chinese currency did not depreciate, important for the recovery in Southeast Asia. In the recent global financial crisis China was the main driver of global recovery.

Many famous economists, working at the frontiers of economic research, participated in the reforms in the former Soviet Union and Eastern Europe. Why couldn't they predict and explain the difficulties of shock therapy, and why were they pessimistic about China's prospects? They did not fully understand the history or the mechanisms behind a planned economy. Nor did they understand the essence of economic transformation in the formerly socialist countries. Their failures are also due to the fact that the current neoclassical theory has some congenital limitations in analyzing economic transitions.

Viability and reflections on neoclassical theories

The implicit assumptions and inferences of modern economics

Theories should be able to explain and predict phenomena. If not, the theories must have some fundamental flaws.[10] The mainstream neoclassical economic theories have arisen mostly for the purpose of explaining what happens in the developed countries, but they have an inherent limitation in explaining what happens in transitional economies and developing countries. Neoclassical economics has a well-known basic assumption of rationality: given all possible choices, a decision-maker will always choose to maximize his or her objective function. This should be applicable as an approach for explaining economic behaviors in socialist and transitional economies, as I demonstrated in the previous chapters. But there is another implicit assumption – the "viability" assumption as I call it – that is taken for granted in the existing theories.

I define viability in relation to the expected rate of profit of a firm in a free, open, and competitive market. If, without any external subsidy or protection, a normally managed firm is expected to earn a socially acceptable normal profit in a free, open, and competitive market, that firm is viable. Accepting the viability assumption in their analyses, most economists will conclude that an enterprise must lack normal management if it does not achieve acceptable profitability in a competitive market. They will infer that the problems must come from corporate governance, incentive mechanisms, excessive government interventions, or property rights arrangements that impede the enterprise's normal management. These problems did show up in SOEs in socialist economies. So, in this theoretical framework, the success of the socialist economic transition depends on eliminating the problems of property rights, corporate governance, and government intervention. "Shock therapy" is based on this theoretical foundation.

A theoretical summary of viability

Neoclassical theories, originating in developed economies, try mainly to explain what happens in developed countries. It is reasonable to assume that enterprises in those economies are viable, since – except for a few minor sectors, such as defense for national security and agriculture for rural employment – governments in these countries rarely give subsidies and other types of support to enterprises. An enterprise with normal management that is not expected to earn acceptable profits will not attract investment in the first place. If such an enterprise is established due to misleading information, investors can also withdraw their investments so that the enterprise will not survive.

But in transition and developing countries, many enterprises are not viable – they cannot earn acceptable profits even with normal management. Why? The answer depends on whether the sector the enterprise operates in, the products it produces, and the technology it chooses in production are consistent with the economy's comparative advantages. If the sector is not consistent with the economy's comparative advantages, the enterprises cannot earn acceptable profits even with normal management, and their survival depends on the state's protection and subsidies.

A good example is agriculture in Japan. The Japanese agricultural sector is dominated by small farms, with farmers being both owners and operators of the farm, so there are no problems of property rights and corporate governance. But Japan has limited land and no comparative advantage in land-intensive agricultural products such as grain. It is also a high-income, high-wage country with no comparative advantage in labor-intensive agricultural products such as vegetables and fruits. Although Japan's agriculture is famous for its delicate, intensive cultivation, the survival of Japanese farms relies on high levels of government tariff protection and fiscal subsidies, without which most Japanese farms could not continue to function.

Many SOEs in transition economies face the same problem of viability as Japanese farms, due to the fact that these enterprises, especially the large ones in heavy industries, are established by governments with the aim of surpassing the industries in advanced countries, thus running against the comparative advantages of their economies. Transition economies such as China and Russia were capital-scarce, backward, agrarian economies before they implemented a socialist planned economy.

In a capital-scarce developing country the development of capital-intensive heavy industrial projects must overcome numerous difficulties through the price distortions, administrative allocation of resources, and direct intervention of management, as discussed in Chapter 4.

In this kind of planned system, if enterprises are in the priority sectors, they enjoy cheap inputs and can be guaranteed profits. By contrast, if they are in sectors that produce necessities for living or intermediate goods for heavy industrial sectors, their product prices will be artificially depressed in the government's plan, and they could incur losses even with good management. So, profitability, to a large extent, depends not on management but on the position of enterprises in the industrial chain.

The various institutional arrangements – such as price distortions in capital, foreign exchange rates, raw materials, wages, and commodity prices, the replacement of market mechanism by plan allocation, and the absence of enterprise autonomy – are all endogenous to the fact that the enterprises prioritized by government development strategies are not viable in a free, open, and competitive market. In the terms of neoclassical economics these arrangements are considered "second best." Under these distortions the decentralized economic surplus in different sectors can be mobilized to the greatest extent and invested in priority sectors by the government. So a backward agricultural economy such as China can develop an atomic bomb and satellite technology in a short time. But resource allocation is inefficient, and incentives in enterprises are low, owing to a lack of autonomy – enterprises and workers are not rewarded for performance.

Many enterprises in socialist planned economies are not viable because they are in the wrong sectors. But most economists working in the developed countries, with the implicit assumption of enterprise viability, only see the distortions in the market and government's interventions in resource allocation and firm management – and assume these distortions and interventions are the main reasons for the poor firm performances in the socialist and transition economies.

Reality and the development of theory

It is true that many distortions and specific institutional arrangements in socialist countries – such as ineffective corporate governance, cronyism, soft budget constraints, and government intervention in enterprise operation, finance, and foreign trade – create an inefficient economic system. However, to a large extent, these interventions and institutional arrangements are endogenous to the fact that the enterprises prioritized by government development strategies are not viable. If non-viability is not addressed, and if the government is unwilling or unable to let enterprises go bankrupt, the distortions will not be eliminated.

Understanding the real world is limited by the model of the world in the observer's mind.[11] The assumption of enterprise viability is implicit in economic theories. Trained under such a framework, economists tend to think that the existing economic theories are appropriate for the analysis of transition economies, particularly when they see the familiar problems of corporate governance, property rights, and government interventions that have proven harmful to economic efficiency in the existing theoretical frameworks and practices in their economies.[12] But they ignore the endogeneity of these problems to the non-viability of priority enterprises in the transitional economies' development strategy. Invited by transition economies to design their transition policies, many distinguished economists often reached a consensus about the desirable reforms and emphasize only privatization, elimination of government intervention, and complete liberalization.[13]

The Washington Consensus and its main tenets

The most prevalent reform package in the 1990s was the Washington Consensus. It called for strengthening fiscal discipline, increasing public investments to improve income distribution (most notably in previously ignored sectors with high rates of return), enlarging the tax base, unifying exchange rates, liberalizing trade, removing barriers to foreign direct investment, privatizing SOEs, lifting regulations on market entry, and protecting private property rights.[14] The shock therapy proposed by economists for transition economies was based on this Washington Consensus.[15] So, we can understand why, in the 1990s, views were more optimistic for reforms in the former Soviet Union and Eastern Europe that implemented shock therapies, but less so for the piecemeal, gradualist reforms in China.

The viability assumption in the existing theories not only has an impact on the views of economists working on issues related to developed economies. It also influences the views of economists working on issues related to other economies. For example, in the debate over socialism in the 1930s, economists such as Oscar Lange believed that the socialist planned economy could increase allocation efficiency by simulating markets.[16] And Friedrich Hayek believed the socialist economy was doomed to fail due to information problems.[17] All took the viability of enterprises in a socialist economy as an implicit precondition in their analyses.

The existing assumption also influences the view of economists living in other economies when they analyze their own problems. János Kornai of Hungary is perhaps one of the most eminent economists specializing in socialist economic problems. His most prominent contribution is the concept of the "soft budget constraint."[18] In many socialist countries, enterprises suffering from poor management can ask for preferential treatment and subsidies, while similar enterprises in market economies have no choice but to go bankrupt.

Kornai proposed that the soft budget constraint is the main reason for a lack of incentive to improve production and for the high prevalence of moral hazard in and among SOEs. He attributes the soft budget constraint to the paternalism of socialist governments toward SOEs. Therefore, reform in property rights and the severance of enterprise–state connections must be carried out to eliminate the soft budget constraint and to promote enterprise efficiency.

Kornai's theoretical framework also unconsciously assumes the viability of SOEs in socialist countries. But the soft budget constraint in socialist economies emerges essentially from enterprise non-viability. In a free, open, and competitive economy, these enterprises would not attract investments and would cease operation. To establish these non-viable enterprises, governments must take on the responsibilities of protecting and subsidizing them.[19]

Enterprises always have incentives to attribute their losses to insufficient government support and protection, even when the losses are due to incompetent operation and faulty management. But due to information asymmetries, governments never know what level of protection and subsidy is adequate. So, they cannot resist enterprise requests for more support, and the enterprise budget constraints become soft.[20]

The soft budget constraint of SOEs thus results essentially from the problem of non-viability rather than the paternalism of socialist governments. Even in non-socialist countries, the soft budget constraint can exist for the non-viable enterprises that governments promote, like the defense industry in the developed countries.

The reform failure of the former Soviet Union and Eastern Europe

With the foregoing reasoning, reforms in property rights, government intervention, and corporate governance – according to the existing theories that neglect enterprise viability – usually cannot achieve the goal of policy reforms and often lead to further deterioration of enterprise performance.[21] In the former Soviet Union and Eastern Europe the socialist governments were removed, and shock therapy and privatization were implemented. But the soft budget constraint of enterprises still existed, and the incentives of privatized enterprise managers to bargain for more support became much greater than those of SOEs. The subsidies that enterprises received from governments did not fall – in some cases they even rose.[22] At the same time the shock therapy weakened taxation capacities. This, combined with high subsidies to enterprises, led to extremely high inflation.

China's reform failure

Since 1978, when China initiated its reform, the two most significant changes, summarized by Deng Xiaoping as the two "unexpected results," were the success of the household responsibility system as discussed in Chapter 7[23] and the remarkable growth of TVEs as discussed in Chapter 8.[24] These reforms were not designed by policy-makers – they were spontaneously adopted by peasants.

In the process of China's reform many of the policies designed by the Chinese government suffered the same fate as the shock therapy in the former Soviet Union and Eastern Europe. Take the reform of SOEs. As discussed in Chapter 8, at the beginning of reform in the early 1980s it was believed that the problems of SOEs lay in the lack of autonomy for SOE managers, with subsequent incentive incompatibility stemming from the absence of rewards for performance. So, decentralization was carried out to promote managerial autonomy and allow SOEs to retain a share of profits for their own purposes. These measures were effective in pilot programs, but became ineffective when they were instituted nationwide (productivity improved but profitability fell). Many scholars thought the problem lay in property rights, with the enterprises owned by the state but operated by the managers, who were not the owners and lacked incentives to care about the returns on capital.

Until the late 1980s and early 1990s, reforms were directed toward drafting a clearer definition of property rights and promoting modern corporate governance with boards of directors and supervision boards. The best arrangement of property rights and corporate governance was considered to be the publicly listed company, since the value of the enterprise would be evaluated before it went public, and after being listed the company would be publicly owned with shares held in both state and private investors. In addition to the board of directors, private individual shareholders would have incentives to monitor enterprise management and operation since they were concerned with the returns to their private investments.

After a few years the financial performance of listed companies did not differ from those of non-listed companies.[25] At first, it was thought that this was due to the fact that the public shares were owned only by small, individual, and diverse investors, who had little capacity and incentive to monitor the managers because the returns to small individual stockholders' efforts would be negligible. These small shareholders were thought to be interested in the short-term price changes in stocks, which led to a highly speculative stock market with high turnover.

Then it was thought that shareholding companies in developed countries were mostly held by institutional investors, with the capacity to hold a substantial portion of the total shares of a listed company. In addition, the institutional investors could afford professional analysis of listed companies' financial statements, allowing them to supervise enterprises more effectively. To achieve this, China's institutional funds were introduced in 1998. But the speculation in stock markets took a turn for the worse, with institutional funds manipulating stock prices.

How could this happen? The reason again lies in the non-viability of these listed companies. Without the ability to earn acceptable profits in a free, open, and competitive market, they cannot distribute dividends to shareholders, so the small individual shareholders can profit only by speculating on stock prices. Although institutional investors own a large amount of shares, they cannot benefit by holding the stocks for a long time due to the non-viability and unprofitability of those listed companies. With large amounts of money in their command and a small portion of stocks in circulation for each listed company, institutional investors manipulated stock prices to get their profits.[26]

So, the failures of copying developed country experience or of designing reform policies according to the existing theories lie in the fact that viability is a precondition for existing enterprises in developed countries and an implicit assumption in the existing theories. But most enterprises in transition economies are not viable.

The failure of other countries' CAD strategies

The problem of viability is not only the key problem in transition economies – it is also widespread in developing countries. As discussed in Chapter 3, on seeing the decisive role of industrialization in the economic and political strengths of developed countries, many leaders of the developing countries that achieved independence after World War II attempted to build advanced sectors comparable with those in developed countries – defying their comparative advantages. They did so by intervening in factor prices, the financial system, international trade, and investment without realizing that the industrial structures of developed nations were endogenously determined by their particular factor endowment structures.[27] As a result, enterprises in the developing economies were not viable in a free, open, and competitive market, and government interventions in prices, resource allocation, and market competition were required to keep them afloat. Those interventions inevitably led to rent-seeking and crony capitalism, which finally resulted in highly unequal income distributions, low efficiency, and rising social and economic instability.[28]

In market economies the protective measures taken toward non-viable enterprises are similar to those in socialist economies: depress interest rates, manipulate the direction of loans dished out by banks and the financial system to provide cheap funds to non-viable enterprises, and establish various barriers to imports to prevent competition from developed countries. The surplus-earning enterprises that are consistent with the economy's comparative advantages were discriminated against and found it hard to develop, which led to a drying up of funds that could be mobilized for development purposes. If external borrowing was ruled out, those economies stagnated. If external borrowing by enterprises or governments was permitted, as in Latin America, a debt crisis ensued.[29]

When a debt crisis broke, countries had to resort to IMF rescues, usually associated with a series of reforms and structural adjustments. The concept of conditionality, based on the Washington Consensus, requires that macroeconomic policy distortions be corrected, that government intervention in banks and enterprises cease, and that corporate governance be improved.

The Washington Consensus, based on the existing theories, assumed that enterprises are viable. So the conditionality aims to eliminate protectionism and subsidization without any attempt to solve the enterprises' viability problem. If non-viable enterprises constitute only a small share of the economy, as in Korea in the East Asian financial crisis or Bolivia in the 1980s, shock therapy is possible, and growth can quickly resume when rising efficiency offsets the shock of bankruptcy suffered by non-viable enterprises in the wake of Washington Consensus measures. But if non-viable enterprises constitute a large share of the economy, as in transition economies, they could produce an L-shaped rather than a J-shaped pattern of GDP growth.[30]

Since non-viable enterprises are a common problem in socialist, transition, and developing economies, it is inappropriate to implicitly assume that enterprises are viable in the analysis of and solutions to the problems in these economies. Viability should be taken explicitly into account in analyzing economic development and transition.

Introducing the concept of viability to development economics and transition economics

Economic theories are like maps. A map is not the real world, but it is a tool for understanding more about the surrounding environment and what will be seen in different directions. Maps, by their nature, must be abstract and simplified, but if some important signs are ignored or incorrect, they will mislead. And when we find out the mistakes, we must correct them. Due to the viability problems in planned transition economies and developing economies, the implicit assumption of viability should be abandoned in analyzing economic problems and designing policies for these economies. With many enterprises not viable, transition and reform should be designed with the understanding that their success also depends on creating conditions that make non-viable enterprises viable, rather than unconditionally following shock therapy and Washington Consensus reforms.

In addition, the objectives pursued in national development must be reoriented. Traditionally, political leaders, economists, and social elites in developing countries aimed to develop advanced technologies and industries similar to those of the developed countries as soon as possible. But the structures of industries and technologies that are consistent with an economy's comparative advantages are determined by the economy's structure of factor endowments. A developing country's attempt to build up the industries and technologies of developed countries makes enterprises in the priority sectors non-viable and unable to survive in free, open, and competitive markets. So, governments have to subsidize and protect them through price distortions, interventions in resource allocation, and so on. Rent-seeking, soft budget constraints, macroeconomic instability, income disparities, stagnation, and crisis are the frequent consequences of government attempts, despite the initial good intentions.

With viable enterprises, the ultimate objective of economic development should be to upgrade its endowment structure, because if it can do that, enterprises in an open and competitive market will have to upgrade their industrial, product, and technological levels accordingly to ensure their competitiveness in the market. Because the endowment of land (and natural resources) in a country is given, upgrading the endowment structure means increasing the amount of capital per worker.

Capital comes from the accumulation of economic surplus. To quicken the upgrading of the endowment structure, a maximum economic surplus should be produced in each period, and a large part of this surplus should be saved. If an economy develops its industries, products, and technologies in line with its comparative advantages at every point, it will achieve maximum competitiveness and generate maximum surplus, have the highest possible returns on capital, and possess the highest possible incentives to accumulate capital. Consequently, the upgrading of its factor endowment will occur most rapidly.

Entrepreneurs care about product prices and production costs, not about the structure of factor endowments in the economy. Only when product prices reflect the prices of international markets, and factor prices reflect the relative scarcity of various factors in the endowment structure, can entrepreneurs automatically make the industrial, product, and technological choices consistent with the economy's comparative advantages. And only in free, open, and competitive markets can the product and factor prices perform these functions. So, maintaining openness and competition in the market becomes the basic economic function of government in targeting the maximal upgrading of factor endowment structure.

As the factor endowment structure is upgraded, previously viable enterprises must upgrade their choices of industry, product, and technology accordingly to maintain their viability in competitive markets. That upgrading involves innovation, requiring enterprises to acquire the latest information about industries, products, and technologies. Such information shares the nature of a public good: collecting and processing it can be costly but disseminating it is basically cost-free. The government can thus help collect information on the latest industries, products, and technologies and provide it free of charge to the enterprises as part of industrial policy. The government should also facilitate industrial upgrading by helping private firms to overcome the coordination and externality issues, as discussed in Chapter 6.

Such policies aim to develop a country's economy according to its particular comparative advantage and can help developing countries make full use of the technological gap between themselves and developed countries and accelerate their economic development through low-cost transfers of technology. This approach will help developing countries converge with developed countries on incomes, industries, and technologies.[31] Note that industrial policy can be used in development strategies aiming at either upgrading the endowment structure or directly promoting advanced industries, products, and technologies. In the former case the enterprises to be supported must be viable, and subsidies should be limited in amount and duration – sufficient only to compensate for information externalities. In the latter the enterprises to be supported are non-viable and, accordingly, require large and long-term subsidies and protection from the government.

The enterprises in heavy industries prioritized by government in traditional planned economies are not viable in open and competitive markets. The objective of the transition from a traditional planned economy is to establish open and competitive markets. But in the transition the enterprise's viability problem becomes explicit. Whether the transition will be stable and successful very much depends on how the viability problem is solved.

Since non-viable enterprises cannot survive in open and competitive markets without government subsidies, the shock therapy that aims to jump over the huge gap between planned economies and market economies will inevitably lead to widespread bankruptcy and unemployment, producing economic collapse and social instability, both unacceptable. So, the government has to continue to subsidize the non-viable enterprises, resulting in an embarrassing shock without therapy.

China's reform is a gradual dual-track process. The Chinese government has relaxed strict controls on resource allocation and allowed new entrants to sectors of the Chinese economy's comparative advantages. This has enhanced the efficiency of resource allocation, created new resources, and provided conditions for the reform of traditional sectors. But the state has continued to protect and support enterprises in traditional sectors to buffer them from the threat of bankruptcy and create conditions for their viability. This dual-track approach can maintain social and economic stability, achieve relatively high growth, and make the transition efficiently without inflicting losses.

After the problems of SOE viability are solved, whether an enterprise can return a profit becomes a problem of management, which is determined by corporate governance and market competition, as discussed in neoclassical economics. The government will no longer be responsible for enterprise performance. Only then can the reform of institutions inherited from the traditional system with the functions of subsidizing and protecting SOEs be carried out thoroughly, and the transition from a planned system to a market economy completed.[32]

References

Asian Development Bank. 1999. *Key Indicators of Developing Asian and Pacific Countries 1999*, 30 vols. Oxford: Oxford University Press.

Balcerowicz, Leszek. 1994. "Common Fallacies in the Debate on the Transition to a Market Economy." *Economic Policy* 9(19): 16–50.

Blanchard, Oliver, Rudiger Dornbusch, Paul Krugman, Richard Layard, and Lawrence Summers. 1991. *Reform in Eastern Europe*. Cambridge, MA: MIT Press.

Boycko, Maxim, Andrei Shleifer, and Robert Vishny. 1995. *Privatizing Russia*. Cambridge, MA: MIT Press.

Brada, Josef C., and Arthur E. King. 1991. "Sequencing Measures for the Transformation of Socialist Economies to Capitalism: Is There a J-Curve for Economic Reform?" Research Paper Series No. 13. Washington, DC: Socialist Economies Reform Unit, World Bank.

Chenery, Hollis B. 1961. "Comparative Advantage and Development Policy." *American Economic Review* 51(1): 18–51.

Dabrowski, Marek. 2001. "Ten Years of Polish Economic Transition, 1989–1999." In Mario I. Blejer and Marko Škreb (eds.), *Transition: The First Decade*. Cambridge, MA: MIT Press, 121–52.

Friedman, Milton. 1953. "The Methodology of Positive Economics." In *Essays in Positive Economics*. Chicago: University of Chicago Press, 3–43.

Gregory, Paul, and Robert Stuart. 2001. *Russian and Soviet Economic Performance and Structure*, 7th edn. New York: Addison Wesley.

Hayek, Friedrich A. (ed.). 1935. *Collectivist Economic Planning*, London: Routledge & Kegan Paul.

Kolodko, Grzegorz W. 2001. "Postcommunist Transitions and Post-Washington Consensus: The Lessons for Policy Reforms." In Mario I. Blejer and Marko Škreb (eds.), *Transition: The First Decade*. Cambridge, MA: MIT Press, 45–84.

Kornai, János. 1986. "The Soft Budget Constraint." *Kyklos* 39(1): 3–30.

1990. *The Road to a Free Economy*. New York: Norton.

Krueger, Ann O. 1974. "The Political Economy of the Rent-seeking Society." *American Economic Review* 64(3): 291–303.

1992. *Economic Policy Reform in Developing Countries*. Oxford: Basil Blackwell.

Lange, Oscar. 1936. "On the Economic Theory of Socialism." *Review of Economic Studies* 4(1): 53–71.

Lin, Justin Y. 1992. "Rural Reforms and Agricultural Growth in China." *American Economic Review* 82: 34–51.

1998. "Transition to a Market-Oriented Economy: China versus Eastern Europe and Russia." In Yujiro Hayami and Masahiko Aoki (eds.), *The Institutional Foundations of East Asian Economic Development*. New York: St. Martin's Press in Association with International Economic Association, 215–47.

2001. "Four Issues on China's Stock Market." Peking University CCER Newsletter 7.

2003. "Development Strategy, Viability and Economic Convergence." *Economic Development and Cultural Change* 53(2): 278–309.

2005. "Viability, Economic Transition and Reflections on Neoclassical Economics." *Kyklos* 58(2): 239–64.

2009. *Economic Development and Transition: Thought, Strategy, and Viability*. Cambridge: Cambridge University Press.

Lin, Justin Y., and Zhiyun Li. 2008. "Policy Burden, Privatization and Soft Budget Constraint." *Journal of Comparative Economics* 36: 90–102.

Lin, Justin Y., and Guofu Tan. 1999. "Policy Burdens, Accountability, and the Soft Budget Constraint." *American Economic Review* 89(2): 426–31.

Lin, Justin Y., and Yang Yao. 2001. "Chinese Rural Industrialization in the Context of the East Asian Miracle." In Joseph E. Stigilitz and Shahid Yusuf (eds.), *Rethinking the East Asian Miracle*. Oxford: Oxford University Press, 143–96.

Lin, Justin Y., Fang Cai, and Zhou Li. 1996a. *The China Miracle: Development Strategy and Economic Reform*. Hong Kong: Chinese University Press.

  1996b. "The Lessons of China's Transition to a Market Economy." *Cato Journal* 16(2): 201–31.

  2001. *State-owned Enterprise Reform in China*. Hong Kong: Chinese University Press.

Lin, Yixiang. 1999. "The Third Institutional Innovation in Security Market and the State-owned Enterprise Reform." *Jing Ji Yan Jiu* [Economic Research] 10: 46–52.

Lipton, David, and Jeffrey Sachs. 1990. "Privatization in Eastern Europe: The Case of Poland." *Brookings Papers on Economic Activities* 2: 293–341.

Murphy, Kevin, Andrei Schleifer, and Robert Vishny. 1992. "The Tradition to a Market Economy: Pitfall of Partial Reform." *Quarterly Journal of Economics* 107(3): 889–906.

Murrell, Peter. 1991. "Can Neoclassical Economics underpin the Reform of Centrally Planned Economies?" *Journal of Economic Perspectives* 5(4): 59–76.

National Bureau of Statistics of China. 2010. *China Statistical Yearbook*. Beijing: China Statistics Press.

North, Douglass. 2002. "The Process of Economic Change." *China Economic Quarterly* 1(4): 787–802.

Qian, Yingyi, and Chenggan Xu. 1993. "Why China's Economic Reforms Differ: The M-Form Hierarchy and Entry/Expansion of the Non-state Sector." *Economics of Transition* 1(2): 135–70.

Sachs, Jeffrey D., and Wing Thye Woo. 1994. "Structural Factors in the Economic Reforms of China, Eastern Europe and the Former Soviet Union." *Economic Policy* 9(18): 101–45.

  1997. "Understanding China's Economic Performance." Manuscript (May).

Sachs, Jeffrey D., Wing Thye Woo, and Xiaokai Yang. 2000. "Economic Reforms and Constitutional Transition." *Annals of Economics and Finance* 1(2): 435–91.

Summers, Lawrence H. 1994. "Russia and the Soviet Union Then and Now: Comment." In Olivier Jean Blanchard, Kenneth A. Froot, and Jeffrey D. Sachs (eds.), *The Transition in Eastern Europe*, vol. I. Chicago: University of Chicago Press, 252–55.

Wiles, Peter. 1995. "Capitalist Triumphalism in the Eastern European Transition." In Ha-Joon Chang, and Peter Nolan (eds.), *The Transformation of the Communist Economies*. London: Macmillan Press, 46–77.

Williamson, John. 1997. "The Washington Consensus Revisited." In Louis Emmerij (ed.), *Economic and Social Development into the XXI Century*. Washington, DC: Inter-American Development Bank, 48–61.

Woo, Wing Thye. 1993. "The Art of Reforming Centrally-Planned Economies: Comparing China, Poland and Russia." Paper presented at the Conference of the Tradition of Centrally-Planned Economies in Pacific Asia, San Francisco, CA, May 7–8.

World Bank. 2002. *Transition, the First Ten Years: Analysis and Lessons for Eastern Europe and the Former Soviet Union*. Washington, DC: World Bank.

Notes

1. This chapter draws on Lin (2005).
2. Balcerowicz (1994); Qian and Xu (1993); Sachs and Woo (1994, 1997); Woo (1993).
3. Murphy, Schleifer, and Vishny (1992); Sachs, Woo, and Yang (2000).
4. Blanchard *et al.* (1991); Boycko, Shleifer, and Vishny (1995); Lipton and Sachs (1990).
5. Brada and King (1991); Kornai (1990); Lipton and Sachs (1990); Wiles (1995).
6. Gregory and Stuart (2001).
7. *Ibid.*
8. Dabrowski (2001).
9. National Bureau of Statistics of China (2010).
10. Friedman (1953).
11. North (2002).
12. Murrell (1991).
13. Summers (1994).
14. Williamson (1997).
15. Kolodko (2001).
16. Lange (1936).
17. Hayek (1935).
18. Kornai (1986).
19. Lin and Tan (1999).
20. *Ibid.*
21. Lin and Li (2008).
22. World Bank (2002).
23. Lin (1992).

24. Lin and Yao (2001).
25. Lin Yixiang (1999).
26. Lin (2001).
27. Chenery (1961); Krueger (1992); Lin (2009).
28. Krueger (1974); Lin (2003); Lin and Tan (1999).
29. Krueger (1992).
30. Lin (1998).
31. Lin (2003).
32. Lin (2009); Lin, Cai, and Li (1996a, 1996b).

APPENDIX

Global imbalances, reserve currency, and global economic governance

There currently is substantial discussion in the press and in the policy community about global economic imbalances. Commonly accepted hypotheses for the root cause of these imbalances are: East Asian economies' export-led growth strategy, the self-insurance motivation for foreign currency reserve accumulation after the East Asian financial crisis, and China's exchange rate policy. These hypotheses are all theoretically plausible. But are they consistent with the empirical evidence?

The export-led growth hypothesis

The trade surpluses in East Asian economies increased dramatically in recent years (see Figure A1). But the East Asian economies have had export-led growth strategies since the 1960s. In fact, a sustainable export-led growth strategy is not based upon targeting an ever-expanding trade surplus. It is based on integration with international markets. That leads to an expansion of both exports and imports, generating higher quality jobs in the tradable sector. In East Asia this process has been successful in producing rapidly rising

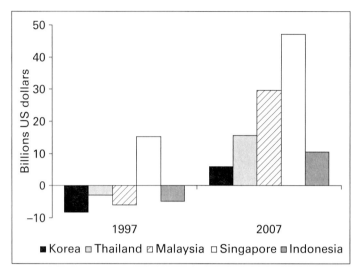

Figure A.1 East Asian trade surpluses
Source: World Bank.

living standards and rapidly declining poverty rates over the last few decades. But the East Asian economies' trade accounts were roughly balanced before 2000. As a result, an export-led growth strategy cannot be the main cause for the emergence of large global imbalances in 2000 and thereafter.

Self-insurance motivation for foreign currency reserve accumulation

After the financial crisis in the late 1990s, emerging market economies in East Asia increased their current account surpluses substantially, and they experienced rising international reserves, as the hypothesis suggests. Note, however, that Germany and Japan also had large current account surpluses over this period (see Figure A2). Yet these countries have "hard" currencies, so they do not have the need for self-insurance. Moreover, the surpluses and reserve accumulation in China after 2005 are too large to be justified by

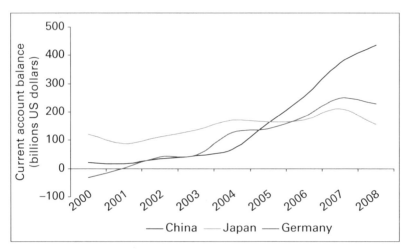

Figure A.2 Three current account surplus countries
Source: World Bank.

the self-insurance motivation. It is difficult to conduct a precise calculation, but in all likelihood the current reserves far surpass an optimal level for self-insurance needs.

China's exchange rate policy

The global imbalances started to grow in 2002, and China has been accused of causing the imbalance by sustaining a large undervaluation of its real exchange rate since 2003. Several key facts tend to contradict that claim. First, China's trade surplus did not become large until 2005, and its trade surplus in 2003 was smaller than it was in 1997 and 1998 (Figure A3). It was commonly believed that the Chinese currency was substantially *overvalued* in the late 1990s. Clearly, other factors, beyond just the exchange rate, influence China's trade balance.

Second, China's currency appreciated against the US dollar by 20 percent in 2005–08, but the global imbalances, especially the US–China imbalance, continued to grow. Third, most other developing

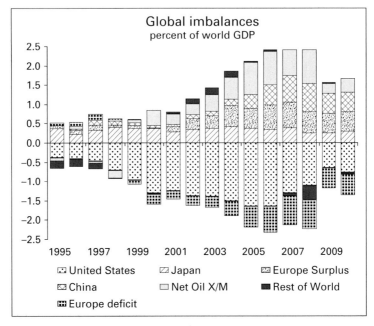

Figure A.3 Global imbalances
Source: World Bank.

countries also increased their current account surpluses and reserves substantially in the same period (see Figure A4). If China's exchange rate was the cause, then the other developing countries that compete with China in the global market would have experienced declining trade surpluses and reserves. So, there must be other factors driving the recent global imbalances.

The need for an alternative hypothesis

The foregoing three hypotheses all imply that the East Asian economies are driving the global imbalances. But this storyline is not consistent with the basic statistics. While the US trade deficits with China did increase substantially, the share of the US trade deficit due to East Asian economies as a region actually declined significantly (see Figure A5).

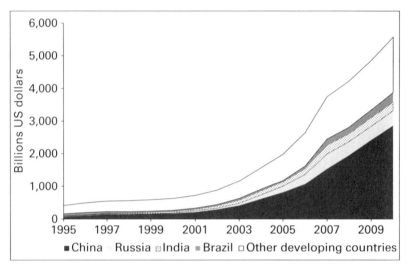

Figure A.4 Foreign exchange reserves of developing countries
Source: World Development Indicators. World Bank.

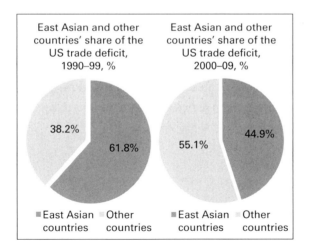

Figure A.5 US trade deficit due to East Asia has declined
Source: World Bank.

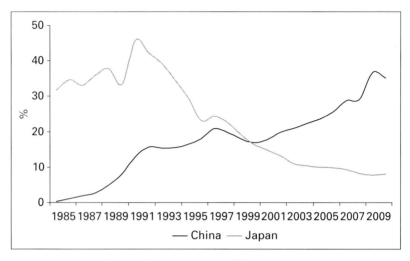

Figure A.6 Share of US–Japan and US–China trade deficits in total US trade deficit
Source: UN Comtrade Database.

The evidence here indicates that the three commonly accepted causes may have contributed but cannot be the main cause of the global imbalances.

By the way, the increase in the US trade deficit with China reflected the relocation of light manufacturing production from East Asian economies to China, as well as regional integration through production networks. This can be seen in the changing patterns of the US trade deficits with Japan and China from 1985 to 2009 (see Figure A6).

An alternative hypothesis consistent with the data

An alternative hypothesis focuses on the structure of international financial assets and policy actions in the United States. More specifically, the global imbalance was a result of the status of the US dollar as the major global reserve currency, combined with the following two policy changes:

- The lack of appropriate financial sector regulation due to deregulation in the 1980s.
- The Federal Reserve's low interest rate policy following the burst of the "dotcom" bubble in 2001.

These policy changes led to excessive risk-taking and higher leverage, producing excess liquidity and "bubbles" in both housing and equity markets in the United States. The wealth effect of these bubbles enabled US households to overconsume, which together with the public debt arising from the Afghanistan and Iraq wars, increased the US current account deficits. As China had become the major producer of labor-intensive processed consumer goods by 2000, the United States ran an increasingly large deficit with China, which in turn ran trade deficits with many other East Asian economies that provided intermediate products to China.

The excess liquidity also led to the large outflow of capital to developing countries, rising from $200 billion in 2000 to $1.2 trillion in 2007, contributing to investment-led growth in many developing countries in the same period. The growth rate of developing countries as a whole in 2002–07 was at a record high (Figure A7). The investment-led growth in developing countries in turn resulted in large trade surpluses in many advanced capital-goods exporting countries, such as Germany and Japan. The accelerated growth in many countries resulted in a sharp increase in demand for – and prices of – natural resources, as well as trade surpluses in natural resource exporting countries. Since the United States is the reserve currency issuing country, the foreign reserves accumulated through trade/capital account surpluses in other countries would return to the United States. And this led to the US capital account surplus.

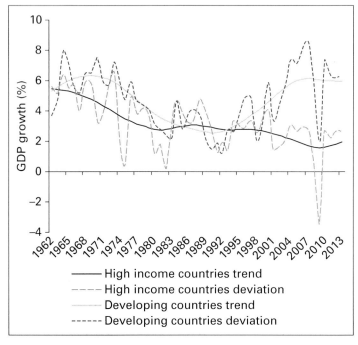

Figure A.7 Trend and cyclical GDP growth
Source: World Bank.

Why did China stand out in the global imbalances?

The undervaluation of the real exchange rate is often attributed as a main reason for China's large trade surplus. The argument is as follows: China's tradable sector's productivity increased rapidly in recent years. Based on the Balassa–Samuelson Theorem, the tradable sector's productivity increase will raise the wage rates in both the tradable and non-tradable sectors, increasing the price of non-tradable goods and services and the appreciation of the real exchange rate. In China the increases in the wage rate and prices of non-tradable goods and services were very small, giving support to the above suspicion. But China still has considerable surplus labor in the rural sector. Before the depletion of surplus labor, the productivity increase in the tradable sector would expand employment

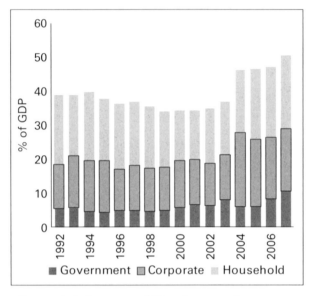

Figure A.8 Structure of China's national savings
Source: World Bank.

in the sector not the wage rate. Therefore, the Balassa–Samuelson Theorem is not applicable, and the real exchange rate in China is likely to be close to equilibrium.

The large current account surplus in China in fact reflects high domestic savings. There are several commonly accepted hypotheses about China's high saving rate: such as the lack of a well-developed social safety net and the demographics of an aging population. These explanations focus on incentives for household saving behavior, but they cannot be the main reason for China's high savings, because household savings in China are about 20 percent of GDP – the same level as India.

The uniqueness of China's savings is the large share of corporate savings (see Figure A8). Corporate savings behavior is driven by the excessive concentration of the financial system that serves the big firms, low taxation on natural resources, and monopolies in some sectors, as discussed in Chapter 12. Reforms to remove the above

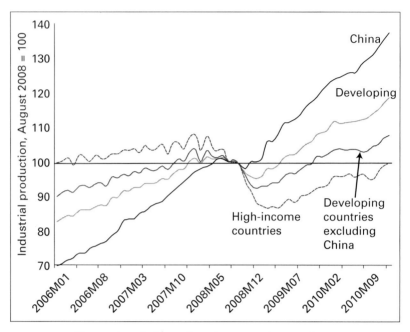

Figure A.9 Industrial production volume indices
Source: World Bank.

distortions are required for increasing consumption and reducing saving in China.

The role of the reserve currency in global imbalances

It is only because the US dollar is a major reserve currency that it is possible for the United States to run such a large current account deficit for so long. The status of the dollar as the major global reserve currency, combined with the financial deregulation of the 1980s and the low interest rate policy of the 2000s, led to the emergence of global imbalances. To prevent the recurrence of global imbalances, the ultimate solution is to replace national currencies as global reserve currencies with a new global currency. The International Monetary Fund's special drawing rights could be a transitional arrangement for a new global currency. But such an

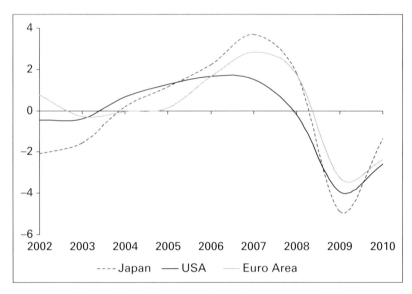

Figure A.10 Output gap (actual versus potential)
Source: World Bank.

arrangement may not be feasible because a major reserve-currency country is unlikely to voluntarily give up its reserve-issuing privilege to a global body. A more likely scenario is the emergence of a basket of reserve currencies with some changes in the basket's composition and weights.

A win-win solution for the global recovery

The most urgent global challenges are high unemployment and the large excess capacity in high-income industrialized countries (Figures A9 and A10). The weakening of the US dollar is at most a zero-sum game among the high-income industrialized countries, because they produce and export the same categories of goods. An increase in US exports and employment will be at the cost of other high-income industrial country exports and employment.

An increase in consumption and a reduction in saving/invest-ment in emerging markets could add to the slack demand for exports and unemployment in high-income countries. These countries are predominantly producers of capital goods, so slower investment growth in developing countries would slow demand for high-income country exports.

Win-win solutions for the global recovery and long-term growth could be based on new international financial arrangements along with structural reforms in both high-income and developing countries. On the financial front one solution would be to create a global recovery fund, supported by hard-currency countries and large-reserve countries and managed by multilateral development banks. This fund could finance investments to release bottlenecks and enhance productivity in developing countries. Such investments would increase the demand for capital goods produced in high-income countries, reduce their unemployment now, and enhance the developing countries' growth in the future. Some of the investment projects could also be in high-income countries. The key is the quality of the investment. The fund itself could be complemented by structural reforms in high-income and developing countries to create space for investment and to improve the efficiency of investment.

Index